"Anyone wanting the facts about priest r
decades should read this book. Based (led
with even-handed judgments, the book ıl
studies that demonstrate that the Catho
is hardly down and out. To the contrary
productive, and happy. CARA, NFPC, ... are to be congratulated
for this useful and up-to-date study."

> — Ronald D. Witherup, SS, Superior General of the Sulpicians
> and author of *Gold Tested in Fire: A New Pentecost for the
> Catholic Priesthood*

"This thorough and thoughtful study compiles responses, by both diocesan
and religious priests, to questions on the impact of such factors as changing
demographics, collaboration patterns, and satisfaction levels on their ministry.
The responses will confirm your intuitions, encourage you with some positive
perspectives, challenge some of your presuppositions, unsettle you with
implications, and offer you substantiated insights into generational
differences. This readable and enlightening text deserves a reflective reading
by laity, religious, priests, and bishops alike."

> — Fr. John Pavlik, Executive Director of the Conference of
> Major Superiors of Men

"*Same Call, Different Men* is an important book. It describes a number of
trends among priests (e.g., they are getting older), probes specific issues
(the effects of the sexual abuse scandal on other priests), spots emerging
concerns (the demands of serving multiple parishes), and suggests ways to
address these challenges (training in collaborative ministry). The book
clearly documents to the complexities of the priesthood and the real-life
experiences of priests, such as the personal satisfaction that can accompany
a life of service in the Church and the working conditions that can limit that
satisfaction. It offers readers a balanced interpretation of good news and
bad news, an honest mixture of predictable findings and surprising results,
and an even-handed inventory of problems and signs of renewal. The
thoughtful reflections of Archbishop Gregory Aymond, Sr. Katarina Schuth,
Msgr. Jeremiah McCarthy, and Dr. Dianne Traflet are a bonus. *Same Call,
Different Men* proves, once again, that, when it is conducted by competent
professionals, social research is a valuable resource for everyone who wants
to understand and strengthen the Church."

> — James D. Davidson, Professor Emeritus, Department of
> Sociology, Purdue University

Same Call, Different Men

The Evolution of the Priesthood since Vatican II

Mary L. Gautier, Paul M. Perl,
and Stephen J. Fichter

LITURGICAL PRESS
Collegeville, Minnesota

www.litpress.org

3	4	5	6	7	8	9

Library of Congress Cataloging-in-Publication Data

Gautier, Mary, 1952–
    Same call, different men : the evolution of the priesthood since Vatican II / Mary L. Gautier, Paul M. Perl, and Stephen J. Fichter.
      p.   cm.
    Includes bibliographical references (p.   ) and index.
    ISBN 978-0-8146-3429-5 — ISBN 978-0-8146-3430-1 (e-book)
      1. Catholic Church—United States—Clergy—History—20th century.
2. Catholic Church—United States—History—20th century.   3. Priesthood—Catholic Church—History of doctrines—20th century.   4. Vatican Council (2nd : 1962–1965) I. Perl, Paul M. II. Fichter, Stephen J. III. Title.

BX1407.C6G38 2012
262'.1427309045—dc23

                                        2011051749

Contents

Foreword   vii

Introduction and Background   ix

Chapter 1: Demographic Changes and Changes in
   Priestly Ministry   1

Chapter 2: Satisfaction in Priestly Life and Ministry   18

Chapter 3: Challenges in Priestly Life and Ministry   48

Chapter 4: Collaboration in Ministry   70

Chapter 5: The Multicultural Reality of Priestly Ministry Today   92

Chapter 6: Effects of the Sexual Abuse Scandal   112

Chapter 7: The Sexual Abuse Scandal and the Stories of
   Nine Priests   148

Chapter 8: Looking to the Future: Who Is Encouraging the
   Next Generation of Priests?   184

Commentaries:

   Reflections from an Archbishop   204
     Most Rev. Gregory M. Aymond
     Archbishop of New Orleans

   Reflections from a Former Seminary Rector   209
     Msgr. Jeremiah McCarthy
     Executive Director, Seminary Department, National Catholic
     Educational Association

   Reflections on a Changing Ministry and Changing Ministers   217
     Katarina Schuth, OSF
     Endowed Chair for the Social Scientific Study of Religion, Saint
     Paul Seminary School of Divinity, University of St. Thomas

Reflections on the Happiness of Priests and the Impact
on Parishes   225
   Dianne M. Traflet
   *Associate Dean, Immaculate Conception Seminary School of
      Theology, Seton Hall University*

References   233

Index   237

Foreword

This study conducted by the Center for Applied Research in the Apostolate (CARA) at Georgetown University continues the commissioned work of the National Federation of Priests' Councils (NFPC) as detailed in the book *Evolving Visions of the Priesthood: Changes from Vatican II to the Turn of the New Century* (Liturgical Press, 2003), by Dr. Dean Hoge and Jacqueline Wenger. In the 1990s NFPC initiated a process of research that would become a "trends study" to provide the Church in the United States with data on the priests of the country over the last forty years. This is the third such research that NFPC commissioned, repeating portions of the initial 1970 landmark priests' survey conducted by the National Opinion Research Center (NORC) at the University of Chicago.

These are important dates because they serve as benchmarks in the movement of the Church across the changing pastoral landscape. In this research, attention is given to the diminishing number and aging population of Catholic clergy, the implications of the sexual abuse scandal that has gripped our nation over the past ten years, the increased numbers of international clergy that now serve alongside native clergy, the burgeoning immigrant church, and the increased participation of laity as priests seek to maintain vibrant faith communities. All of these factors have implications for the shifting and changing pastoral landscape in which priests exercise their pastoral ministry.

For the purposes of the NFPC, the data presented here offer issues for the setting of an agenda. The clearly identified challenges that surface from this latest study and are reported here give the NFPC and the bishops a clear picture of what the priests are feeling and thinking, how they are disposed to lead local faith communities, and what specific problem areas need further research, clarification, and attention.

As in previous companion volumes, commentaries in this book provided by distinguished scholars and pastoral leaders will assist in furthering the discussion we hope this book will provoke.

I commend *Same Call, Different Men: The Evolution of the Priesthood since Vatican II* for your reflection and study. It is the wish of the NFPC that the findings of this work will further the research into and understanding of priestly life and ministry in the United States today.

The NFPC offers special thanks to Sr. Mary Bendyna, former CARA executive director, and Mary Gautier, senior research associate at CARA, for guiding the project when Dean Hoge's health no longer permitted him to continue journeying with us. We are also indebted to our anonymous donor, whose assistance has made this project possible.

Rev. Richard Vega
President, The National Federation of Priests' Councils

Introduction and Background

This book is the latest in a long line of research on priestly life and ministry in the United States that stretches back some forty years and involves five major surveys of priests. These surveys were all carefully designed and analyzed to track trends over time in the composition, ministry, attitudes, and behaviors of priests in the United States.

The first study in this series was called the *American Catholic Priesthood Study*. The study was undertaken in 1970, when the number of priests in the United States was close to its peak. Record numbers of men had entered seminaries in the 1940s, 1950s, and 1960s, in the boom years following the Second World War. These were the sons and grandsons of hardworking Catholic immigrants, for whom having a cleric in the family was a real status symbol.

At the same time, 1970 was a time of turmoil, both for American society in general and for the Catholic Church in particular. Effects from the civil rights movement, the Kennedy assassination, the War on Poverty, the feminist movement, the hippies, and other rapid social and moral changes were rocking American society. The Catholic Church was grappling with the changes that emerged from the Second Vatican Council, which involved not just liturgy and language but also a fundamental change in the way clergy and laity interact. By 1970, seminary enrollments were falling off and large numbers of priests were leaving the priesthood.[1]

Concerned about these rapid changes and their impact on both the clergy and the Church, the United States Conference of Catholic Bishops (USCCB) commissioned a major study of priesthood. They engaged

---

[1] The *American Catholic Priesthood Study* would later report that 3 percent of diocesan priests in the United States were preparing in 1970 to leave the priesthood and another 10 percent were uncertain about their future.

Fathers Andrew Greeley and Richard Schoenherr of the National Opinion Research Center at the University of Chicago to survey a national sample of active and resigned priests. The purpose of the study was to learn the facts about priestly life and ministry—to understand priests' satisfactions, dissatisfactions, motivations, and problems. The findings were published as *The Catholic Priest in the United States: Sociological Investigations* (Greeley, 1972).

Fifteen years later, in 1985, Professor Dean Hoge and colleagues replicated questions from the 1970 study and drew an equivalent sample to survey. They repeated the process in 1993, so that they could begin to track some trends among active priests. The findings from these studies were published by Dr. Hoge in a series of articles in academic journals. The findings were also described in a report titled *Project Future Directions*, published by the NFPC in 1994. In 2001, another eight years later, the NFPC again commissioned a study, this time funded by Duke Divinity School's Pulpit & Pew Research on Pastoral Leadership Initiative. Findings from the 2001 study were published by Hoge and Wenger in *Evolving Visions of the Priesthood* (2003).

In 2009, the NFPC again sought funding, this time from an anonymous foundation, for a fifth study in the series. Due to the untimely death of Dr. Hoge shortly after the funding was announced, the NFPC contacted CARA at Georgetown University to conduct the research.[2] This current research replicates many of the questions that were on the original 1970 study, particularly those that were repeated in 1985, 1993, and 2001. Thus, we have valuable trend data on US priests that now extends nearly forty years.

Methodology

In the same collaborative spirit as the earlier studies, CARA drew on the expertise of others to ensure that the 2009 study would accurately track trends in the life and ministry of priests in the United States. CARA senior research associate Dr. Mary Gautier and representatives from NFPC examined all four previous questionnaires to develop the 2009

---

[2] CARA is a Catholic social science research center started by Church leaders in 1964. It compiles data and conducts surveys, demographic studies, and focus groups for Church organizations of all types. In a number of places, this book cites CARA findings from research projects other than this study for the NFPC. Among these findings are results from previous studies of priests, both national-level surveys and surveys conducted for individual dioceses.

questionnaire. The team developed a twelve-page questionnaire of approximately 150 items, with an open-ended question at the end that invited participants to reflect on any recommendations they would have for a young man who is discerning a vocation to priesthood.

The questionnaire was designed to replicate a number of important items from previous waves of the study. Where possible, tables in this book present the responses to these identical items from each wave of the study, so the reader may examine changes across time. In addition to the important demographic and current ministry questions, many items relating to priestly satisfaction, problems faced in ministry, and attitudes about specific aspects of ministry are also included from previous surveys. New questions were developed to address issues in priestly life and ministry that were unheard of in 1970, such as sharing ministry with laity, multicultural ministry, working with international priests, and ministry in the wake of the clergy sexual abuse crisis.

The next step was selection of a sample. In the 1970 study, Greeley and Schoenherr determined that a mailing list of priests obtained from *The Official Catholic Directory* had too many inaccuracies to use as a sampling frame. Instead they stratified dioceses and religious communities into four size groups, according to the number of priests contained in them, and further divided them according to the four major US census regions (Northeast, Midwest, South, and West). They then selected 85 dioceses and 87 religious institutes by sampling within each size and geographic cluster. These 172 units were asked to provide a complete list of priests, from which priests were randomly selected and then mailed a printed questionnaire. The final data set was then weighted to compensate for this stratified sample. Hoge followed approximately the same methodology for the 1985, 1993, and 2001 versions of the survey.

For the 2009 survey, CARA already had in its possession a relatively clean mailing list of approximately 24,000 diocesan priests and more than 13,000 religious priests from every diocese and religious order in the United States. Rather than stratifying by size and geography and then weighting to ensure a nationally representative sample, CARA randomly selected 2,400 diocesan priests and 800 religious priests to receive a mailed copy of the questionnaire. CARA mailed a survey packet consisting of the twelve-page questionnaire booklet, a cover letter (on NFPC letterhead signed by its president Father Richard Vega for diocesan priests; on letterhead of the Conference of Major Superiors of Men (CMSM) signed by its executive director Father Paul Lininger, OFM Conv, for religious priests), and a return envelope addressed to CARA.

Each packet also contained a postcard addressed to CARA that was to be signed by the responding priest and returned by separate mail at the time he completed and returned his questionnaire, thus ensuring the confidentiality of the survey response and eliminating each responding priest from further follow-up mailings.

CARA mailed the survey packets in summer 2009 and randomly selected a replacement for any packets that were returned undeliverable or that had been mailed to a priest who was ineligible for the survey (through death, laicization, or infirmity). CARA conducted follow-up with nonrespondents throughout the fall of 2009 and cut off data collection at the end of 2009. When all collected surveys were entered into the database, the final data set consisted of 960 respondents, for a response rate of approximately 30 percent.[3] Of these, 678 are diocesan priests and 282 are religious order priests, for a ratio of about seven-tenths diocesan priests and three-tenths religious priests—close to the same proportions that exist in the overall priest population in the United States.[4] A sample of 960 from a population of approximately 37,000 priests yields an overall margin of sampling error of + or -3.1 percentage points, meaning that the characteristics of priests represented in the poll can be assumed to be within 3.1 percentage points of the characteristics of all Catholic priests in the United States.

In addition to the surveys, CARA researchers also conducted focus groups and interviews with priests, to obtain more detailed information about their ministry experiences. CARA research associate Father Stephen Fichter[5] conducted three focus groups of approximately ten priests each,

---

[3] This response rate of 30 percent is considerably lower than that attained by prior studies in this series (68 to 89 percent), all of which used two-stage sampling procedures in which dioceses and religious orders were sampled first. True national samples of priests have generally obtained relatively low response rates. For example, the 2002 *Los Angeles Times* mailed survey of priests and the 2002 CARA telephone poll of priests each obtained a response rate of 37 percent. Lower response rates may be caused in part by inaccuracy in national lists of priests. Additionally, in the case of two-stage sampling, researchers can typically appeal to diocesan and religious institute leaders to encourage participation among their clergy, but this was not an option for this survey.

[4] Nevertheless, for all survey results presented in this book, we have weighted the data to match the exact national percentages (68 percent diocesan and 32 percent religious).

[5] Father Fichter's grand uncle, Rev. Joseph Fichter, SJ, was a member of the US bishops' Ad Hoc Committee for the Study of the Life and Ministry of the Priest, the group that commissioned and collaborated in the design of the original 1970 study of priests. Both priests earned a PhD in sociology.

in winter and spring 2010. Each group consisted of both diocesan and religious priests. One group was in a medium-sized archdiocese in the Northeast, one was in a small diocese in the Southwest, and one was conducted at the National Organization for the Continuing Education of Roman Catholic Clergy (NOCERCC) annual conference in 2010, with priests from across the United States.

To obtain a broad spectrum of interviews, CARA randomly selected fifty names from all priests that had been mailed a copy of the survey and sent them a postcard inviting them to be interviewed by phone for the project. CARA research associate Paul Perl contacted priests to be interviewed from among those that returned the postcard and also contacted other priests that were known to have particular expertise or experiences of interest to the project. In all, thirty-one of the priests who were interviewed have been quoted in the book.

Organization of This Book

This book builds on the broad shoulders of the previous researchers described above, who have systematically tracked the characteristics, behaviors, and attitudes of priests in the United States since 1970. The historical context of the priesthood during this period of the last quarter of the twentieth century was laid out in some detail in *Evolving Visions of the Priesthood* (Hoge and Wenger, 2003), the previous book on this subject. In chapter 1 of that book, Professor Hoge outlined some of the changes in priestly life that evolved out of the documents of the Second Vatican Council, such as a new emphasis on the role of the priest as a servant-leader in the community and the struggle to clarify the role of the priest in a changing ecclesiology that recognized emerging forms of leadership—permanent deacons and lay leaders.

In addition, Hoge described changes in Catholic culture and in American society that had an important impact on priestly life. Catholics in the final quarter of the twentieth century were fully assimilated into American society; they were no longer an immigrant subculture struggling to find a place in the broader society. As a result, they were no longer concentrated in the immigrant neighborhoods and villages of the Northeast and Upper Midwest but had followed jobs and opportunities to settle in the South and West, many of them in areas that were not traditionally Catholic. They took advantage of all the cultural and economic opportunities that were open to them in American society and, partly as a consequence, the numbers of Catholics responding to a call to priesthood or religious life dropped precipitously. At the same time, Catholics were also affected by changes in the broader society, such as increasing cultural diversity, decreasing trust in institutions, increasing acceptance of discourse about sexuality in society, and a move away from hierarchical leadership and toward more collaborative decision making in organizations.

Figure 1
Catholic Population by Census Region

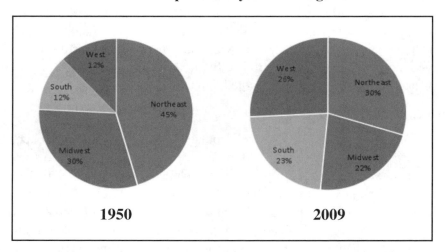

These trends have persisted into the twenty-first century and their influence continues to affect the priesthood in the United States. In addition, several other emerging factors have also had an impact on the priesthood:

- The number of seminarians has stabilized over the last twenty-five years, to about 3,500 seminarians enrolled in theology each year (Gautier, 2009). In the last decade, the United States has averaged about 450 ordinations to priesthood per year, with little variation from year to year. However, this number is still only about a third as many new priests as are needed to compensate for those who are retiring, dying, or otherwise absent from active priestly ministry. Bishops in many dioceses are struggling to find ways to stretch fewer priests to assume responsibility for more than one parish and are bringing in priests from outside the United States to help out as well. This puts additional pressure on newly ordained priests to accept responsibility for a parish, even if they feel called to some other aspect of priestly ministry, and to become pastors before they have had the years of mentoring as a parochial vicar (associate pastor) that has been traditional (Bleichner, 2004).

- The number of Catholics continues to grow at a rate of about 1 to 2 percent a year, approximately keeping pace with the growth of the US population, but these Catholics now are increasingly located in the suburbs and cities of the South and Southwest, in areas that lack the Catholic infrastructure (parishes, schools, seminaries, and colleges and universities) and personnel (priests and religious) of the Northeast and Upper Midwest. The effect of this trend is that dioceses in the Northeast and Upper Midwest have to close parishes and schools that no longer have enough parishioners to sustain them, while dioceses in the South and Southwest are under increasing pressure to build more and larger parishes and schools to accommodate the demand. Priests in some parts of the Rust Belt are experiencing a Church in decline, while priests in the Sun Belt states more often serve a Church that seems to be "bursting at the seams."

- In addition, the Catholic population, mirroring the US population, is becoming increasingly diverse as a result of immigration from Catholic population centers around the world. Latinos, in particular, are underrepresented in the priest population relative to their presence in the Catholic Church in the United States. For priests, this means that they are sometimes challenged to accommodate a variety of cultures and language groups within a single parish.

- Finally, the clergy sexual abuse crisis that erupted in the national media in 2002 and resulted in the US bishops issuing their Charter for the Protection of Children and Young People in Dallas in June 2002 has had an impact on priestly life and ministry in recent years. Although research has shown that most of the allegations involved sexual abuse of minors that occurred from the mid-1960s through the mid-1980s, the repercussions continue to affect priestly life and ministry today.

With this most recent wave of data, collected in a national survey of priests in fall 2009, we explore some of these areas of change in the priesthood in the United States during the last forty years as well as ways that priests today are remarkably similar to the generations before. Some of the questions on this survey were also asked on previous surveys of priests in 1970, 1985, 1993, and 2001. The 2009 wave gives us four national surveys of priests at eight-year intervals, plus a 1970 baseline survey from which to compare our findings.

The first chapter of this book explores demographic trends, such as the aging of priests in the United States, men entering seminary after college and getting ordained later in life, priests from other countries coming here for ministry, and the increasing diversity of men entering the priesthood. It also describes an emerging phenomenon of retirement from priestly ministry as well as other changes in priestly ministry. Chapter 2 describes some of the sources of satisfaction with priestly life and ministry and documents a trend of increasing satisfaction among priests with their chosen vocation. In counterpoint, chapter 3 discusses some of the major problems priests face in their life and ministry. It then tracks changes in those problems over time and discusses the relationship between problems and happiness in priestly life.

In chapters 4 and 5, we turn our attention to a couple of specific issues that are in some ways both a challenge to priestly ministry and an opportunity to minister more effectively in a rapidly changing Church. Chapter 4 deals with collaboration with others in ministry. It examines priests' attitudes about the emerging phenomena of permanent deacons and lay ecclesial ministers assuming more leadership in parishes. Priests also describe their attitudes related to working with international priests in ministry as well as attitudes about working with women. We conclude the chapter with a look at how priests' attitudes about the priesthood and the Church have changed over time. Chapter 5 examines the multicultural reality of priestly ministry in the United States today. The chapter first explores priests' attitudes about the challenges of expanding multicultural diversity in parish ministry as the US Catholic population grows increasingly diverse. We then turn to a discussion of the multicultural character of the priesthood and explore how priests born in the United States compare to their brother priests from other countries in their experiences and attitudes about priestly ministry.

Chapters 6 and 7 explore the effects of the 2002 clergy sexual abuse scandal on priests and their attitudes about their life and ministry. Chapter 6 lays out a brief history of the scandal as well as the development and implementation of the Charter for the Protection of Children and Young People. It then describes some of the reactions of priests to the Charter as well as their attitudes about the scandal and the effects it has had on their ministry. Chapter 7 presents the stories of nine priests in more depth and describes how their lives and ministry were affected by the scandal.

Chapter 8 discusses what priests are saying about priestly ministry to young men who may be considering a vocation to priesthood. In light of all the changes and all the challenges, priests tell us what recommendations they have for someone discerning a vocation to priesthood today.

Finally, just as Hoge and Wenger did in the 2001 study, CARA and NFPC requested commentaries on the written chapters from a number of distinguished scholars and pastoral leaders who are familiar with the struggles and joys of priestly ministry in the United States. These commentaries are included at the end of this book in the hope that their insights will assist in furthering the discussion about these trends in priestly life and ministry.

Acknowledgments

The authors benefited from remarkable cooperation throughout this project. We would like to thank the National Federation of Priests' Councils for initiating the project and obtaining the funding from a foundation that wishes to remain anonymous. In particular, we thank NFPC president Rev. Richard Vega and executive director Vic Doucette for entrusting the project to CARA when it became clear that Dean Hoge was too ill to carry it out. We thank the late Dean Hoge, whose meticulous notes from previous waves of the survey were a valuable resource that guided the current project and we thank his wife, Josephine Hoge, who made those notes available to us.

We thank all the priests who participated in focus groups and shared their insights in interviews throughout the project. We especially thank all the priests who took the time to complete the survey and share their ministry experiences with us. We have tried to be faithful to the spirit of what they said to us. We thank Linda Ferrara and Eleanor Jetter of Sacred Heart Parish in Haworth, New Jersey, for transcribing the focus groups for us and C. Joseph O'Hara and M. Connie Neuman of CARA for compiling the index.

Finally, we are grateful to the commentators who read the manuscript and reflected on its findings for the benefit of all the Church. Their comments will help further the conversations that need to take place so that this research becomes a useful tool for those who are concerned about the future of priestly ministry.

Chapter 1

Demographic Changes and
Changes in Priestly Ministry

Certainly, responsibility has its own crosses. Here I am, not even forty, and my goodness, who would have thought that I would be a pastor for ten years now? That's ridiculous! Who becomes a pastor when they're thirty?

—*Priest in an interview*

One area of the priesthood that has experienced significant change is in the demographics of the priesthood itself. In this chapter, we explore the demographic characteristics of priests today and show how those characteristics have changed over the last forty years. We also examine how priestly ministry has evolved to meet the changing needs of the Catholic population in the United States.

Age and Generation

By far the most striking trend to come from these data, and probably the one trend that is having the most immediate impact on priestly life in the United States, is the aging of the priesthood. The average age of priests in the United States has been increasing steadily over the last forty years, in large part because the total number of priests in the United States reached its peak in 1969. The figure here shows the rapid growth in the number of priests during the first half of the twentieth century as well as the marked decrease in numbers over the last forty years.

Far fewer men have been entering seminaries since the 1940s, 1950s, and 1960s, and the men preparing for priesthood are entering seminary later in life, on average. The effect of this pattern is that the average priest in active ministry today is much older than his counterpart of forty years

Figure 1.1
Priests in the United States

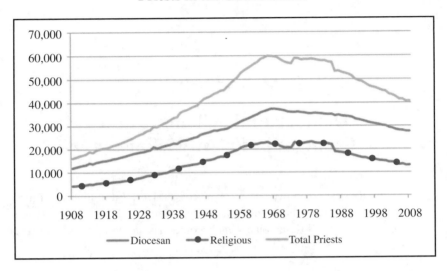

ago. In 1970, at the time of the first study in this series, the median age of active diocesan priests was 45 (Schoenherr and Young, 1993). Although slightly older than the general labor force, they were about the same age as other professionals, according to data from the US Bureau of Labor Statistics.

By 2009, the median age of the general labor force increased just slightly (5 percent) from 39.8 to 41.8. Doctors and attorneys followed the same pattern, with their median ages increasing by 3 and 5 percent, respectively. Active diocesan priests, by contrast, have a median age in 2009 of 59, an increase of 31 percent from the 1970 figure. They are much older today than these comparable professionals with graduate degrees. This shrinking pool of increasingly older active diocesan priests is being experienced as a shortage of priests available to staff parishes in dioceses across the country.

The median age of *all* priests in this study is 64, which means that half of those responding to the survey were at least within a year of eligibility for Social Security! Dioceses and religious institutes are facing increased financial pressure to provide for greater numbers of elderly and infirm clergy. In fact, diocesan priests average about five years younger than religious priests and this gap has been consistent over time. In the 1970 survey, the average age of diocesan priests was 34 and for religious priests it was 37. By 2001, the average age of diocesan priests

Figure 1.2
Median Ages Compared

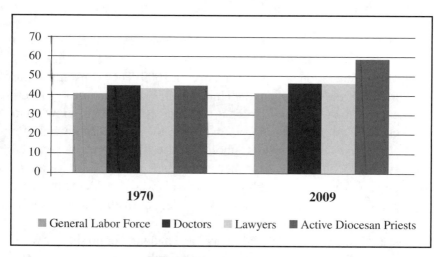

was 59 and religious priests averaged 64 years of age; in 2009, diocesan priests average 62 years of age and religious priests average 66 years.

Table 1.1
Average Age of Priests[1]

	1970	1985	1993	2001	2009
Mean age (in years):					
All priests	35*	52	57	61	63
Diocesan priests	34	51*	55	59	62
Religious priests	37	55*	60	64	66

* Imputed from data provided

[1] The 1970 data set from the *American Catholic Priesthood Study* is not publicly available. Therefore, the 1970 data reported in this book come from Greeley, 1972, and other published sources. In some cases, the sources have only reported separate percentages for diocesan and religious priests; when necessary we derived estimates for all 1970 priests by weighting based on the numbers of diocesan and religious priests. We obtained the data sets for the 1985, 1993, and 2001 studies from the Association of Religion Data Archives (ARDA) and employed the weights provided with those data sets. These numbers may vary by 1 or 2 percentage points from results reported elsewhere, due to the particular weighting variables employed.

Priests also came of age during different periods of time and were influenced by the prevailing culture of the times. The three generations described below will be used later as the basis for comparison.

- Priests of the pre–Vatican II generation were born prior to 1943 and most were ordained well before the Second Vatican Council. Priests of this generation are age 67 and over in 2009. They constitute more than half of all priests in the United States and remain a key reference group for priests. These priests, for the most part, grew up in ethnic Catholic neighborhoods where they were immersed in a supportive and nurturing Catholic culture. They typically received strong encouragement for their vocation from other family members, parishioners, neighbors, and friends who considered the local parish priest a respected and trusted leader of the local Catholic community. Most of these priests entered the seminary in high school or directly from high school and had little or no secular work experience. When they entered the priesthood, rectory life was a formal, hierarchical community of several priests with defined roles and a relatively light workload. As is true for their secular counterparts, institutional loyalty is a key value for members of this generation. Forty-four percent of priests in the 2009 survey are of the pre–Vatican II generation.

- Priests of the Vatican II generation were born between 1943 and 1960 and are between the ages of 49 and 66 in 2009. The Catholic neighborhoods in which these priests grew up tended to be more suburban and affluent, as the children and grandchildren of immigrant Catholics assimilated into American society and moved into the middle class. They were encouraged in their vocation by family members and communities who looked up to the priest as a "servant-leader" who is active in promoting social justice in society. These priests witnessed the impact of the Council during their formation years and were often directly affected by the resulting changes in seminary life and priestly ministry. Rectory life gradually became more communal and less hierarchical than it was for the previous generation. As part of the "baby boomer" generation, these priests tend to place greater value on change and questioning institutions and structures than other generations. Priests of this generation are 41 percent of those surveyed in 2009.

• The post–Vatican II generation, born after 1960, includes those who are age 48 or younger in 2009 and have come of age after the Second Vatican Council. For them, the Council is a historical fact, not something they personally experienced. These priests grew up with few of the experiences of the "Catholic subculture" that so influenced the generations before Vatican II. Immersed in American culture, they had to seek out their Catholic identity in parish life, Catholic schools, and Catholic organizations. Compared to previous generations, fewer of them attended high school seminary or college seminary. They are more likely to have completed college and held jobs before entering the seminary. Once ordained, though, they are more likely than the generations before them to be assigned to parishes immediately and to be made pastors in just a few years. Rectory life for this group is more likely to mean living alone. With many demands on their time and few opportunities for socializing with other priests, they tend to place greater value than the generations before them on priestly identity and fraternity. Priests of this age group make up 15 percent of the sample.

Age at Ordination and Ordination Cohort

As mentioned earlier, priests today are also entering the priesthood later in life and getting ordained at an older age than they were in 1970. In 1970, high school seminaries enrolled about 12,000 young men who were considering a vocation to priesthood, according to statistics reported by seminaries to CARA. The trajectory they followed typically included four years of college seminary and another four years of theology, culminating in ordination on average at age 27.

Table 1.2
Age at Ordination by Ordination Cohort

	Average age at ordination
Pre–Vatican II (ordained before 1964)	27
Vatican II (ordained 1964–77)	28
Post–Vatican II (ordained 1978–91)	31
Millennial (ordained 1992–present)	37

The average age at ordination for all priests in the 2009 survey is 30. This average is misleading, however, because we know from other research that priests are being ordained later in life. We can see this changing age at ordination even within this sample of priests by comparing the average age at ordination among priests who were ordained at different periods in history (see table 1.2). This same pattern of later average age at ordination has been reported in annual surveys of ordination classes for the last twelve years (see Bendyna and Gautier, 2010).

Just as we separated priests according to age into generational categories, we have also subdivided priests into analytically meaningful ordination cohorts. Priests who were ordained in a particular period in history often exhibit attitudes and behaviors that are similar to other priests who also shared similar formation experiences. The four ordination cohorts shown above in table 1.2 had the formation experiences described below.

- The pre–Vatican II ordination cohort is composed of priests who were ordained before 1964, the year that marked the midpoint of the Second Vatican Council. These men average 79 years of age and have been in priestly ministry for an average of more than 50 years. Their seminary formation often began at the high school or college seminary and followed a monastic tradition that included instruction in Latin, rigid separation from the secular world, and a formal hierarchy of priestly roles. Many, though certainly not all of them, tend to have a more hierarchical view of priesthood and see the priest as "a man set apart" from society by his ordination. Most of these men are white (98 percent) and were born in the United States (92 percent), and all are members of the pre–Vatican II generation. About a third of this cohort is still in active ministry, a fifth is semiretired from ministry, and almost half are currently retired from ministry. These priests are a quarter of all responding priests in 2009.

- The Vatican II ordination cohort is composed of priests who were ordained during the Second Vatican Council and in the turbulent years following. Like the pre–Vatican II ordination cohort, many of them entered seminary in high school or in college. Their seminary formation took place in a period of great flux in the Church, when the theological renewal engendered by the Second Vatican Council was being implemented, new models of being Church were advanced (Dulles, 1974), and expectations of reform were high. Seminaries moved away somewhat from the traditional monastic model and toward a more academic model. Some seminaries began to include lay students alongside priesthood candidates in classes. Instruction was in English and seminarians were encouraged to see themselves as "servant-leaders" ministering within the world rather than as men set apart from the world by their ordination. Nearly all priests of this cohort are white (95 percent). Nine in ten were born in the United States and they are equally split between the Vatican II generation and the pre–Vatican II generation in terms of age. Most are still in active ministry (85 percent), although 7 percent are semi-retired and another 7 percent are retired from active ministry. A third of all responding priests in this study are members of this cohort.

• The post–Vatican II ordination cohort is composed of priests who were ordained during the first half of the pontificate of John Paul II (1978–91). Unlike the two cohorts before them, these men entered during a time of decline and reorganization for seminaries—there were half as many priesthood candidates studying in theologates in the mid-1980s as there were in the mid-1960s (Schuth, 1988). As the numbers of priesthood candidates declined, more and more seminaries opened their programs to lay students, who shared in the academic formation that was formerly reserved for priesthood candidates. These men were also older, on average—the first seminary experience for most of this cohort came after college, at the post-graduate level. Many of these men had college and work experience before entering the seminary. Priests of this cohort are nearly all US-born (91 percent) but are more diverse than previous cohorts. Nine in ten are white, but 5 percent are African or African American, 3 percent are Hispanic, and 2 percent are Asian or Asian American. Most of these are men of the Vatican II generation (82 percent), but 13 percent are post–Vatican II generation and 5 percent are men of the pre–Vatican II generation. These priests are nearly all in active ministry (97 percent), although 2 percent are retired. About a quarter of responding priests (23 percent) is in this cohort.

• The millennial ordination cohort is also sometimes referred to as the John Paul II priests. The entire lived experience of Church for most of these men was during the post–Vatican II period. Many were just coming of age when John Paul II was elected pope in 1978. Seminaries during this period were reacting to the Vatican-mandated seminary visitations of the 1980s, an international synod on priestly formation in 1990 with the ensuing apostolic exhortation *Pastores Dabo Vobis* (1992), and the fourth edition of the *Program of Priestly Formation* (PPF, 1993). Each of these emphasized preparing priesthood candidates in all areas of their formation apart from other students and focusing more attention on the norms for priestly formation as set out in the PPF. Thus, especially among those ordained in the latter half of this cohort, as seminarians they were more likely to define themselves as "a man set apart" than were the two cohorts that preceded them. A quarter of these priests were born outside the United States and they are much more diverse than previous cohorts. Three in four are white (76 percent), 12 percent are Hispanic, one in ten is Asian or Asian American, and 3 percent are African or African American. Two in three are members of the post–Vatican II generation (65 percent), but one in three is of the Vatican II generation (30 percent) and 5 percent are of the pre–Vatican II generation. About a fifth (18 percent) of responding priests in this study are in this cohort.

Nativity, Race, and Ethnicity

One demographic characteristic that is beginning to change among priests is their nativity and ethnic heritage. Most priests (89 percent of this sample) were born in the United States, although the proportion is gradually changing as more bishops bring in priests from outside the United States to compensate for the dwindling local supply. The 1970 survey only asked priests whether they were born in the United States. The question was not asked in the 1993 or 2001 surveys. Comparing the 1985 survey to the 2009 survey, one can begin to see the trend toward more priests serving in the United States who were born outside North America and Europe.

It is becoming more common for bishops in some US dioceses to develop relationships with bishops and seminary rectors in other countries to compensate for fewer indigenous vocations. Among priests in the 2009 survey that were born outside the United States, a little more than half (54 percent) were ordained for the diocese (or religious institute) in which they now serve. The remainder came to the United States after

Table 1.3
Nativity of Priests over Time
(Percentage in each category, by year)

	1970	1985	1993	2001	2009
Born in the United States	90%	93%	n/a	n/a	89%
Born in Europe or Canada		6			6
Other international		1			5

ordination. About a quarter of all seminarians now studying in US theologates are foreign-born and three in ten newly ordained priests are born outside the United States (Bendyna and Gautier, 2010).

In the 2009 survey, this trend becomes clearer when we separate responding priests by age group. While more than nine in ten priests of the Vatican II and pre–Vatican II generations are born in the United States, the proportion drops to seven in ten among post–Vatican II priests.

Table 1.4
Nativity by Generation
(Percentage in each category)

	Pre–Vatican II	Vatican II	Post–Vatican II
Born in the United States	91%	93%	70%
Born in Europe or Canada	7	2	9
Other international	2	5	21

This trend to look beyond national borders for priests to serve in the United States is having another effect as well—it is gradually increasing the racial and ethnic diversity of priests in the United States. Generations ago, the German, Italian, and Irish Catholics who immigrated to the United States more often than not brought their own priests with them and petitioned the local bishop for permission to build a "national church" to serve their ethnic group (Morris, 1997). This practice of establishing national parishes for ethnic groups gradually declined, though, in favor of multicultural territorial parishes. And while the Catholic population in the United States has grown increasingly diverse, particularly in the second half of the twentieth century, the priest population has not kept

Figure 1.3
Race/Ethnicity of Catholics and Priests

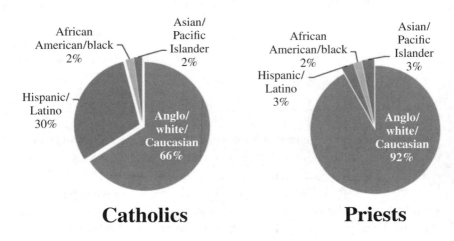

Catholics   **Priests**

pace. Among the adult Catholic population in the United States, about two-thirds identify as white, one in three is Hispanic/Latino, and 2 percent each are Asian/Pacific Islander, black/African American, or other (*U.S. Religious Landscape Survey*, 2007). More than nine in ten priests in the 2009 survey (92 percent) are white, 3 percent are Hispanic/Latino, another 3 percent are Asian or Pacific Islander, and 2 percent identify as black, African American, or African.

Once again, if we compare the priests in the 2009 survey according to their age group, we can show how priests are also gradually becoming more diverse. Younger priests, who are more likely than older priests to be born in a country other than the United States, are also more racially and ethnically diverse than the previous generations.

Table 1.5
Race and Ethnicity by Age Group
(Percentage in each category)

	Pre–Vatican II	Vatican II	Post–Vatican II
Anglo/white/Caucasian	97%	91%	75%
Hispanic/Latino	<1	2	15
Asian/Pacific Islander	2	3	8
African American/black/African	<1	4	2

Figure 1.4
Percentage Retired, by Year

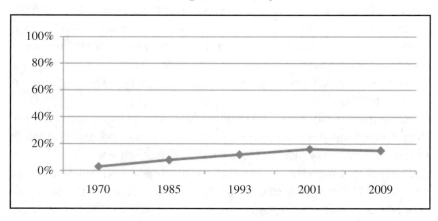

Retirement

Retirement is another factor that is affecting priestly life and ministry today more than it did forty years ago. In 1970, only 3 percent of responding priests were retired. By 2001 the proportion had grown to 16 percent. More than a fifth of the priests responding to the 2009 survey (22 percent) are either retired or semiretired from active ministry (15 percent are retired and 7 percent say they are semiretired).

Table 1.6
Ministry Status
(Percentage in each category)

	All	Diocesan	Religious
What best describes your current ministry status?			
In active ministry	78%	79%	75%
Semiretired (receiving at least partial retirement)	7	4	14
Retired (receiving full retirement benefits)	15	17	11

As figure 1.4 shows, priests that responded to the survey in 2009 are no more likely to say they are retired than they were in 2001. However, the reality is more complex than this simple figure can show. First, none of the surveys before 2001 asked priests about semiretirement; they only offered "retired" as a category in a question about their current ministry position. It is likely that the clarification in question wording in 2009 may have affected this distribution. Second, many dioceses are increasing the age of retirement for priests in response to the reality of fewer priests available for active ministry. Increasingly, bishops are also asking priests who are eligible for retirement to continue in ministry for a number of years, as "senior priests" to relieve the burden on active priests. These conditions are likely suppressing the number of priests who might otherwise be retired.

Retirement is still a concept that is more common in the secular world than it is among priests. More than half of diocesan priests who are of retirement age (66 or older in the secular world) are still active in ministry (52 percent). Likewise, nearly six in ten religious priests of that age (58 percent) are still active in ministry. In a recent CARA study of diocesan priest retirement issues (Gautier and Bendyna, 2009), one active priest described the practice in his diocese as follows:

> Currently, our diocese has no set age for retirement. We are able to receive our full pension at age 68. Many of our number are then elevated to "senior priest" at that time and continue working three to five more years. "Retirement" is a slippery word in our diocese.

Two other priests, now retired, took some offense at the use of the word "retired" to describe priestly life:

> Do not use the term "retired priest"! Use "senior priest," active or inactive.

> I think that many diocesan priests have adopted the attitude that we are members of a professional elite, like lawyers and academics, to the virtual exclusion of the truth that we were called to companion a suffering and despised Savior and privileged to die for him.

Yet another priest noted the difficulty of retiring from priestly ministry because one's identity as a priest is so intertwined with priestly ministry:

> Too often priestly identity is formed by particular assignments, but to understand more the inner meaning of priesthood without assignment is a great challenge.

In contrast, a priest who is still active in ministry noted his frustration with the administrative responsibilities of running a parish and expressed his desire to retire from that burden so that he could devote more time to the pastoral aspects of his ministry:

> By "retire" I mean leave behind administrative duties and return to full-time ministry. If I win the lotto I'd "retire" tomorrow—and do ministry until I dropped dead.

In fact, 78 percent of the priests who described their ministry status as semiretired agreed at least "somewhat" with the statement, "I would be happy to attend primarily to the sacramental life and let the laity assume responsibility for most other functions." Although canon law stipulates that the bishop must provide suitable housing and support for pastors upon their retirement from active ministry, most continue in ministry for years after they become eligible for Social Security. These semiretired priests often serve as "supply priests" who assist active priests in parishes or take over assignments temporarily while others are on vacation or on retreat. CARA surveys of diocesan priests found that semiretired priests typically work five days a week, averaging thirty hours a week, and retired priests still work an average of four days a week, averaging fourteen hours a week.

Ministry

Most priests today are assigned to a parish as their primary ministry. Three in four diocesan priests and 38 percent of religious priests are currently assigned to at least one parish.

Table 1.7
Parish Ministry
(Percentage in each category)

	All	Diocesan	Religious
Are you currently assigned to a parish?			
Yes, one parish (with or without a mission church)	53%	63%	33%
Yes, more than one parish (e.g., clustered parishes)	10	12	5
No, but I help out in a parish	21	18	29
No, not engaged in parish ministry at this time	16	7	33

It is also becoming more common for priests to be assigned to more than one parish as the Catholic population continues to grow while the population of priests keeps declining. Ten percent of the priests responding to this survey are assigned to more than one parish in a situation that is most often referred to as clustered, paired, twinned, yoked, or linked parishes. In these arrangements, which can be short-term or long-term, a priest is assigned administrative and pastoral responsibility for more than one parish. This is a relatively recent accommodation that many bishops are using to forestall having to close parishes; the question was not even asked on previous waves of this survey. While we do not have trend data on this yet, we are confident that this proportion will increase in the next twenty-five years (see Gray, 2010).

Even priests that are not assigned to parishes regularly help out in parishes. One in five priests in this survey say they are not currently assigned to a parish but they help out, most often by providing daily Mass or by celebrating one or more weekend Masses at a nearby parish. Among semiretired priests, almost one in four report that they are assigned to one or more parishes and another half say that they help out in a parish. Only about a quarter of semiretired priests say that they are not engaged in parish ministry. Even among the retired priests, one in ten responded that they are assigned to a parish and more than half (54 percent) say that they help out in a parish.

Just one priest out of six in this sample is not engaged in parish ministry at this time. Religious priests are much more likely than diocesan priests to say that they are not engaged in parish ministry. Many of these religious priests are involved in leadership in their religious community, teaching, writing, retreat work, formation work, or spiritual direction. The diocesan priests who are not engaged in parish ministry are most typically involved in campus ministry or chaplaincy at a nursing home or hospital.

Removing retired and semiretired priests from the analysis and examining only active priests, table 1.8 further reinforces the point that most active diocesan priests are engaged in parish ministry. In fact, close to nine in ten active diocesan priests are involved in a parish in some way as their primary ministry and almost three in four are pastors—47 percent are pastors who are serving in a parish with no other priests assigned to help them. Very few diocesan priests have assignments outside of parish ministry.

Religious priests are much less likely than diocesan priests to be involved in parish ministry. More than half of religious priests are involved

Table 1.8
Current Primary Ministry (among active priests only)
(Percentage in each category)

	All	Diocesan	Religious
What best describes your current ministry?			
Pastor without a parochial vicar (associate pastor)	37%	47%	14%
Pastor with a parochial vicar (associate pastor)	25	29	16
Educational apostolate	9	3	21
Full-time parochial vicar (associate pastor)	7	7	8
Other nonparish ministry	7	2	17
Full-time diocesan or religious community administration	6	3	12
Other parish ministry (e.g., helping out in a parish)	5	5	6
Hospital chaplaincy	2	2	<1
Parochial vicar with special work outside parish	2	1	1
Social service apostolate	1	<1	3
Prison chaplaincy	<1	<1	<1

in education, administration within their religious community, or some other nonparish ministry. Nevertheless, three in ten active religious priests are pastors in parishes and another sixth are associate pastors or help out in parishes in some other way. We would expect that the proportion involved in parish ministry is substantially higher than it would have been in 1970.

These changes mean that priests are less likely to be seen in settings other than parishes, such as teaching in schools or serving as campus ministers, serving as prison or hospital chaplains, working in soup kitchens, shelters, or social service agencies, or working in diocesan or other church-related administrative positions. Among the diocesan priests still active in ministry who responded to this study, 89 percent are in parish ministry, 8 percent are engaged in some type of social service outside of parish ministry, and just 4 percent are involved in some type of nonparish administrative position (such as a vicar for clergy in a diocese or executive director of a Catholic nonprofit organization). For religious priests in this study, 45 percent are in parish ministry, 43 percent are in social service outside of a parish setting (including positions such as retreat director, writer, and spiritual director), and 12 percent are in administration (most often within their religious community).

Another effect of the changing demographics among Catholics in the United States is that priests today are being made pastors, with primary administrative and pastoral responsibility for parishes, much earlier than had been the case in earlier generations. In the 1970s, a newly ordained priest commonly served as a parochial vicar (associate pastor) under the supervision of a pastor in one or more assignments for a number of years, to gain practical experience before receiving a parish of his own.

Table 1.9
Pastor by Ordination Cohort (among active diocesan priests only)
(Percentage in each category)

	Pastor without a Parochial Vicar	Pastor with a Parochial Vicar
Pre–Vatican II (ordained before 1964)	56%	22%
Vatican II (ordained 1964–77)	49	32
Post–Vatican II (ordained 1978–91)	46	32
Millennial (ordained 1992–present)	42	20

Today's newly ordained priests have little time to "learn the ropes" as parochial vicars before taking on the responsibilities of pastors. Many of them will have five years or less as parochial vicars in parishes with pastors before they are placed as pastors. About three-fifths (62 percent) of the diocesan priests who have been ordained since 1992 (the millennial ordination cohort) are already pastors. As recently as 1993, the equivalent proportion was only about two-fifths (39 percent). Even if we restrict the 2009 sample further and look only at those who have been ordained in the last ten years (after 1998), more than half of these diocesan priests (55 percent) are already pastors (compared to 29 percent in 1993). Almost all of them (96 percent) are in parish ministry in some capacity and one in ten already has responsibility for more than one parish!

Conclusion

Priests that responded to the survey in 2009 differ in several important respects from priests who responded in 1970 and in each of the three surveys in between. On average, priests in the United States are older and they are getting ordained later in life. This means that they are more likely to bring life experience with them into priesthood, but it also means that they may be less likely to celebrate their golden jubilee of fifty years of priesthood than priests who were ordained at age 25 in 1970. More priests today are retired from active ministry, although most stay involved in ministry to some extent, often serving as "supply priests" for priests in parish ministry.

Priests today are also somewhat more diverse in their race and ethnic background, although they do not represent the diversity that is the Catholic Church in the United States. More of them were born outside the United States, too, particularly among the youngest generation of priests.

Finally, diocesan priests today are engaged in parish ministry to the exclusion of nearly everything else. Even among priests in religious orders, who have traditionally been more involved in other apostolates such as education, hospitals, and social service, almost half of those responding to this survey are involved primarily in parish ministry at some level.

In the next three chapters we will explore how these demographic changes are playing out in the lives and attitudes of priests today. Chapter 2 examines satisfaction among priests and finds that priests remain very happy in their lives and ministry despite these changes.

Chapter 2

Satisfaction in Priestly Life and Ministry

> I truly love being a priest. Not that I haven't had struggles like we all do, but what a joy this road has been for me. I'm only sad about not having too many more years left, but I will use each day to embrace the Lord more deeply in my own life and share that presence with any who seek Him in my work as a priest.
>
> —*A respondent to the survey*

General Satisfaction

Some of the challenges facing the US Church and its priests a decade into the Church's third millennium are so familiar, they hardly need enumerating. A decline in vocations since the 1960s has already led to a 31 percent drop in the number of priests in the last thirty-five years. And the oldest priests of the Vatican II generation will start reaching retirement age this decade, further reducing the overall number available for ministry. Meanwhile the number of lay Catholics continues to rise with population growth and with immigration from Latin America. Bishops have tried to address ministry pressures in a number of ways, including unpopular rounds of parish closures and reorganizations. But the bulk of the ministry burden has fallen on priests themselves. Pastors are increasingly leading larger parishes and, most often, doing so without the benefit of associate pastors. In a 2002 CARA poll, nearly one-fifth of nonretired priests reported that they worked *over eighty hours* in a typical week, a response that was particularly common among those serving in large parishes (Perl and Froehle, 2002). Despite mounting administrative responsibilities, priests often place great pressure on themselves to be available to the people they serve. In the same poll, three-quarters of diocesan parish priests reported that they were on call for their parishioners twenty-four hours a day.

Table 2.1
Questions Regarding General Satisfaction
(Percentage in each category)

	All	Diocesan	Religious
Which of the following statements most clearly reflects your feeling about your future in the priesthood?			
I will definitely not leave	86%	86%	88%
I probably will not leave	11	11	9
I am uncertain about my future	3	3	3
I probably will leave	0	0	0
If you had your choice again, would you enter the priesthood?			
Definitely yes	76%	74%	80%
Probably yes	19	21	17
Probably not	4	5	3
Definitely not	1	1	1
How happy are you with your life as a priest?			
Very happy	61%	59%	66%
Pretty happy	36	37	33
Not too happy	3	3	1
Not at all happy	<1	<1	<1

Given such challenges and a rather bleak outlook for future ordinations, can we presume that satisfaction among US priests languishes at an all-time low? Not at all. Priests express quite high levels of satisfaction with their lives and ministry. Table 2.1 shows responses from the 2009 survey to questions that reflect general satisfaction with one's life and ministry. The priests were asked if they are likely to leave the priesthood in the future. Out of all respondents, 86 percent report that they "will definitely not leave." Not a single priest responding to the survey said he "probably will leave." Next, about three-quarters of priests report that if they had the choice again, they would "definitely" enter the priesthood. Just 5 percent say they would "probably" or "definitely" not enter the priesthood again. Finally, respondents were asked how happy they are with their lives as priests. Sixty-one percent describe themselves as "very happy" and 36 percent as "pretty happy." Of course, this is not to deny that there are very real problems and frustrations in priestly life—we will discuss those in the next chapter—but by and large priests are considerably happier than one might expect. And, in fact, our findings are consistent with others; in recent decades virtually all studies of priests have found relatively high levels of satisfaction (Hoge and Wenger, 2003:29; Greeley, 2004:49–53).

The *Los Angeles Times* conducted a national survey of Catholic priests in 2002, just a few months after the clergy sexual abuse issue first erupted in large scale on front pages across the country. If ever there was a time when morale might be low in the priesthood, surely this was it. The *Times* asked, "All things considered, would you say you are satisfied or dissatisfied with the way your life as a priest is going these days?" Seventy percent said they were "very satisfied" and 21 percent said they were "somewhat satisfied" (Watanabe, 2002). The wording of the *Times* question differs from the wording of the question in our survey about happiness and for that reason our purpose here is not to compare the exact percentages. But the *Times* findings demand essentially the same conclusion. Even at the height of the scandal—when priests might understandably be tempted to question the life to which they had committed themselves—most reported relatively high satisfaction.

In their own words, priests often reaffirm what the numbers suggest. An open-ended question in the survey asked, "What recommendations would you have for a young man who is discerning a vocation to priesthood today?"[1] There is a great deal of variety among the responses, ranging from very practical steps for discernment and spiritual growth to philosophical reflections on the priesthood. Many priests, however, respond by sharing a sense of the joy they experience in their lives and ministry in spite of the accompanying difficulties:[2]

> It's a challenging and sometimes very difficult vocation. However, it is, without a doubt, extremely rewarding!

> I would tell him it is a good life, very fulfilling.

> Priesthood is a great and wonderful way to serve the Lord. While being a priest is very challenging, it is very fulfilling.

> I would wholeheartedly encourage him—it is a great, very fulfilling life—awesome!

---

[1] This question was repeated in focus groups, and a few of the responses transcribed below come from that setting.

[2] Here and throughout the book, when indented quotations are separated by a blank line, the quotations come from different individuals.

Many other responses to this open-ended question urge caution and reflection for men considering the priesthood. Yet from over seven hundred total responses, only eleven are entirely discouraging of a vocation. These discouraging opinions, some of which are transcribed in chapter 8, generally allude to topics such as celibacy, the structure of the Church, and the leadership of the hierarchy—exactly the kind of issues that previous research has found to inhibit some priests from encouraging vocations (Los Angeles Times Poll, 2002). But do such discouraging opinions mean the priests themselves are unhappy? Though a few are unhappy, most are not. We examined the attitudes of those eleven priests and found that four describe their lives as priests as "very happy" and five as "pretty happy." Only two say they are "not too happy."

In his book on the 1970 survey of priests, Greeley began a chapter by observing, "It is frequently said that the Catholic clergy in the United States are going through a very serious morale crisis" (1972:215). He then proceeded to analyze data on priests and college-educated men of equivalent ages and observed that priests "seem to be happier than comparable groups of men" (1972:22). Twenty-three years later, Hoge and colleagues examined self-reported happiness among diocesan priests in the 1993 survey, concluding, "Observers claiming that priests today are in the midst of a morale crisis are wrong" (Hoge, Shields, and Griffin, 1995:201). As real and significant as the problems priests face are, by now there can be no basis for questioning whether Catholic priests are really happy in their lives. They are. We should focus instead on understanding why this is the case.

A first step is to ask whether priests are relatively unique in comparison to other clergy in the United States. In 2001, a national survey of congregation leaders (pastors, excluding associate and assistant pastors) was reported by Jackson Carroll and several colleagues for Duke University's Pulpit & Pew National Survey of Pastoral Leaders (Carroll, 2006). Table 2.2 compares responses of Catholic priests to those of clergy in three other religious traditions: mainline Protestant, conservative Protestant, and historically black. The Catholic priests are most likely to describe themselves as very satisfied with their current ministry, although differences among the traditions are not particularly large. Differences are also relatively small on satisfaction with one's spiritual life. There is more variation among the four religious traditions when it comes to considering leaving the ministry and having doubts about being called to the ministry, but priests are neither highest nor lowest on these items. The most important point of these findings is that Catholic priests do not differ greatly from clergy of other faiths. Clergy of all major faith traditions in the US appear to be relatively satisfied.

Table 2.2
Satisfaction of Pastors, by Religious Tradition

	Catholic	Mainline Protestant	Conservative Protestant	Historically Black
"Very satisfied" with current ministry position	79%	72%	74%	75%
"Very satisfied" with spiritual life	40	37	44	49
Has "never" considered leaving pastoral ministry in the last five years	76	62	70	84
Has "never" doubted being called by God to the ministry in the last five years	56	44	69	78

Source: 2001 Pulpit & Pew National Survey of Pastoral Leaders

Comparing clergy to other occupations can provide a clue to the sources of their satisfaction. Tom Smith of the National Opinion Research Center analyzed job satisfaction among people who responded to the General Social Survey from 1986 to 2006 (University of Chicago News Office, 2007). Clergy exhibited higher satisfaction than members of any other occupation included in the study. Asked, "On the whole, how satisfied are you with the work you do?" 87 percent of clergy described themselves as "very satisfied," compared with 47 percent of the population as a whole. Moreover, clergy's relatively high satisfaction was not limited just to their work. Clergy were also most likely to describe themselves as "very happy" with their lives generally. What other occupations join clergy near the top of the satisfaction scale? Smith lists several: firefighters, physical therapists, education administrators, painters and sculptors, teachers, authors, psychologists, and special education teachers. While there is variety in this list, one notable thread is the number of helping professions represented. A career spent in service to others—like that lived by physical therapists, teachers, psychologists, and clergy—tends to make people happy.

Another probable reason clergy generally and Catholic priests specifically tend to express great satisfaction and happiness is that they are
doing work they find immensely meaningful. Finding one's work meaningful is very important in job satisfaction (Brooks, 2008:168–69). For
a religious person, what can be more central to life than building and
leading a community of people toward greater love and service of God?
And indeed, it is important to emphasize that the parish is a *community*.
For priests, the people they serve are not "clients," as other kinds of social
service providers might call them, and priests' jobs are not nine-to-five
activities separate from the rest of their lives (as indicated by the fact
that a multitude are on-call twenty-four hours a day). Many think of
themselves as belonging to their parish in just the same way that other
parishioners do. And despite all the pressures that accompany service to
their parishioners, many priests receive support from parishioners in
return. Catholic priests, more than clergy in other denominations, may
also build community with each other. Lacking spouses and children,
there is a particular incentive to lean on each other for support and
camaraderie. The ties of community among priests are, of course, most
evident in religious orders. But even diocesan priests often share a special
bond and sense of fraternity with one another.

Of these three possible sources of happiness in priestly life—service,
meaning, and community—one is very strongly reflected in responses
to the open-ended survey question (recommendations for a young man
discerning a vocation). The importance of entering the priesthood for the
purpose of serving others is heavily stressed by priests. And many of
them overtly link service to others with their own personal happiness:

> If you are thinking about your own happiness you will be disappointed.
> If you are thinking about the happiness and spiritual well-being of others,
> you will be happy yourself and be spiritually enriched.

> Be with the people, spend time with them. Enjoy the people of God; they
> are great! Show them you love them and will care for their needs.

> A great life, vocation. Like marriage, the more you give (serve), the more
> you receive (are fulfilled).

> It can be a great life; be sure you become a priest to serve, not to become
> somebody important or so that you can tell others what to do.

> Be realistic about the vocation of a priest. Realize there will be many
> challenges, some loneliness and frustration. But also many rewards and

it can be a very satisfying life of service. Service is the key. Don't try to become a priest unless you want to serve God and His people.

Love the people you are ordained to serve—love them the way Jesus loves you. If you have any other motivations or agendas you will be a poor priest and unhappy.

Get involved in service work that is not in the sanctuary. Visit the sick, teach kids, build houses for Habitat, work in a soup kitchen. If you don't love serving, don't consider priesthood.

Fully understand the meaning of: "To serve and not to be served."

Priests are less likely to mention the rewards of community and meaning in their responses to the question about advice to a young man considering priesthood, but they do occasionally appear. For example, a few priests mention fellowship and fraternity with other priests. A number of priests also mention importance of pursuing a life one finds meaningful. These responses, like many of those transcribed above, often emphasize the happiness and fulfillment that accompanies these aspects of priestly life:

The fraternity among priests really brings them together, and they really admire each other.

There is no doubt in my mind that I would recommend the seminary. I tell the high school kids that serve our church that there are great days and bad days, wonderful experiences, horrible experiences. But by and large you are going to be happy. What attracted me to the priesthood was a seminarian who worked at a summer camp I was at. What struck me was how happy they [he and the other seminarians] were. I was struck by their fraternity, and I wanted a part of that. I try to expose the kids to that fraternity. I always try to expose the kids to our seminarians. They are a blast.

It is a great life. Develop one's own spirituality that can be used throughout priesthood. Be a part of a priestly fraternity group.

Priesthood is a most meaningful and satisfactory life for yourself and those you serve.

"You want to make a real difference in this world in your life." When I had my twenty-fifth jubilee, I stood up (and had rehearsed what I was going to say): "If there is one thing I know I am doing exactly what God wants me to do after twenty-five years." That's a great thing. "You want to make a difference. You want your life to really mean something in this world. Think about this."

Accept the challenge. It is a wonderful and meaningful vocation.

It is a meaningful life, working with people to form hearts and minds in the spirit of the Gospel.

Increasing Satisfaction over Time

Not only are priests relatively satisfied with their lives and ministry but satisfaction actually has been increasing over time (Hoge and Wenger, 2003:29), even as the decline in priests available for ministry has accelerated and the sexual abuse issue has emerged. For example, the 91 percent of priests who described themselves as either "somewhat" or "very" satisfied in response to the 2002 *Los Angeles Times* survey of priests, conducted at the height of the sexual abuse scandal, was actually up slightly from 89 percent in 1993 (Greeley, 2004:50). Table 2.3 compares responses from our survey on two questions—the likelihood of leaving the priesthood and whether one would choose the priesthood again—to responses from previous surveys in this series. Today, as we have seen, 97 percent of priests say they will "probably" or "definitely" *not* leave the priesthood. This proportion has risen steadily from 88 percent when the question was first asked in 1970. Similarly the percentage who would "probably" or "definitely" choose the priesthood again, currently at 95 percent, is up from 79 percent in 1970. Table 2.3 also shows that the proportion of priests who describe themselves as "very happy" was rising from 1970 to 2001.[3]

Table 2.3
Satisfaction of Priests Over Time

	1970	1985	1993	2001	2009
"Definitely" or "probably" will not leave the priesthood	88%	93%	93%	95%	97%
Would "definitely" or "probably" choose the priesthood again	79	—*	—*	88	95
Is "very" happy**	28	37	39	46	—**

* Not asked

** Question wording: "Taking things all together, how would you say things are these days? Are you very happy, pretty happy, or not too happy?" The 2009 question is not comparable due to wording changes.

[3] Due to wording differences, results for the happiness question in our survey cannot be compared to those from prior surveys.

Figure 2.1
Increasing Satisfaction Across Time
among Priests Who Were in Their 30s in 1985

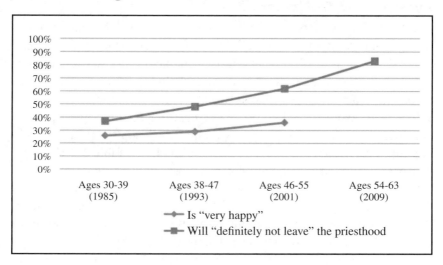

Why might satisfaction be increasing? One explanation we have heard is that the priesthood went through a transition period in the aftermath of Vatican II. According to this argument, changes associated with the Council brought about a temporary crisis of identity in the priesthood that coincided with a large outflow of men from the priesthood. The theology of Vatican II tended to deemphasize the special nature of priestly life vis-à-vis the laity. This made it easier for doubts to arise about one's vocation and led to a period of adjustment. Men who were dissatisfied with their lives as priests left the priesthood and the priests who remained eventually became more comfortable with the newer understanding of the role of the priest in Church life. However this is essentially an argument about events that took place in the aftermath of the Council, the late 1960s and 1970s. It is hard for us to imagine that the process of readjustment among priests would have lasted to the present day. More than four decades have now passed since the end of Vatican II, and satisfaction continues to rise.

The changing age distribution of priests represents another possible reason satisfaction has risen among priests. Priests tend to become more satisfied as they grow older.[4] As an example, let's look at the priests who

---

[4] Age differences largely explain the small satisfaction differences between religious and diocesan priests seen in table 2.1.

Table 2.4
Satisfaction, by Year and Age

	1985	1993	2001	2009
Percentage who will "definitely not leave" the priesthood				
30s	37%	52%	64%	88%
40s	44	50	57	73
50s	69	66	70	81
60s	91	87	84	85
70s and older	96	97	97	95
All priests	62	72	79	86
Percentage who are "very happy"				
30s	26%	37%	47%	
40s	32	31	40	
50s	40	33	41	
60s	42	42	47	
70s and older	53	53	53	
All priests	37	39	46	

were in their 30s when the 1985 survey took place. (See figure 2.1). At that time 26 percent described themselves as "very happy," and 37 percent reported that they would "definitely not leave" the priesthood. In the 2001 survey, these figures had changed considerably among priests of this cohort (who were by that time 46 to 55 years old). Thirty-six percent described themselves as "very happy," and 62 percent said they would "definitely not leave."[5] In the 2009 survey, 82 percent of these priests (now 54 to 63 years old) say they will "definitely" not leave. Some of this increased satisfaction, of course, reflects resignations of priests who were originally among the least happy; they are no longer available to be surveyed. But for present purposes, the degree to which the age-satisfaction relationship reflects resignations versus "real" change among priests who remain is not the important point. We are interested, rather, in how this relationship can lead to an overall increase in satisfaction over time. As we saw in chapter 1, the mean age of priests in the United States continues to ascend, as it has for several decades now. In 1970,

[5] These percentages exclude priests ordained after 1985.

less than 10 percent of priests were over the age of 65 (Hoge and Wenger, 2003:21). Now it is more than 40 percent of priests. Table 2.4 shows that satisfaction has generally remained steadily high among older priests (those ages 60 and over) since the mid-1980s. Given these trends, overall satisfaction among priests could be expected to have risen over time, even if nothing else had changed.

Table 2.4 shows that something else has changed. Today's younger priests are more satisfied than younger priests were in years past. The table also reveals a relatively large increase of priests in their 40s who say they will definitely not leave the priesthood. Thus, to fully understand why satisfaction among priests as a whole has increased over time, we must understand why it has done so among younger men.

This could be related to changes in ministry. In the 1960s, Joseph Fichter conducted a survey of associate pastors that revealed frustration with their ministry. The associates often chafed under the supervision of their pastors and the mundane tasks they were assigned. Many would have preferred, at minimum, better use of their talents and, ideally, promotion to positions with greater autonomy and responsibility for parish leadership (Fichter, 1968). Due to the declining numbers available for ministry, priests are increasingly being assigned to full pastor positions at ages much younger than they were just a few decades ago.[6] Though it may play some role, we find, in fact, that the rise in general satisfaction of younger priests cannot be attributed solely to quicker promotion to full pastor positions. Even *among* associate pastors, general satisfaction has increased substantially. In 1985, 44 percent of full-time associate pastors said they would "definitely not" leave the priesthood. By 2009, this proportion had risen to an astounding 93 percent.

Alternately, changes in vocations may provide a clue to increasing satisfaction among younger priests. Far fewer young men are entering the priesthood than in the past. The number of Catholic men who report having ever considered the priesthood has dropped among the youngest generation, though not nearly as precipitously as seminary enrollment and ordinations.[7]

---

[6] In the 1985 survey, 60 percent of priests in their 30s were associate pastors and 14 percent were pastors. In the 2009 survey, the percentages have nearly equalized; 37 percent are associate pastors and 34 percent are pastors.

[7] In the 2001 CARA Catholic Poll, a national telephone survey of self-identified Catholics, 18 percent of men of the Vatican II generation (born 1943 to 1961) reported that they had considered becoming a priest or brother at least "somewhat seriously." Among men of the post–Vatican II generation (born since 1961) 9 percent reported this, including only 6 percent of those born since 1970.

There are almost certainly multiple causes of the vocation decline (a controversial topic that lies beyond the scope of this book), but one of these might be freer and more informed self-selection among young men who consider the priesthood. In other words, men who once might have joined the priesthood and wound up being unhappy may now consider a vocation but ultimately decide not to pursue it, either because they feel less pressured to do so or because they are better able to judge priesthood as a poor fit for them. This is a difficult hypothesis to test, but we can do so indirectly by comparing priests ordained at different ages. Men choosing the priesthood today are often being ordained at somewhat later ages, typically after having worked in the secular sphere (Gautier et al., 2010). In our sample, about half the men ordained since 1995 were over 35 when they were ordained. Such priests may have the life experience to make more informed decisions about whether they want to enter priesthood in the first place and, later, to better evaluate whether they would have been any happier in a life outside their priestly ministry. However, we do not find evidence to support this supposition. Controlling for current age, the age at which priests were ordained does not significantly predict their satisfaction.

Finally, we consider another possible reason that satisfaction has increased so much among the young: the greater orthodoxy among priests of the millennial ordination cohort (a cohort that of course includes some older members, but two-thirds of which consists of priests currently in their 30s and 40s). By greater orthodoxy we mean the more "traditionalist" positions they take on theology, ecclesiology, liturgy, sexual morality, faithfulness to the magisterium, and related topics. Why might such beliefs among younger priests be associated with satisfaction? One possibility is that today's younger priests find more affirmation for their beliefs from the Church's hierarchy and the general movement toward traditionalism in recent decades. This may translate into a feeling of greater support from Church leadership. In our survey, 73 percent of priests under 40 report receiving "strong" support from the Vatican. In the 1993 survey this was the case for just 33 percent of priests under 40. Today's young priests are also more likely to report strong support from their own bishop (79 percent of those under 40 in 2009 compared to 52 percent of those under 40 in 1993).[8]

---

[8] As we will see in the next chapter, today's priests under 40 also seem slightly more hopeful about the future of the Church than today's older priests. But they do not differ in this regard from young priests of the mid-1980s.

Another possibility lies not so much with the beliefs themselves but the zeal and certainty with which they are held and their connection with a sense of obedience to God. Hoge and Wenger extensively discussed the relative orthodoxy of young priests and described it as springing from "a longing for the time-tested, the true, and the authoritative in knowing God's will" (2003:121). A priest in his 30s talks about the outlook of younger priests today and speculates about its relationship with satisfaction:

> There's really a different sense of spirituality among priests of my generation in terms of doing God's will and really trying to develop a prayer life. . . . I think that brings peace and satisfaction. So we're happy doing God's will. Let's say, I'm just guessing, in the 1970s, if you're in rebellion mode, ultimately that doesn't make you very happy. If all you're thinking about is: "The Church is evil. The rules are bad," you sound like an immature little brat. It's the immature Church. At least that would be one theory I have. So no wonder you're not fully happy because, you know, you think your Mom is evil. Well we, this age group, tend to think Holy Mother Church is a good Mom, and She knows what's best to give Her children. It may be difficult. It may be difficult to do your homework or eat your vegetables, but Mom knows what's best for us. It really is for our benefit. Trying to do it the best we can, we find real peace and satisfaction.

From a social scientific standpoint, the certainty with which beliefs are held represents a very plausible explanation. Research has shown that people who are more certain of their political positions (typically those at the two extremes of the political spectrum) tend to express greater happiness with their lives (Brooks, 2008). It seems likely that the same is true of religious certainty. There is a reason that doubts are said to "nag" people. They erode one's sense of purpose and commitment. Earlier, we discussed the significance of leading a life of meaning for priests' satisfaction. Experiencing their lives and priestly ministry as meaningful is surely much easier if they are certain about their beliefs. Today's youngest priests may be more likely to feel such certainty than were the young priests of prior decades. Unfortunately, there is not extensive survey data that would allow us to measure doubt or uncertainty among priests. So this possibility, though it strikes us as quite plausible, must remain speculative.

Hoge and Wenger did demonstrate, however, that beliefs about priestly identity, or what they call the "ontological status of the priest" (2003:114), are related to satisfaction. Those who believe more strongly in maintaining a clear distinction between priests and laity tend to express greater happiness and tend to be less inclined to leave the priesthood. Hoge and Wenger reasoned this may be because the alternative leaves priests with "a less distinctive priestly identity, providing them with less affirmation and self esteem" (126). Whatever the case, the researchers found that younger priests tend to place more emphasis on maintaining such a distinctive priestly identity (125–26); it is one, though by no means the only, aspect of their more traditionalist beliefs.[9]

The results from our survey confirm the Hoge and Wenger findings. Using a number of questions about priestly identity, we recreated the "cultic model index" developed by Hoge and colleagues in previous research (Hoge and Wenger, 2003). Put simply, this is a scale that aligns the survey respondents according to how strongly they believe that priestly identity should remain distinct from that of the laity.[10] Hoge summarized the cultic model of priesthood as being concerned with maintaining the view of the priest as "a man set apart." He labeled the other end of the spectrum as the servant-leader model, the idea that the priest is a leader serving from within the community of believers, more of a leader among equals than a man set apart. Certainly there is truth in both models and no priest is consistently or unilaterally one or the other. In several places in this book we use the cultic model index as shorthand for broad "traditionalist" versus "progressive" religious beliefs, but again it is important to keep in mind that the index is actually constructed using attitudes on the specific issue of priestly identity.

---

[9] Have we then come full circle? Above, we addressed and then dismissed the idea that a temporary crisis in priestly identity resulting from Vatican II can explain the rise in satisfaction among priests. We stand by this conclusion; we do not believe that beliefs of younger priests today represent a return to a supposed equilibrium that existed prior to the Council. They are an unrelated phenomenon.

[10] The questions used by Hoge and colleagues were five agree-disagree statements (2006:175–76): (1) Ordination confers on the priest a new status or a permanent character that makes him essentially different from the laity within the Church. (2) The priest is the man in society who proclaims God's word and provides for sacramental encounter with God in Christ. (3) I feel that I am most a priest when I am saying Mass and hearing confessions. (4) As a priest, I feel that I am a member of the bishop's team. When I am doing a job that has the local bishop's approval, I am doing priestly work. (5) The idea that a priest is a "man set apart" is a barrier to the full realization of true Christian community (reverse coded).

We divided priests into four roughly equal groups according to their position on the index. Of those who are in the bottom quartile of the scale—the fourth of all priests who most strongly adhere to the servant-leader model—44 percent describe themselves as "very happy." But of priests who are in the top quartile—those most strongly adhering to the cultic model—77 percent describe themselves as "very happy." This confirms a link between more traditional views of priesthood and satisfaction. Our results also provide further evidence that today's younger priests are embracing the cultic model of priesthood—although differences between these young men and their older counterparts are not as dramatic as one might imagine. As shown in table 2.5, 68 percent of priests who are in their 30s score in one of the top two quartiles of the cultic model scale. This proportion gradually falls as age increases until it bottoms out at 33 percent for priests in their 60s. (It then rises among those 70 and older to 50 percent.) Thus, while we would not describe the differences between younger and older priests as an extreme polarization, the data are consistent with the conjecture that a relationship exists between traditional views of the priesthood and general satisfaction among today's younger priests.

In summary, we believe there are at least two important reasons that general satisfaction has risen among priests in recent decades: the aging of priests and the tendency toward orthodoxy among the members of the millennial ordination cohort.

Table 2.5
Cultic Model of the Priesthood, by Age
(Percentage who fall into each approximate
quartile* of the cultic model index)

	Lowest Quartile ("Progressive")			Highest Quartile ("Traditionalist")
30s	9%	23%	31%	37%
40s	14	32	18	36
50s	22	32	24	22
60s	33	34	19	14
70s and older	22	28	26	24
All priests	24	31	23	23

* As the "All priests" row shows, the categories are not exactly 25 percent each. This is due to an imperfectly smooth distribution of the index scores.

Specific Sources of Satisfaction

Table 2.6 explores some of the specific sources of satisfaction in priestly life and ministry. The survey asked priests to indicate how important each is to them on a scale ranging from "no importance" to "great importance." The table lists the percentage who describe each as being of "great importance." At the upper end of the scale, 94 percent of priests say that the "joy of administering the sacraments and presiding over the liturgy" is a great source of satisfaction for them. Not far behind, at 83 percent, is preaching the Word, which is obviously closely tied to

Table 2.6
Sources of Satisfaction
(Percentage saying each is of "great" importance as a source of satisfaction)

	All	Diocesan	Religious
Joy of administering the sacraments and presiding over the liturgy	94%	95%	91%
Satisfaction of preaching the Word	83	82	83
Being part of a community of Christians who are working together to share the Good News of the Gospel	73	71	76
Opportunity to work with many people and be a part of their lives	71	71	70
Sense of well-being that comes from living the common life with like-minded priests*			71
Opportunity to exercise intellectual and creative abilities	58	57	59
Serving as an *alter Christus* to the faithful	54	55	52
Sense of well-being that comes from working with like-minded priests	51	47	60
Challenge of being the leader of a Catholic Christian community	50	54	42
Organizing and administering the work of the Church	30	32	27
Engaging in efforts at social reform	25	24	26
Respect that comes to the priestly office	22	24	16

* Asked of religious priests only

celebrating the Eucharist. These results are perhaps unsurprising. The sacraments are at the heart of Catholic spirituality, priestly ministry, and indeed priestly identity itself. In the survey 80 percent of priests agree with the statement, "I feel that I am most a priest when I am saying (celebrating) Mass and hearing confessions." Further, the frustrations, challenges, and administrative stresses that accompany other aspects of priests' work are probably comparatively rare in these areas of ministry. Administering the sacraments and preaching the Word remain more purely spiritual activities. Perhaps most important, celebration of the sacraments often coincides with important moments in the lives of Catholic laypeople.

When asked in interviews and focus groups about the greatest sources of joy in their lives, priests often talked with us about the sacraments and preaching. Following are some examples:

> As it relates to my ministry as a religious priest, the greatest joy of my life is celebrating the sacraments, the special moments in people's lives. Because I am an ordained priest in the Catholic Church, I'm invited into the most sacred moments of people's lives: when their loved ones are dying, when they're burying their loved ones; when people are marrying and committing their lives together forever; when they're bringing their children into the Church after they've conceived them in love. That's phenomenal grace in my life—to be trusted by someone who has a deep understanding of how they have sinned and wants to reconnect with God and God's people through the sacraments. And to be invited to pray with them during those moments of grace, that's the greatest gift. . . . That's a huge joy. Another one would be preaching the Gospel, especially on Sundays. I really would like to think that I work hard preparing my homilies and gathering people for prayer and celebrating the Eucharist in a way that gives people experience of God's grace in their lives. That, too, is a rich blessing for me.

> I often tell students when that question arises, that the greatest joy is being invited into people's lives because I'm a priest, not because of who I am, whether it's in joyful times or sad times. It could be anointing someone in the hospital or in their home. Or working with a family after death. Or it can be a couple's first baby, a wedding, a fiftieth wedding anniversary, different things like that where I've truly felt a part of people's lives.

> I have a great passion for preaching. Since I was ordained a deacon, preparation for preaching has been the cornerstone of my prayer life. My prayer life pretty much goes from one homily to the next. I've gotten very

strong feedback that God seems to be at work in me when I preach. . . .
Many times after Mass you stand outside and you shake hands with people.
Most people just say, "Nice homily." But many times I've had people
come to me and say, "Oh Father, thank you. That homily was for *me*.
Thank you so much for that." I once had an old woman come up and grab
my arm and say, "You have to start a homily school." I said, "Okay." She
grabbed my hand even tighter and said, "No, I really mean it." She walked
away and then ran back. She said, "Don't forget!" "Oh, okay, I'll write it
down." . . . And then offering Mass, to be able to bring the Eucharistic
Word to people and to have that experience of intimacy in Christ. Offering
Mass is the capstone of my priesthood.

One is the Sacrament of Penance or Reconciliation, especially when I hear
a penitent say, "Father, my last confession was thirty years ago." It just
breaks me to pieces and melts my heart because the prospect of coming
home, coming back to God's embraces, is just amazing.

The kids always ask, "What's your favorite part of priesthood?" and I always say, "hearing confessions." That always kind of shocks them because
most people think I should say the Mass and Eucharist, which *are* a joy,
but to me are second to confessions. There's just nothing like that one-
on-one personal, intimate moment of being an instrument of God's mercy.
You can say to someone, "Your sins are forgiven. You have a new beginning. You can leave here a new man, a new woman." . . . To be able to
help heal somebody from their wounds is just absolutely powerful and
very humbling. It's just awesome. Individually, you really feel like you're
making a difference when you bring a soul back to the Lord, especially
somebody who's been gone a long time. This past Lent I had a lot of big
fish, a lot of people who said their last confession was *forty* years ago.
And of course it entails a lot of tears, a lot of weeping. They're just cleans-
ing themselves of their sins, and the Lord says, "You're forgiven." That
is the best.

After that, the most satisfying thing is always the Mass, the Eucharist—changing bread and wine into the Lord's body and blood. Incredible.
It's the focus of every day, of course. That's the focal point of spiritual
life. And then the other sacraments. It's just wonderful to be a part of
Baptisms and weddings. And the Sacrament of the Anointing of the Sick.
There have been some beautiful moments of anointing somebody. In the
past five years, I've actually been with two people when they've died. It's
kind of a unique experience. In the case of one man, he was breathing. I
was anointing him. We were praying the Litany of the Saints. Then he
stopped breathing. . . . Just to be there at those moments.

"Being part of a community of Christians who are working together to share the Good News of the Gospel" is also a relatively important source of satisfaction for priests, with 73 percent reporting that it is of "great" importance. So is the "opportunity to work with many people and be part of their lives," at 71 percent. There are many potential sources of community and relationships in priestly life, though comments in focus groups and interviews tend to point to the bonds that are forged in parishes and other places of ministry. Below are further examples of responses priests gave when asked about their greatest sources of joy and satisfaction:

> One of my greatest fulfillments is to see the people rallying behind me, the Spirit in the parish. Seeing people working together and achieving one goal for the parish. That, to me, is amazing.

> The relationship with my parishioners. I have wonderful parishioners. Most of them are seniors because it is a winter vacation place. There's a lot of terminal life issues. . . . I also enjoy the relationship I have with an incredible diversity of people who are wonderful to be with. And that makes up for a lot of the other stuff that goes on.

> At my high school the demography of the student body is that a majority, about 60 percent, is Latino. Of the remainder, about 35 percent is of African descent, either African or African American. The people are very expressive in their relationships. We're not just school staff members to them. They want friendships with us. They invite us to their homes at key moments in the lives of family members—all family members, not just the kids who attend the school. They ask us to come bless their houses. We accompany them in their whole lives, not just in the education of their children.

> I really appreciate the time that I can pray with my people in all different forms. We do the Liturgy of the Hours before Mass. I enjoy that rather than praying by myself. . . . I also enjoy being with people who are in a crisis, to be a source of comfort for people.

> Very often I'll get a knock on the door in the middle of the night from students because I live in a dorm. They'll say, "Hi, you don't know me, but my roommate says you're good to talk to when everything turns to shit. My life is turning to shit, so I'm here to get your help." So when kids are in crisis they know they can come to me. One of the students introduced me at a talk and said, "Look, there are a lot of priests on this campus but when one says to another, 'You should go and talk to the Father,' we

all know that we're talking about you." So, yeah, I've had a really deeply satisfying experience of spiritual fatherhood. . . . And the students really, really want to have a father. . . . Things like that have been very rewarding. It shows that young people are willing to accept me as a spiritual father.

Though service to others is a central motivation for priests' vocations and ministry, they readily spoke with us about the blessings, affirmations, and inspiration they receive from the communities of laypeople they serve:

> Just the interaction with people, seeing their faith. I've been hearing confessions at [a shrine]. You get all kinds of people coming in there. The faith of people and their attempts and willingness to lead good lives is really a source of inspiration.

> Working with the poor evangelizes *me*. . . . It teaches me about what it means to be a believer. A lot of people in the world can depend on things, or degrees, or jobs, or titles for their identity. People who don't have any of those things still find their identity as sons and daughters of God. I find that that's a challenge to me. It teaches me the Good News, that God is not one who wants us to acquire those things for our identity but basically asks that we get all of our identity from God.

> Satisfaction with the priesthood really comes from the affirmation of the people, the love of the people. I thank God every day I am so loved. In the parish, people are always giving me feedback on how they like my homilies, things like that. . . . So that's where I get all the satisfaction.

For diocesan priests, the question about being part of a community of Christians is a better predictor of how happy they are in their lives than any of the other satisfaction items in table 2.6 (though none is a particularly great predictor). Of course, religious priests share a special community with the brother priests of their orders. Seventy-one percent of religious priests say they find great satisfaction in the "sense of well-being that comes from living the common life with like-minded priests."

> My religious community is definitely a blessing for me. It's a source of support. I mean, it's no utopia or Shangri-la. I am definitely, at times, challenged by living with and among my brothers because we don't all think alike all the time. We have different understandings or viewpoints. . . . But I definitely like sharing life on a daily basis with men and doing so in a way that is grounded in prayer, ministry, and a common

life. It's a place where I can be challenged and sometimes stretched, be repeatedly welcomed to the human race in terms of humility where my brothers invite me to grow. I'm grateful for that.

I know I wasn't meant to live alone. I do enjoy solitude some times; there are days when I just want to lock the door. But I'm an extrovert. I want to share my life with others. I enjoy the camaraderie of community and the shared core values—not that we're all robots or anything like that. There is a diversity of opinion. But what is essential is what people share. We are a group of people who look out for each other. When moving to a new city where I don't know anybody else, there will be a community there for me. There is a group of brothers anywhere you go. And it's nice to be able to give to my brothers too. It's not just about what you get from the community. I like being able to give to my brothers—in a different way than I give in my ministry.

"Organizing and administering the work of the Church" is a source of "great" satisfaction for 30 percent of priests. In interviews, priests in administrative positions typically told us that what they most enjoy about their work is the opportunity to help many other priests in their ministry, or more broadly, interacting with a wide variety of people. A religious priest who has been a provincial and is currently a college administrator describes why he finds his ministry satisfying:

I have liked it. The jobs that I've had are heavily people-oriented. As provincial you spend a huge amount of time interacting intimately with the people who are members of your province. You have colleagues that assist you with the other sorts of things, for example overseeing finances. Ultimately the buck stops on your desk, but I've always found it helpful to work closely with a team of people on such matters and delegate. . . . The modern administration of an educational institution is also very people-focused and you're dealing with a great variety of constituencies. That I suppose has played well to my strengths. What I thought I would never want to do, for example fund raising, I've actually really enjoyed.

Do priests who tend to enjoy administrative work gravitate toward it as a full-time ministry? On the contrary, priests whose ministry is in full-time diocesan or religious community administration are *less* likely to receive great satisfaction from administration than priests in parish ministry (26 percent of diocesan or religious community administrators, compared to 36 percent of pastors and 44 percent of full-time associate pastors). Perhaps many of those who are in full-time administrative work do it partly because they recognize that it must necessarily be carried out for the sake of the Church and not because it is their ideal preference. Indeed, this fits with what a number of priests in administrative positions told us in interviews. A religious priest who is an administrator for his order reflects,

> I guess I'm good at it or they wouldn't keep asking me to do it. To a certain extent I do enjoy it. After a while you get sick of it and you'd rather be dealing with "real" people than other [members of the order]. . . . I've been doing this for nine years straight. It's time to switch gears again. But there is certain satisfaction in it, particularly getting to see the good work being done by your men around the country, even around the world. That's the plus of being in leadership.

A priest whose current ministry is primarily diocesan administration describes missing his former parish ministry:

> I have some strong administrative gifts and talents. My preference is to be in a parish and to be a pastor. Certainly I realize that my gifts have been recognized, so it's a burden, I guess, that I have to embrace for a while. I'm not going to do it for my whole career. I do want to get back to a parish eventually. Even in parishes, I've had some great success in organizing and turning things around. I've been at parishes that have been in trouble, and I have the ability to bring people together and fix the problems and heal the community. . . . However, I miss terribly the relationships and being part of people's lives—the incredible, awesome gift it is to be welcomed into people's lives like no one else is . . . to really be that presence of God in those traumatic and joyful and sad times of life. I miss that terribly because I don't get a lot of that any more with administration. I minister to priests, so I try to consider them my parish. They're less receptive because usually when I show up it's bad news or some issue's being addressed and I'm spokesperson for the bishop. So they don't usually like to see me come.

As the above quote suggests, another possible reason that parish priests express more satisfaction with administration is that the administrative tasks required of them—besides being just one portion of their ministry—are tied to the needs of a community of parishioners. Indeed, "the challenge of being the leader of a Catholic Christian community" is a great source of satisfaction for half of priests, considerably more than for administration and organizing. In this case, the degree of satisfaction parish priests experience appears related to the amount of responsibility they hold. Forty-seven percent of full-time associate pastors report great satisfaction, compared to 52 percent of pastors with an associate pastor and 66 percent of pastors without an associate.

The "respect that comes to the priestly office" is a great source of satisfaction for just 22 percent of priests. And one-third (32 percent) say it is of "little" or "no importance" at all. In a sense, this is not surprising; many priests understand their vocation as a call to serve, to be an instrument of God for others, not to elevate themselves in the eyes of the laity. As one priest puts it,

> Any respect that comes from the priestly office has very little to do with me and everything to do with Christ. So there is a respect I see with the priestly office; it's a respect that lay people are showing to Christ and not to me as an individual. I would list that as low in terms of personal satisfaction.

Perhaps a better indication of how many priests find fulfillment in their role as a man set apart is in responses to the item about "being an *alter Christus* to the faithful." Slightly over half of priests experience great satisfaction from this, more than twice the proportion who gain great satisfaction from the respect that comes to the priestly office. It's not hard to see why. Being "another Christ" carries connotations of shepherding and caring for the flock that the respect of the office by itself does not. Younger priests are particularly likely to experience satisfaction from being an *alter Christus*. Eighty-three percent of those in their 30s report that this is a great source of satisfaction for them, as do 64 percent in their 40s. A religious order priest in his 40s reflects on being an *alter Christus*:

> Yes, that's important to me. I was once at a large parish where there was a regional celebration of the Sacrament of the Anointing of the Sick. I had never anointed that many people in one day. I knew that they weren't coming to me because it was Father [Name] but because it was Christ working through me. Likewise I was doing some missionary work in the third world and we had an outdoor Mass. The priests processed past people on the ground. The people would reach out and touch the hem of my alb and then kiss their fingers. It wasn't because this guy who was born in [my hometown] came to them. It was because I was *alter Christus*. People do have that expectation of meeting Christ in me. That's thrilling. It's very humbling too because I'm very acutely aware of my own flaws and weaknesses. Somehow God in His providence is able to use me.

Many priests also report finding great satisfaction in the opportunity to exercise intellectual and creative abilities (58 percent). This is especially common among priests who have earned a doctoral degree since ordination (71 percent) and those whose ministry is in education (76 percent). A priest who teaches high school says,

> I enjoy the chance to be creative in presentations in classrooms. I try to be creative in my preaching at Mass too, but the opportunity is much more limited. People start shuffling at about twelve minutes into a homily, and at fifteen minutes you're really pushing it. When teaching, I can use video in classes, group discussion, and other ways to engage students. It's a point of satisfaction for me.

A college professor and medical ethicist talks about the intellectual fulfillment that accompanies his ministry:

> The greatest satisfaction in my ministry as a professor is using all my abilities, including intellectual talents. I love teaching. I have my doctorate. Thanks to the diocese I was given the opportunity of having a great education and all these things that stimulate me, the research and the publications. And because of that background I'm the medical moral theologian for the diocese. In fact, I have to call up the hospital now [about a medical ethics issue]. . . . Even though it's a Catholic hospital, most of the people on the ethics committee are not Catholic. Many times I have to try to defend Catholic teaching. The only reason I'm respected in that by them is because of the degree. Those ethical meetings sometimes drive you up a wall, but again the collegiality is where I find satisfaction. You're accepted by the professional community because you taught so many of them and they have such high regard for you. And your degree and publications mean something to them. With any other priest, they would think, "He's just saying the priest line, what the Church says." But with me I think they realize that it's a little more of an informed decision in support of the Church.

The "sense of well-being that comes from working with like-minded priests" is a great source of satisfaction for about half of survey respondents. A diocesan priest describes a recent time when he found satisfaction among like-minded priests:

> I just got back from our diocesan vocation camp. I've been ordained a little over a decade now, and everybody else was ordained after me, so younger than me, in ordination years at least. We all worked together very

well. There was a sense of satisfaction in that there weren't tensions about the way to celebrate Mass or the theology of the Church. We're all on the same page theologically . . . morally . . . liturgically. So the Masses were beautiful. . . . The teachings were beautiful. It was great. There was definite satisfaction in those situations. We had to work together in this. Boy what a change it's been from even ten, twelve years ago, when there was so much tension between the priests. Because I remember being at the camp when I was a seminarian. . . . There's a lot of satisfaction in working with these like-minded priests that have the same theological, moral, and liturgical beliefs.

The college professor, who earlier discussed using his intellectual abilities in his work, describes the sense of solidarity between himself and other priests at his college:

We have a few other diocesan priests on the faculty. It seems like we're all on the same track. Even though we have a huge age span among us, we more or less agree on the way the Church is going. I think that's so important. We want to make sure we uphold the Catholic identity of the university. We help one another, like if something comes up and I can't have one of the Masses, one of the others will do it. So yes, there's great satisfaction being like-minded.

As seen in table 2.6, religious priests are more likely than diocesan priests to report receiving great satisfaction from the sense of well-being that comes from working with like-minded priests (60 compared to 47 percent). This difference cannot be attributed to religious priests being more likely to have a shared or collaborative ministry. Even when the comparison is limited to those who serve in a parish with another priest (i.e., limited to associate pastors or pastors with an associate), the diocesan priests report receiving significantly less satisfaction from working with like-minded priests.[11] In fact, for religious order priests, the "sense of well-being that comes from working with like-minded priests" and

[11] Diocesan priests are more likely than religious priests to report receiving satisfaction from the challenge of being the leader of a Christian Catholic community (54 compared to 42 percent). In this case the difference is attributable to the types of ministries in which religious and diocesan priests are engaged. Religious priests are less likely to be pastors and therefore the question probably doesn't apply to them as well as it does to diocesan priests. When limiting the comparison to pastors, diocesan and religious priests report very similar levels of satisfaction from the challenge of leading a Christian Catholic community.

the "sense of well-being that comes from living the common life with like-minded priests" better predict how happy they are in their lives than any of the other sources of satisfaction listed in table 2.6. Thus, having rewarding relationships *with other priests* is more important for the general happiness of members of religious orders than is satisfaction in other specific aspects of their lives and ministry. A religious priest discusses working in high schools with other members of his order and the support they have provided for his ministry and understanding of his vocation:

> There's always some variety of viewpoints in my community, but the core values are the same. We're all working for the salvation of the young. We share the same spirituality and charism. . . . By the time I was ordained I had already been teaching high school for five years. When I began, I was teaching religious education and I hadn't even had much theology myself. I had to seek input from older priests at the school on what to teach. Other teachers were invaluable guides and resources when I began, and they continue to be models. Immediately after ordination, a challenge I faced was that I was returning to the same environment and ministry. I was still teaching high school. I questioned: "What am I doing now that is different than before? What integrates my priesthood into my teaching?" I had to learn what that means. Why did I have to be ordained to keep teaching? The older priests at the school were helpful as I was working through these questions.

Aside from a few we have already mentioned, sources of satisfaction differ little based on age. However, one case warrants discussion. In 2000, the *New York Times* ran an article titled, "Priests of the 60's Fear Loss of Their Legacy" (Schemo, 2000). It included interviews with priests ordained in the wake of Vatican II who treasure the teachings of the Council and the social justice awakening of that era. The priests expressed concern that, among other things, priests ordained more recently are not as interested in pursuing social justice causes. Our survey data do not reveal how much time and effort priests put into working for such causes, but they do show the amount of satisfaction they receive from "engaging in efforts at social reform." Among all responding priests, 25 percent say it is of "great" importance as a source of satisfaction and another 47 percent that it is of "some" importance. Whether looking at generation or ordination cohort, Vatican II era priests are not particularly distinctive. The only notable variation we find is that priests who are currently in their 30s tend to report less satisfaction from efforts at social reform than all other priests. Forty-six percent of priests in their 30s say these efforts give them either some or great satisfaction, compared to 73 percent of those who are at least 40. Thus the data suggest that any divide on social concerns is not so much between Vatican II era priests and all those ordained after them but rather between the very youngest priests and all others.

We have seen that overall satisfaction among priests has been increasing over time. Does this mean that there have also been increases in satisfaction from particular aspects of their lives and ministry? Table 2.7 shows responses since 1970 to selected satisfaction items included in previous surveys. There have been definite increases for two items: the joy of administering the sacraments and presiding over the liturgy, and

Table 2.7
Selected Sources of Satisfaction, by Year
(Percentage saying each is of "great" importance
as a source of satisfaction)

	1970	1985	1993	2001	2009
Joy of administering the sacraments and presiding over the liturgy	80%	87%	92%	90%	94%
Satisfaction of preaching the Word	—*	—*	82	80	83
Being part of a community of Christians who are working together to share the Good News of the Gospel	63	65	69	62	73
Opportunity to work with many people and be a part of their lives	72	72	74	67	71
Opportunity to exercise intellectual and creative abilities	52	46	53	55	58
Challenge of being the leader of a Catholic Christian community**	38	39	46	47	42
Organizing and administering the work of the Church	31	32	33	34	30
Engaging in efforts at social reform	22	20	23	23	25
Respect that comes to the priestly office	23	21	23	25	22

 * Not asked
** Prior to 2009, the question asked about "the Christian community" rather than "a Catholic Christian community."

being part of a community of Christians who are working together to share the Good News of the Gospel. Even these increases are relatively small (the largest is for administering the sacraments and presiding over the liturgy, an increase of 14 percentage points from 80 to 94 percent). And neither of these two increases extends across each survey-to-survey period in the series.

Still, the increases in satisfaction from these two areas make intuitive sense. Because they are so central to priestly ministry and happiness, one might predict that these two items would have risen in tandem with overall priestly satisfaction.

Arguably there has also been an increase in satisfaction from the opportunity to exercise intellectual and creative abilities—though since the 1980s only. Why has this proportion grown? One possibility is that the increase reflects changes in the ministerial positions held by priests. In 1985, 26 percent of nonretired priests were associate pastors and 47 percent were pastors. As of 2009, just 7 percent are associate pastors and 62 percent are pastors. Has the shift toward positions as pastor—which might involve more responsibility and decision-making[12]—increased intellectual and creative outlets for priests? It seems not. Pastors and associate pastors gain about equal amounts of satisfaction from intellectual and creative opportunities. Indeed, the increase in satisfaction from intellectual and creative opportunities has taken place among all ordination cohorts and age groups of priests except the very oldest, who are mostly retired. If the increase reflected the kinds of positions priests hold in parishes, it would have been greatest among those who are relatively recently ordained, as they are now moving into pastor positions much more quickly than in the past.

Another explanation is possible. Among the other satisfaction items, the opportunity to exercise one's intellectual and creative abilities is most strongly correlated with the challenge of being the leader of a Catholic Christian community. The correlation suggests a link between feeling challenged in one's ministry and deriving intellectual and creative satisfaction from it. Perhaps the growing challenges faced by nearly all active priests in an era of reduced vocations place them in a position where they must increasingly find creative ways to effectively meet the needs of

---

[12] It is worth noting that self-perceived autonomy, responsibility, and decision-making ability increased substantially among associate pastors from 1970 to 1993, though associates still lagged behind pastors in this regard (Hoge, Shields, and Griffin, 1995).

their parishioners.[13] If ministerial demands have indeed given some priests a greater outlet for their creative gifts, with accompanying satisfaction, then this is likely one of the few positive outcomes to be found in the priest shortage. The next chapter, which discusses problems in priestly life and ministry, addresses in greater detail some of the challenges associated with fewer priests.

Conclusion

Probably the most important reason that priests, along with clergy of other faiths, are so highly satisfied (University of Chicago News Office, 2007) is that they are members of a helping profession, having dedicated their lives to the service of others. It is a truism that money can't buy happiness. In actuality, that's a little misleading; there is generally a positive correlation between income and happiness (e.g., Easterlin, 2001). But nowhere is the imperfect nature of this correlation more evident than among members of the helping professions. Some priests may occasionally have regrets about giving up romantic relationships and marriage, but it is rare indeed that any complain about having missed the opportunity to amass wealth in their lives.

> I was dean of [a professional school] in California until our new bishop made me come back home from sunny southern California. I've been back many years now and I've lost about two million dollars in salary. But you know what? I don't care a bit. I'm just happy in my priesthood, being able to function as a priest.

> I was born at the beginning of the financial depression. My parents were poor. . . . I was offered free tuition, books, housing, and food for five years at the university by a wealthy banker [to join him in banking]. I was to pay back nothing. My bishop invited me to go to the seminary and to become a priest. I accepted the bishop's invitation to become a priest. . . . It has been a *great* life as a priest. I often invite young men to consider the priesthood.

Among priests, the factors from table 2.6 that most strongly predict the degree to which they are happy are the following:

---

[13] If this explanation is correct, it could be expected that satisfaction from the challenge of "being the leader of a Catholic Christian community" would also have risen over time. The percentage in the final column of table 2.7 suggests that is not the case. However, this result could be due to changes in the question's wording in 2009.

- For diocesan priests, "Being part of a community of Christians who are working together to share the Good News of the Gospel."

- For religious priests, "The sense of well-being that comes from working with like-minded priests" and the "sense of well-being that comes from living the common life with like-minded priests."

These findings strongly suggest that having satisfying relationships is central in priests' overall satisfaction. However, as the next chapter reveals, the experience of certain problems is even more strongly related to priests' happiness than any of the sources of satisfaction in table 2.6. At the end of chapter 3 we explore the relationship between happiness and problems in priestly life. First, though, we examine the problems themselves.

Chapter 3

Challenges in Priestly Life and Ministry

These are difficult times to be a priest. I have come to the realization that the priest shortage is not my fault and I can't fix it. All I can effectively do is stay in my parish, fly below the radar of the chancery, and don't expect any support from them. And try not to get burned out!

—A survey respondent

As we saw in chapter 2, priests tend to be very satisfied with their lives and ministry. They are not merely content; they are happy. From among 960 survey respondents, the ones who are "not at all happy" can be counted on the fingers of one hand. So just how salient are the problems and challenges that priests face? At the outset of the three focus groups, we asked, "When you think about the Catholic priesthood today, what words or phrases come to mind?" Following are selected responses, which are generally representative of all those that were shared by the participants:

Overwhelmed with work
Advanced stress
Endangered species
Unpopular
Challenging
Sacrifice
Beloved
Exciting
Multifaceted, like fighting a war,
    going in all directions
No two days are the same

Expectations
Rewarding
Numbers
Growing division
Countercultural
Witness
More administrative
Overworked but happy
Limited support
Isolated

If somebody were to look at these words and phrases without context, not knowing where they came from, what is the likelihood he or she would guess the source is a group of people who are among the most satisfied of any profession in our society? About half the total responses include at least some ambivalent or negative connotations, and many are quite negative indeed: *advanced stress, endangered, overwhelmed, isolated, unpopular*. As happy as priests are, it seems the problems that do exist in their lives are not submerged far below the surface. This is the seeming paradox, that priests are satisfied even though the problems in their lives are not trivial. One response in particular succinctly sums up related themes from the previous chapter and this one: *overworked but happy*. We saw the happiness of priests in chapter 2. We will get to the overworked part shortly.

The survey asked priests about twenty-one potential problems in their daily lives. Table 3.1 presents the twelve that were rated most problematic. The first column shows that relatively few priests describe any particular issue as being a "great" problem for them. However, a majority of priests describe several issues as at least "somewhat" of a problem. Differences between diocesan and religious priests (not distinguished in the table) are relatively small, with a few exceptions that will be mentioned later.

The Way Authority Is Exercised in the Church and Relationships with Superiors

Three in ten priests say that "the way that authority is exercised in the Church" is a "great" problem for them in their daily lives, with nearly two-thirds saying it is at least "somewhat" of a problem. Based on responses to other questions in the survey, we find that most of the priests who experience authority as a problem belong to two (partially overlapping) groups. Members of the first group express dissatisfaction with their relationships with superiors. Not every priest who is dissatisfied with superiors experiences authority as a problem, but a disproportionate number do. Among those who report receiving "little or no support" from their bishop, 59 percent say the way authority is exercised in the Church is a great problem for them. (By way of comparison, recall that among all priests the percentage is 30 percent.) Among those who disagree strongly that they are "a member of the bishop's team," the proportion is even higher, 71 percent. The second group includes priests who are not necessarily unhappy with their own bishop or superior but who favor

Table 3.1
Most Common Problems
(Percentage in each category)

	"A Great" Problem	"Somewhat" of a Problem	Combined "Somewhat" and "Great"
The way authority is exercised in the Church	30%	34%	64%
Shortage of available priests	27	39	66
Difficulty of really reaching people today	18	40	58
Too much work	17	33	50
Unrealistic demands and expectations of laypeople	15	38	53
Being expected to represent Church teachings I have difficulty with	15	26	41
Relationship with the bishop of the diocese in which you work	14	21	35
Parish restructuring in the diocese	14	29	43
Uncertainty about the future of the Church	12	29	41
Celibacy or lifelong commitment to chastity[*]	11	23	35
Loneliness of priestly life	11	29	40
Relationships with superiors or pastor	10	23	33
Theological differences in the concept of the priesthood	10	33	43

Note: Due to rounding, the figures in the first two columns may not sum exactly to the third.

[*] Diocesan priests were asked about "celibacy," and religious priests were asked about "lifelong commitment to chastity."

greater democracy in the Church. For example, among those who agree strongly with the idea of priests in a diocese choosing their own bishop, 59 percent say authority is a great problem. Note that support for greater democracy need not reflect only priests' desire to have it for themselves. Consider those who, in the 2001 survey, strongly favored the idea of

Table 3.2
Percentage Who Say "the Way Authority Is Exercised in the Church" Is a "Great" Problem for Them, by Selected Attitudes

Attitudes about Superiors

Receives "little or no" support from the bishop	59%
Has "very little" confidence in the diocesan bishop	68
Disagrees strongly that "I feel that I am a member of the bishop's team. When I am doing a job that has the local bishop's approval, I am doing priestly work."	71

Attitudes about Democracy in the Church

Agrees strongly that "priest members of presbyteral councils need more influence if the councils are to be effective in enhancing priestly ministry."	50%
Agrees strongly that "I think it would be a good idea if the priests in a diocese were to choose their own bishop."	59
Agrees strongly that "I think it would be a good idea if Christian communities such as parishes were to choose their own priest from among available ordained priests."*	64

* From the 2001 survey

parishioners choosing their own priests from among available ordained priests. Nearly two-thirds of these men, 64 percent, said the exercise of authority in the Church was a great problem for them.

Two priests share thoughts about the Church that touch on issues of democracy and decision making:

> There seems to be a tremendous pull to centralize authority in the Church. A question I have—it's not a complaint—I'm just wondering how smart it is that authority be so centralized in Rome. I love being Roman Catholic, and I think it's phenomenal that we have a strong sense of unity with our leadership. But I'm just wondering if there's a way to have—how shall I say this—greater shared authority and shared responsibility for the Church. We are inviting our local churches to take responsibility for themselves, specifically around stewardship and finances. Yet at the same time, it seems that when it comes to questions around leadership and governance, the people who are responsible for stewardship aren't invited into

those types of decisions. I'm just wondering if that could potentially be a problem for us.

The wave [of the sexual abuse scandal] has finally hit Rome, and we are so centralized that we seem to be more concerned about her power and control than resolving what needs to be resolved in a collegial manner.

In a similar vein, a retired priest looks back on his life and ministry:

I never felt respected for my own experience. I felt I had a lot to share and give to the authorities in my life, but they didn't seem to care. I often wondered: why doesn't the Church have more respect for the ground-level experience that we have interacting in ministry with the people we serve? Why isn't that being respected by, like you're doing now, asking me? Yeah, I think this is the first time anybody ever asked me how I felt about my years of ministry. . . . Why don't we take advantage of the rich experience worldwide we have in every culture? Why don't we listen to that and let it influence the decision-making that has to be made for our future? . . . Let people tell us what they're struggling with trying to be good Catholics, like Pope Paul VI did when he had that commission on birth control but ignored it when it came out.

Somewhat in contrast to the quotes above, other priests emphasize that they recognize the challenges facing Church leaders and the need for decisive leadership and decision making from above:

Authority in the Church seems to be exercised very indirectly. . . . Bishops in general don't want to be confrontational. They believe everything has to be done nicely. And yet, I've been in rooms where marines would be discussing something to the point where they looked like they were going to kill each other. But they came to some kind of conclusion, and everybody would be fine. It was a lot of confrontation. It was a lot of what the nuns used to call, "manly talk." It resolved stuff, and everyone continued on. But you look at the bishop's conference, and you want to throw up. Nobody debates anything. Nobody has strong opinions. They are all being very nice. . . . I'm not saying the leaders should be autocratic. [My bishop] is a great leader. You might not agree with him, wherever he is coming from, left or right. But he knows how to lead. If he wants to give a directive, he'll give a directive.

Some people find it difficult to cope with authority. I do. . . . I think [my bishop] has been fantastic. He's very understanding. I find I can talk to him about anything, really. But you know that some of his decisions are sort of secret, behind the scenes. Well, it's got to be like that, doesn't it? . . . We discuss moving people from one parish to another, and then he makes the final decision. Well, he knows the reasons. The vicars and others don't.

As table 3.1 also shows, one's "relationship with the bishop" and "relationship with superiors or pastor" is at least somewhat of a problem for 35 and 33 percent of priests, respectively. Diocesan priests are more likely than religious priests to identify the former as a problem, presumably because religious priests rarely report directly to their local bishop. Whether diocesan or religious, a very high proportion of those who say their relationship with their bishop is a problem also say that the exercise of authority in the Church is at least somewhat of a problem (87 percent among all priests). Similarly, a very high proportion who say that their relationship with their superiors or pastor is a problem also say that the exercise of authority in the Church is a problem for them (an identical 87 percent). A diocesan priest describes having a difficult relationship with a prior bishop:

> We had years in my diocese of an administrative bishop concerned about money. When he was giving me my new assignment, all he was concerned about was the money. He asked the financial officer to come into the office with a portfolio on the finances of the parish. And I wanted to know: how many confessions are being heard? How many Holy Hours are happening? How many Masses are being offered? How many people are joining the church? How many souls are being baptized? . . . He was a total jerk. At priest gatherings he would come up to me and say, "Have you made the annual goal of the diocesan appeal yet?" not, "How are you? How is Lent going for you?" It is a huge difficulty and frustration in the priesthood when the bishop is not on the same page as you. It was a great, great cross. I didn't feel like I had his support.

Another diocesan priest describes feeling unsupported by his bishop when he belonged to a team of priests responsible for a cluster of parishes in a low-income area:

> When you don't have total control and authority to implement your vision, it's frustrating. I'll give you an example. The bishop closed one of the schools in the cluster because he thought it was too costly, so we asked if it could be a charter school. After a year of it being closed, he agreed to that. He was happy because then he wouldn't have to worry about the empty building and so on. The lease of the building, and gym, and classrooms, and so on was [a very large dollar amount] a year. Well, we had hoped that money would be for ministries that we couldn't afford in these parishes. He refused to allow us to have it—not even split it, not even get

a dollar. It's extremely frustrating to do any ministry where you don't have the support and the backing to fulfill the decisions that are made.

Difficulty Reaching People

"The difficulty of really reaching people today" is reported as at least somewhat of a problem by 58 percent of priests. Diocesan priests are more likely to say this than religious priests (63 compared to 48 percent). And among diocesan priests, pastors are more likely to do so than associate pastors (64 compared to 52 percent). In focus groups and interviews, priests discuss the challenges they face inspiring people to devote their lives to God and be fully active in the life of the Church:

> That's an issue in the parish. It's really hard to reach out to people because they are always so busy with their own work. And sometimes they don't even have an interest in practicing their faith. They are very much interested in sending their children to catechism, but that's it. Call them for a meeting, call them for a gathering, and they won't show up. I just don't know how to bridge the gap.

> One of the problems that I see in ministry right now is that so few young adults are participating in the life of the Church. That's a great concern for me. I'm in middle-age. I'm concerned that the twenty-somethings and the thirty-somethings are not membering our Church. . . . That's a big problem. I'm wondering what we as leaders of the Church, priests and bishops, are doing to address that. I'm not seeing a lot of creative responses to that issue.

> You had a much more close tight-knit community back in the 70s, early 80s. Families were tighter. I think now you have many more scattered situations. People are "busier" and less inclined, particularly young folks just getting started, who did not have as solid a background in their faith from their religious education classes as maybe their parents or grandparents did. . . . People bring their children to be baptized who don't go to church and are not interested in it, but grandma wants the kid baptized or something like that. You can't convince them that, "You're coming to baptism with this child. You need to come to church." At one parish, we did first penance in March and first communion was in May. The day of first communion, a mother came up to me and said, "My son needs to go to confession again." I said, "Why?" She said, "Well, he hasn't been to church." I said, "It's not his sin. He can't get here by himself. He's seven." . . . That's the kind of frustration I mean, where people are not even aware they have a responsibility.

Uncertainty about the Future of the Church

A problem farther down in table 3.1—uncertainty about the future of the Church—is sometimes raised by priests when they talk about the difficulties they experience trying to engage Catholics. Asked if they feel uncertain about the future of the Church, two priests reflect:

> The Church will continue going on until the end of time. But what we're seeing now is a decrease in Mass attendance, a decrease in reception of the sacraments. I think we're going down to a low point here, a nadir. What happens there, I think, depends on evangelization. We're starting that "Come Home" program in our diocese here. Hopefully these things will start to bring people back. . . . So it doesn't mean the whole Church will go down the tubes. But the Church is decreasing in its authority and its influence in forming the consciences of people.

> I see the future as both exciting and hopeful. But I also see it as a little bit intimidating because we have to make a lot of changes. . . . I don't think we're overly effective at evangelizing and converting the hearts of the faithful. I think we have too many folks just riding along and not really engaging their faith. We've got to cut them loose and start challenging people to practice their faith. . . . They're disconnected from the community. They come to do their own thing. They're disconnected from the larger Church. . . . The challenge is to reach out to the younger folks who are, I think, very interested in social outreach, social concerns, and the poor. I think they're disillusioned with the institutional Church and formal, ritual practice. We're going to have to help them understand what we do, to engage them to participate and be active members of the faith.

Priests in their 30s are a little less likely than others to report that uncertainty about the future of the Church is a problem for them (26 percent of priests in their 30s say it is at least "somewhat" of a problem, compared to 41 percent of priests who are at least 40 years old). This seems to fit with our speculation in chapter 2 that younger priests may experience fewer doubts about their beliefs. One priest in his 30s says,

> No, that's not a concern of mine. From my standpoint, the Church was built on the rock, and the gates of hell shall not prevail against it, as we hear every year on the feast of Saints Peter and Paul. We know that the Church will remain, so there's comfort in that.

The trepidation felt by some priests about the future of the Church as a whole is relatively minor compared to the pessimism expressed by others with whom we spoke about the future of the priesthood and religious life itself. In response to a question about the priesthood ten years from now, a focus group participant says,

> I have no concerns for ten years from now because I don't think there is going to be a priesthood. The curtain is coming down rapidly. Look at the Sisters of Charity, for instance. A few years ago they had 1,800 nuns. Now they have 400. The Benedictine monks are down to eight people. Jesuits are disappearing. Until we really start taking a look at the priesthood, it is going to die. As long as the world refuses to look to the option of ordaining deacons, marrying priests, and ordaining women, it is going to be over. And I'm an optimistic guy.

Too Much Work and Shortage of Available Priests

We will consider two of the most commonly reported problems in table 3.1 together: shortage of available priests and too much work. Although related, one notable distinction between them is that while the likelihood of reporting too much work drops considerably when priests retire (not surprisingly), concerns about the shortage of priests persist. Retired priests are just as likely as active priests to say the priest shortage is a problem. In general, priests are concerned about the declining numbers, even if their own ministry isn't directly affected at this time.

When priests are asked about the biggest problem in their lives via an open-ended question (i.e., one without predetermined response categories like those shown in table 3.1), workload is the one that they tend to name most frequently (Los Angeles Times Poll, 2002). Thus it was a topic that priests discussed extensively in focus groups when asked about problems in their lives. Three concerns related to workload were frequently expressed by the focus group participants: that important things such as vision are lost amid more immediate demands; that they do not have enough time to meet all of the needs of the people they serve; and, most frequently of all, that overwork takes a toll on their own well-being and sense of balance in life.

> I often feel outnumbered. If there were thirty-six hours in a day and I didn't need to sleep, there still wouldn't be enough hours in the day. There's just a tremendous need for priestly ministry. And I think people really want the ministry of good priests. Making sure that I have the time to exercise, to sleep, to pray on my own, to maintain my health, to maintain contacts with my family—that's a real challenge.

There is no time for vision. I am very busy and do not have time to even make phone calls.

The day is just filled with things. . . . By the time I get home [from a full-time hospital chaplaincy] I am so tired, I fall asleep in the chair and I don't get my breviary read. Or, I will take it in the morning thinking I will read it during the day at the office. But then it is just one thing after another, after another.

I had to give up my days off. It's been a while since I did that, taking my days off. . . . Even then I still had to do some stuff that was related to the church on my days off. But probably for the past few months I haven't had free days. . . . I just got another parish a few months ago and that is another added load for me.

[The declining number of priests] affects my struggle to have balance in free time and work. There are so many people coming at you and from so many different sides. You have to fight harder for balance.

Balance is the greatest problem in my life, balance of my personal well-being and ministry. I get going and I have trouble stopping. At the school where I teach, there is great need. The amount and intensity of the need is overwhelming. . . . I struggle with finding a line between doing as much as I can and knowing when to stop, before it carries over to my personal health, prayer life, and community life.

Who tends to report that too much work is a problem for them? Pastors are nearly twice as likely as associate pastors to say it is at least "somewhat" of a problem (59 percent compared to 30 percent). This could be related to the amount of responsibility they feel for the ultimate well-being of their parishes. For pastors, having an associate does little to reduce feelings of being overworked; those with an associate are actually *more* likely to report having too much work (65 compared to 56 percent). Among both pastors and associates, being assigned to more than one parish increases the likelihood of reporting too much work. However, we were surprised to find that it does so only slightly (62 percent compared to 55 percent of those assigned to a single parish, a statistically nonsignificant difference). Perhaps this is because priests with multiple parishes are often responsible for smaller ones. As mentioned in the first paragraph of chapter 2, pastoring a large parish also brings its own considerable time burdens. Workload aside, responsibility for multiple parishes does significantly predict whether priests feel personally affected by the priest shortage. Seventy-nine percent of those assigned to multiple parishes say that the shortage of available priests is a problem for them, compared to 66 percent of those assigned to one parish.

In addition to challenges of balancing personal well-being and ministerial demands, an often overlooked outcome of a high workload is the potential for festering resentment among priests of a diocese. Many of CARA's diocesan-level surveys of priests have included the following agree-disagree statement: "Too many priests in the diocese do not do their fair share of work or ministry." Typically, between three-tenths and one-half of all priests in a given diocese agree with the statement. The proportion tends to be higher when limited to diocesan priests in parish ministry, and higher still when limited to those working over seventy hours a week.

Unrealistic Demands and Expectations of Laypeople

Slightly over half of priests report that "unrealistic demands and expectations of laypeople" are at least somewhat of a problem for them. There is a relatively strong correlation between reporting unrealistic demands and expectations of laypeople to be a problem and reporting too much work to be a problem. In other words, if a priest says that one of these issues is a problem for him, there is a good chance he says the other is also a problem. From this we infer that the areas in which priests most often experience unrealistic expectations center around their own availability for the people they serve. A priest discusses parishioner expectations regarding his availability for one-on-one time:

> A difficulty with ministry . . . is people who will just call to chat and spend time talking with a priest, aside of course from pastoral needs that come up like sickness or illness. This applies to an awful lot of lonely or widowed people who just need somebody to talk to. I try to be kind and grateful and gracious. But a number of people want to have me over for dinner or join them on a weekend or something like that—not that I'm able to get away for a weekend. There are some people, just a few, who almost want to appropriate you as part of their own life, to sort of become their family priest. There's an expectation on their part that you can spend an awful lot of time with them. And I *can't*. I can't. People don't realize how busy priests are.

In addition to expectations about their availability for one-on-one ministry, priests often mention the tendency for laity to assume that previous experiences of parish life will continue with little change, even as the number of priests continues to plummet and dioceses are forced to reorganize parish ministry. A diocesan priest who is pastor of three parishes says,

> One of the most stressful things is setting the Mass schedules. The prior pastor decided to make everybody happy, and he would change the Mass schedule every month. Do you believe this? Every month the Mass schedule was different. If you're going to bring somebody back to the Church, you have to be able to say, the "Mass in this parish is *always* at ten o'clock. Come and join us sometime," not, "In months that end in a full moon, the Mass is going to be at ten o'clock." There's a lot of resistance from the people. [In a whiny voice:] "We don't have Mass at the time we want." It's very frustrating to me how lazy sometimes the parishioners become. They're not willing to think about 150 years ago when the missionary Jesuit came down once a month and they'd be happy to have Mass that often. Or, if they don't like the time, they can drive fifteen minutes to one of the other parishes. They drive to [the city], forty minutes away, to get groceries, to get an oil change. But they can't drive fifteen minutes to see God.
>
> Besides the Mass schedule, they really want what was in the 1950s, when every parish had its own priest. They expect me to be at [Parish A] 100 percent of the time, at [Parish B] 100 percent of the time, and at [Parish C] 100 percent of the time. So [Parish A] gets frustrated. "You're not staying for our potluck supper after Mass?" "No, I have to go meet with a couple," or, "I have to go to the hospital." I just can't do everything. I wish I could. I wish I could go to every little event.

A priest who took over two small parishes while also holding a position in diocesan administration describes the experience:

> Initially they didn't [understand that my availability would be limited] because both of the places previously had pastors who were there for a long time who were available twenty-four/seven. . . . What was successful for me was to communicate. I wrote in the bulletin in both places. I communicated to the folks about what my schedule was. I had set office hours, so if you needed me, Tuesday mornings I was one place and Thursday afternoons I was another place. Then I'd balance myself on the weekend to get everything covered. And they knew they could always get me at the office downtown. It was after a couple years that they finally realized I *was* concerned about them, I did love them, I wanted to be of service to them. It ended up being a good thing, but it was a very painful process. Because one day they had a fulltime pastor, the next day they had me, and I wasn't around a lot.

Other priests discussed with us the importance of better informing the laity about changing realities in the Church and working to adjust their expectations to an appropriate level. While discussing parish reorganization in his diocese, a priest in a focus group says,

> I have a difficult time convincing people that there is a shortage of clergy and that it is going to get worse before it gets better. . . . I am concerned that we are not moving quickly enough to get people to realize that there may have to be more consolidating of parishes and closing of schools. Some institutions started by their great grandparents may have outlived their usefulness and have to be closed. Dioceses and religious orders are constantly having to adapt to be able to meet the needs of the people as best as they can. Sometimes I get a sense that there is a resistance on the part of the people in the pews, that they don't want to believe it.

A religious order priest talks about helping laypeople understand his limited availability:

> I think people are well-intentioned. They might be initially unreasonable in their expectations, but once I kind of clarify for them, I don't think in any way do they persist in their unreasonableness. . . . We need to be able to say, "I'm not able to help there," if that's the case. One of the ways to do that, to address unreasonable expectations, is to speak to and model an ecclesiology that is not so priest-centered.

Representing Church Teachings

Another relatively common complaint is "being expected to represent Church teachings I have difficulty with," described as at least somewhat of a problem by about four in ten priests. Perhaps not surprisingly, there are substantial age differences among responses for this item. Just 11 percent of priests in their 30s describe it as being a problem for them. This compares to 22 percent of priests in their 40s, 39 percent of those in their 50s, 53 percent of those in their 60s, and falling back to 42 percent of those 70 and over. Among teachings mentioned in focus groups as being especially challenging are those dealing with marriage, contraception, homosexuality, and similar issues. Some priests discuss seeking nuanced ways of talking about such topics with laypeople:

> I get upset about the politicization of homosexuality. People keep making like the Church is teaching that it is "intrinsically disordered."[1] I am never

---

[1] The priest is referring to theological terminology in the *Catechism of the Catholic Church*, which describes homosexual acts this way.

going to give a sermon on something being intrinsically disordered because you need to be a philosopher to understand these distinctions. . . . When I had the privilege of being at [a well-known college] for four years, the kids would say, "What would Jesus do?" And I thought, "Gee, this is simplistic." But ultimately, that's the question. And lots of times you say, "I don't know what the heck Jesus would do."

It was a shame that the birth control prohibition and a few other pronouncements silenced the priests who were working with the people—that you couldn't explore, you couldn't talk openly about these issues. You had to do it all in the confessional or at least outside of the pulpit, if you wanted to stay in the system. It hamstrung us. . . . I never preached on abortion until about four years ago—once—because I didn't like the Bishops' stand on a constitutional amendment. I explained why the Supreme Court couldn't overrule abortion because there was such a huge number of people in favor of it. You can *restrict* abortion, but then that doesn't satisfy Rome.

During a focus group discussion on *Humanae Vitae* (the 1968 papal encyclical about contraception) one priest shares his hesitation to speak about the issue:

There are just some subjects that I won't talk about. If I'm asked to talk about it on an individual basis with a particular case then we'll deal with it. But I will not give a sermon about contraception. I will do a sermon on conscience, but I won't do a sermon on contraception. I don't think it's a Gospel value. . . . That's for a moral theology classroom.

Some of the priests we spoke with said that the challenge for them is not necessarily that they disagree with Church teachings but that it can be difficult presenting those teachings to laypeople who may be disinclined to hear them (at best) or openly hostile (at worst). As a focus group participant puts it during the same discussion on birth control, "I agree with *Humanae Vitae*, but I'm not going to take out an ad in the newspaper." Below are more comments from priests on the difficulty of presenting controversial topics to the laity even when they themselves have no problem with the Church's position:

When people have problems with Church teaching, because so many of these things affect people emotionally, they will bring up the subject and often get very angry about it. Whether it's just a spontaneous gathering of people after Mass or whether it's being out to dinner with a Catholic couple or family, they'll bring up a controversial subject—whether it's a male-only priesthood, or celibacy, or contraception or whatever it might be—and get angry. I never bring it up, but other people do. I really wish that when people bring the subject up with me that they were just a little calmer and a little less angry and a little more open and accepting to what I have to offer on it, rather than putting me on the spot. . . . I wish they would take a deep breath and try to incorporate prayer and faith into their consideration of these controversial teachings.

One of the challenges in priesthood is trying to speak and teach and act in the name of the Church. Obviously that isn't always well received by people on either the so-called left or right. I was working with someone on an annulment case that I thought was going to be easily granted and it wasn't. I had to try to work with that person and her new husband and ask them to be patient with the process because it has to go through the appeal now—even though I really had trouble myself because I didn't think it was necessarily a fair judgment. But being a representative of the Church I can't just circumvent those procedures. Another example would be the bishop's efforts here to speak out against same-sex marriage. I knew a letter from the bishop was coming out. I felt that I should prepare people for it and ask them to be receptive to it. So I did my column on marriage, letting them know that this was coming. I just found out moments ago that because of that letter, a cantor in my parish has decided to leave the Church. So when we take a stand or when I say or teach something, the challenge is to remain faithful even in the face of criticism, sometimes from both sides. In the political season . . . I won't even go to a caucus because I don't want any affiliation I might have to affect my pastoral work.

Along similar lines, other priests emphasize that they refrain from voicing open dissent, even in cases where they themselves may have some doubts about Church teaching:

I feel a tremendous responsibility to represent the Roman Catholic Church in its fullness. I've always said this, and I really believe it: the Church is bigger than I am. It would be both irresponsible and arrogant for me to think my ideas trump 2,000 years of tradition. So while I may struggle at times with an understanding of Church teaching . . . , I'm also not willing to publicly dissent or disagree with it. I just think that would be pastorally and professionally irresponsible. . . . You're at a wedding and somebody might come up and say, "My annulment didn't go through." And I can't speak to that because I don't know their annulment case or the details of it. It certainly *pains* me that somebody can't go to communion. . . . Yet the teaching of the Church says that if you're not in a valid marriage, you're not to do that. That would be one area where I'm in conflict. But again, I'm not going to be disrespectful.

When I was in the final throes of seminary, I had some issues with Church teaching, and I came upon the help of the Holy Spirit for resolution of that. I simply felt: "If what I think is wrong with the Church is really wrong with the Church, nobody wants to change it more than the Holy Spirit, who has a whole lot more clout than I do. So I am going to let the Church be the Church." So, that's been my resolution. . . . I will uphold the Church's teaching as compassionately as I can.

Loneliness and Celibacy

Loneliness is at least somewhat of a problem for 40 percent of priests. Contrary to what might be expected, diocesan priests are only slightly more likely than religious priests to report that this is a problem (42 percent of diocesan priests and 36 percent of religious priests say it is at least "somewhat" of a problem, a statistically significant but rather small difference). However, the extent to which priests are around each other and spend time together does seem to be related to loneliness. For example, loneliness tends to be more common among retired diocesan priests than among active diocesan priests (53 compared to 40 percent), perhaps because the former may tend to be somewhat cut off from the rest of the presbyterate and from parish ministry.

In surveys conducted for diocesan presbyterates over the years, CARA has found other evidence that points to the importance of interactions among priests in reducing loneliness.[2] First, in most, though not all, dioceses, priests who frequently gather with other priests to socialize are less likely than others to report being lonely. Second, in most dioceses, though again not all,[3] foreign-born priests are more likely to report loneliness than those born in the United States. This is particularly true among younger priests, those of the post–Vatican II generation. Obviously, distance from family and friends back home could play a large role in the greater loneliness they feel. It could also be that in many dioceses foreign-born priests are less well integrated into the presbyterate. Third, in a few dioceses, priests who live in small towns or rural areas often report being at least a little lonely. This tends to be the case in dioceses where geographic distances among rural parishes are particularly great. A diocesan priest who lives in a small town describes the greatest challenge he currently faces in his life:

---

[2] The dioceses have self-selected to commission these surveys from CARA; they are not a random sample drawn from among all dioceses in the country.

[3] In at least one diocese surveyed by CARA, foreign-born priests are significantly *less* lonely.

> Coping with loneliness. I'm in a small parish. There isn't too much to do. Sometimes it is very lonely, I find. Thank God I come up to [a city where there are other priests] quite often.

A religious priest, who lives in a college town where no other members of his order currently reside, describes how he feels:

> I'm surrounded by people *continuously*, but very few are my peers. If I have dinner with a family member, for example, I'm still a Father. I can't unburden myself about my stresses. I can really only do that with another member of my order. When I had another priest living with me, we would get together every evening and just talk for an hour, just review the day and compare notes and complain and laugh and cry together. That was a really wonderful experience of community. Now that he's gone, I either have to drive three and a half hours to [a large city] or I have to have long distance phone calls. That can be lonely. As I said, I'm with people constantly. . . . I have genuine friends here, but even so I don't have many local peers with whom I can remove all my filters and speak with full candor.

A final relevant finding from CARA's presbyteral surveys is that diocesan priests are more likely to feel lonely if they live alone than if they live with other priests. This is particularly true if they live alone off-site from their parish. One might infer from this finding that dioceses should consider encouraging their priests to live together, to the extent it is possible. The challenge, however, is that most diocesan priests responding to CARA's surveys say they prefer to live alone. A religious priest describes the situation as he sees it:

> As I look at my diocesan brothers, I think they somehow need to find a way to get support for themselves. A lot of them have it but a lot of them don't. . . . One of the things they tried in [the diocese] was to get pastors to live together, but it didn't work very well. That's a real concern, particularly as there are fewer and fewer priests out there.

Loneliness, along with celibacy, is probably one of the things that comes immediately to mind for many laypeople when they imagine the most difficult aspects of being a priest. Certainly the celibate lifestyle is one that many priests themselves admit is not always easy. But the media and fiction have perhaps oversold this problem through images of the tormented priest, brought to anguish after having forever turned his back on marital companionship and sexual intimacy. In recent years, revelations surrounding the sexual abuse scandal have probably reinforced the popular notion that celibacy is a source of tremendous problems, of which loneliness is just one. Though loneliness is indeed a significant issue in the priesthood—more on this later—we should keep in mind that fewer than half of priests report loneliness to be problematic for them.

> I'm very blessed. I have great family. I'm so grateful to my parents. I have very good priest friends that I talk to frequently, get together with. Their friendship is beautiful. I really don't experience loneliness, at least not to a really intense degree. I just haven't experienced it. For me, I need more solitude in my life. I love to eat alone and to listen to books on tape. I pray: "Lord, please, give me some time alone to pray and be with you!" I feel like Jesus when the crowds were pressing on Him. He retired to the mountain alone to pray. Please, let me go to the mountain alone. . . . Any time you're talking to a young man who's considering priesthood, that's his greatest fear. "I'm going to be so lonely. What am I going to do?" Once you enter into it, it's really not that bad. You discover you are not really alone but there with Christ.

A retired priest whose close priest friends have all died talks about finding relationships in his ministry:

> Loneliness is not an issue. I would say this: the lack of immediate family could make life difficult if I got very sick to the point where I couldn't take care of myself. But then again the diocese would take care of me. I've found out that your friends are where you are. Deep friendships take a long time, but good friendships can be found wherever you're ministering, living, or such. . . . I spent six weeks in a nursing home because I broke my hip. I go back to that same place now once a week and I visit everybody in it. I know all the help and I know most of the patients who are there long-range, those in rehab. It's a great joy to me to be going in, smiling, and spending time. Occasionally I anoint one, but I'm not the chaplain.

A relatively strong correlation exists between experiencing celibacy as a problem and experiencing loneliness as a problem. Of priests who say that celibacy is at least "somewhat" of a problem, 62 percent say that loneliness is also a problem. Priests we interviewed were often reluctant to discuss celibacy in their own lives. Those who did share with us on this issue talked about being aware of the path they did not take in life and, in some cases, having questions about the purpose of priestly celibacy. The following comment, from a priest whose ministry involves working with other priests, exemplifies both concerns:

I don't know that I would say it's a *struggle* for me personally. It's certainly an *issue* for me, trying to understand what celibacy means and how to find appropriate intimacy in my life for nurturing. Part of that has to do with coming on middle age. My nieces and nephews are all starting to go to college. I'm just thinking about life and, "What if I had a wife and kids? How would my life be different?" I think it becomes more present in my work when I'm dealing with guys who are not faithful to celibacy and talking to them about their own struggles. It makes me think about my own life and how I find balance. . . . Do I struggle with celibacy? No. But I'm at that point in life when I keep asking myself, "What is the ultimate value of celibacy?" I guess I'm questioning whether it's necessary for functioning as a Roman Catholic priest in the United States. I would say that I don't believe it's necessary for everyone. I see it as a value for some and certainly some people embrace it a lot easier, but I don't see it as necessary.

Problems over Time

Table 3.3 shows cross-time comparisons of the percentage of priests who identify various issues as "a great" problem for them personally. It reveals a great deal of stability in responses to this series of questions. "The way authority is exercised in the Church" was the most commonly identified problem in 1970, just as it is now. Moreover, the percentage for this item in 2009 is reasonably close to what it was in 1970. Similarly, the percentage for "difficulty of really reaching people today," while having fluctuated over the years, has ended up close to where it was four decades ago.

The one item in table 3.3 for which there has been a steady increase is not surprising. The proportion of priests saying that "too much work" is a great problem has moved up from 8 percent in 1970 to 17 percent at present. In fact, if there is any surprise about this, it's that the increase hasn't been even greater.[4] There has also been a slight increase for "unrealistic demands and expectations of laypeople," from 7 to 15 percent, though the percentage was actually highest in 1993 when it was 18 percent. Thus there has been a doubling since the early 1970s of the propor-

---

[4] The growing proportion of priests who are retired (and therefore less affected by the problem of workload) masks the size of the increase, though only slightly. Among all priests, those reporting too much work as a great problem rose from 11 percent in 1985 to 17 percent in 2009, a difference of 6 percentage points (See table 3.3). Among priests who are *not retired*, those reporting too much work as a great problem rose from 12 to 20 percent during the same time period, a difference of 8 percentage points.

tions of priests identifying these two issues as a "great" problem for them. That workload and lay expectations are becoming greater concerns for priests—and the likelihood that they will only worsen in the future—may account for the intense discussion of them in interviews and focus groups.

Table 3.3
Selected Problems, by Year
(Percentage saying each is a "great problem for me personally")

	1970	1985	1993	2001	2009
The way authority is exercised in the Church	26%	21%	26%	24%	30%
Difficulty really reaching people today	16	7	10	7	18
Too much work	8	11	15	16	17
Unrealistic demands and expectations of laypeople	7	15	18	13	15
Being expected to represent Church teachings I have difficulty with	—*	—*	14	13	15
Relationship with the bishop of the diocese in which you work**	—*	8	11	7	14
Uncertainty about the future of the Church	9	5	11	10	12
Celibacy or lifelong commitment to chastity***	11	15	14	10	11
Loneliness of priestly life	15	14	15	13	11
Relationships with superiors or pastor	12	9	8	7	10

* Not asked

** In 1985, the question asked about the "ordinary" rather than "bishop."

*** Before 2009, the question was "celibacy" only.

Conclusion: The Relationship between Happiness and Problems in Priestly Life

As we saw in chapter 2, satisfaction is higher among priests than among members of most other professions. It has remained high—even risen slightly—despite an increase in problems such as workload and expectations of the laity. Is there a complete disconnect between satisfaction and problems among priests? It turns out that the relative happiness of priests can, in fact, be predicted quite well by the extent to which they say *a few particular* issues are problems. However, these are not the problems that are most common. The one question in our survey that best predicts priests' general happiness is the extent to which loneliness is a problem. Of the one in ten priests who say loneliness is a "great" problem for them, just 23 percent report being "very" happy in their lives as priests. Of priests who say they experience "no problem at all" with loneliness, 86 percent are very happy. As we saw earlier, most priests who say celibacy is a problem for them also feel lonely. But priests may be lonely for other reasons too, for example, if they feel isolated from or unsupported by their fellow priests. Consider two hypothetical priests: one who feels lonely but experiences little problem with celibacy, and a second who struggles with celibacy but nevertheless feels little loneliness. The latter is more likely to feel "very happy" in his life as a priest.[5]

The second best predictor of overall happiness in our survey is the extent to which priests experience a "lack of opportunity for personal fulfillment."[6] (This item is not shown in table 3.1 because it falls outside the top twelve problems.) Questions in the 1985 survey help us better understand what priests mean when they say they "lack opportunity for fulfillment." Such men tend to describe their work as not giving them a "sense of accomplishment" and not being "satisfying." They tend to describe themselves as lacking "autonomy to make decisions" compared to other professionals and as frequently feeling "bored." Finally, they typically feel they are not using "important skills and abilities" in their current assignment. While loneliness reflects the private side of priestly unhappiness, lack of opportunity for personal fulfillment appears to reflect the ministerial side.

While feeling burdened by too much work diminishes priests' overall happiness, it does so to much less of an extent than loneliness or lack of opportunity for personal fulfillment. We find this surprising because workload clearly affects the extent to which priests can meet all the needs of the people to whom they minister, and it harms the sense of balance

---

[5] This does not necessarily mean that loneliness is the strongest predictor of whether priests eventually choose to leave the priesthood entirely. We cannot provide definitive evidence on that topic because our sample includes no resigned priests. Researchers disagree about the single most important factor in priest resignations (Hoge, 2002; Greeley, 1972, 2004), but both celibacy and loneliness are unquestionably important.

[6] Note that in the 1985 survey, lack of opportunity for personal fulfillment was the strongest predictor of happiness and loneliness was a close second.

they feel in attending to their own needs. One possible explanation lies in the importance of relationships. Recall from the previous chapter that the specific sources of satisfaction that most strongly predict overall happiness are (for diocesan priests) "being part of a community of Christians who are working together to share the Good News of the Gospel" and (for religious priests) "the sense of well-being that comes from working with like-minded priests" and the "sense of well-being that comes from living the common life with like-minded priests." And of course loneliness is the problem in table 3.1 that most strongly predicts overall happiness. These items all reflect the extent to which priests have fulfilling relationships with other people. A heavy workload presumably limits the time priests have available for socializing with other priests or spending personal time with family and friends. Other than these challenges, however, overwork may not necessarily harm priests' interactions with others and therefore may not necessarily harm their overall satisfaction. At the least, busy parish priests are pouring their time into a parish community and the web of relationships of which it consists.

There is an exception, however. Among pastors who are responsible for multiple parishes, the problem of workload becomes a somewhat stronger predictor of unhappiness. We suspect that, as priests become spread thin among multiple parishes, it becomes harder to establish meaningful relationships with their parishioners. Priests become less able to feel that they themselves are part of the communities they serve. As one priest we interviewed puts it,

> If you let the workload get out of hand, it can grind you down. . . . I have misgivings about a circuit-rider approach to handling ministry in our Church as we get fewer and fewer priests. . . . You just can't connect well with people that way. There's a satisfaction that I think we derive from the engagement and ministry with people. That's harder to do if you're trying to juggle a number of different parishes on a circuit-rider basis.

As pastoring multiple parishes becomes more common, this concern is likely to grow. Chapter 4, which focuses on collaboration, discusses in greater depth several of the problems that have been touched upon in this chapter, among them, the ministerial challenges that arise in a time of fewer active priests.

Chapter 4

Collaboration in Ministry

I think collaboration is an essential part of priestly ministry, both in parishes and institutions. I rely upon the lay people for a lot of different things, both people on the staff and volunteers, in terms of pastoral council, finance council, consulting trustees, parishioners who help and direct building and renovation projects. I teach in the school, so I collaborate with the principal and teachers in that setting as well. I'd say on the whole it's been a rather positive experience. I couldn't imagine doing what I do without the help of lay people.

—Priest in an interview

In the United States over the last forty years the number of active Roman Catholic priests available for ministry has been declining as the number of Catholics continues to increase. Moreover, priests are neither randomly nor equitably distributed throughout the United States. For example, according to statistics provided by dioceses and published in *The Official Catholic Directory* (OCD), in 2009 there were 1,604 Catholics for every priest in the 194 dioceses and eparchies that are members of the USCCB.[1] However, this statistic masks the reality that 143 dioceses or eparchies had a ratio of Catholics to priests that was lower than this national average (fewer Catholics for each priest) and 51 had a ratio that was higher than this—eight in ten of them located in the South or the West, the areas of greatest growth in Catholic population. In all probability, no bishop would say that he has too many priests to meet the ministerial needs of his diocese and few would boast that they have a sufficient

[1] The Archdiocese for the Military Services, USA, is excluded here because the hundreds of priests and millions of Catholics served by this archdiocese are counted in their home dioceses.

Figure 4.1
Church Leadership Positions over Time

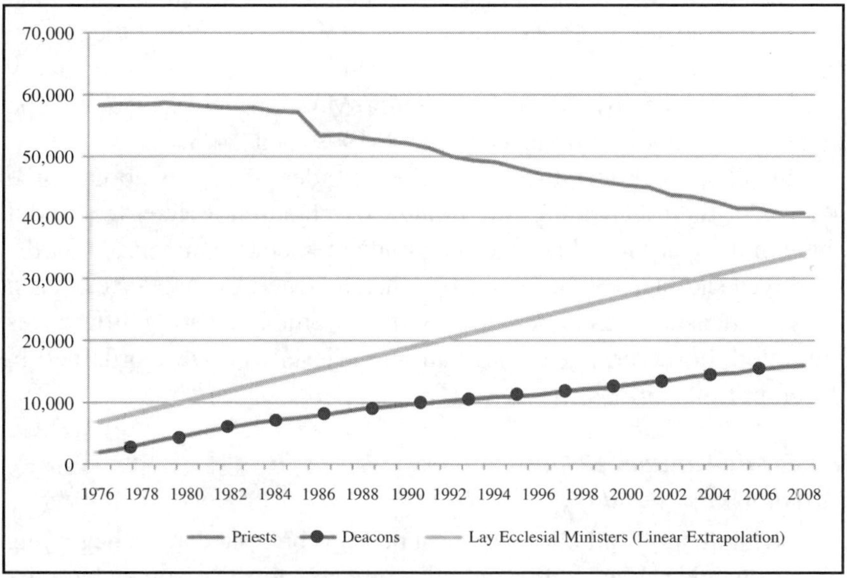

number. A few dioceses, particularly in California, Nevada, and Texas, are experiencing the "priest shortage" as a ratio that is more comparable to the 6,000 Catholics per priest found in Mexico than the 1,600 Catholics per priest average in the United States.

Church leaders have tried a number of measures to alleviate some of the increasing pressure on priests, from reinstating the permanent diaconate —allowing for the ordination of married men as permanent deacons— and employing lay ecclesial ministers, to recruiting priests from other countries and accepting converts ordained in other denominations to be ordained as married priests. Over the same period, attitudes among Catholic laity and ordained leaders about the nature and function of leadership have evolved. Stemming in part from a renewed understanding of the role of the laity in the life of the Church, the documents of the Second Vatican Council emphasized baptism as the source of a universal call to holiness. They promoted an understanding of the Church as the people of God, and they urged the laity to become more actively involved in parish life and to assume more responsibility for leadership. Lay leadership and the restored permanent diaconate flourished at the same time as priestly vocations declined. Figure 4.1 displays the total number of ordained clergy (priests and permanent deacons) as reported in the OCD from 1976 through 2009. Nonordained Church leadership positions, such as lay ecclesial ministers, is an emerging trend in the Church that is not yet tracked by OCD or any other source. Therefore, the line in figure 4.1 that represents lay ecclesial ministers is drawn from survey estimates provided by the late Msgr. Philip Murnion and David DeLambo in a series of studies published in 1992, 1999, and 2005.

This chapter looks at trends in the attitudes of priests about some aspects of their leadership role in the Church and how they feel about some of the measures that have been implemented to compensate for the perceived shortage of priests. We find that, in general, acceptance of each of these measures has increased over time. Some interesting differences are noted, however, particularly among priests who were ordained in different time periods.

Trends in Attitudes Relating to Fewer Priests in Parish Ministry Today

The number of Catholics per priest that was presented at the beginning of this chapter (about 1,600 Catholics for each priest) is somewhat misleading, because it includes all living priests, without taking into account their availability for parish ministry. If we exclude religious priests (because less than a third of Jesuits, Franciscans, and other religious order priests are involved in parish ministry) and only focus on diocesan priests that are not retired or otherwise removed from ministry, we see that the total number of Catholics per active diocesan priest has increased from about 1,500 Catholics per priest in the mid-1970s to about 3,500 per priest now.[2] When polled by CARA recently, two-thirds of adult Catholics say they are aware that there are fewer priests today but half of these say they have *not* been personally affected by the priest shortage (Gray and Perl, 2008). In contrast, two-thirds of the priests surveyed in this study say that a shortage of available priests is a "somewhat" or "great" problem to them on a day-to-day basis (see table 4.1).

---

[2] This is the ratio of the total parish-identified Catholic population to the total number of diocesan priests who are in active ministry—not retired, ill, or otherwise removed from ministry—as reported in the OCD.

Table 4.1
Importance of Selected Problems on a Day-to-Day Basis for Priests

	"Somewhat" or "Great" Problem
Shortage of available priests	66%
Unrealistic demands and expectations of laypeople	53
Difficulty of working with international priests	31
Conflict with parishioners or laity about issues	28
Difficulty of working with women	5

One priest explained his perception of the situation like this:

> Day to day, getting Masses done, hospital visits, funerals, etcetera leaves very little time for vision. Starting new programs and seeing the needs [is difficult] because there are not as many priests and each priest has multiple jobs.

The pressure is experienced most severely by priests who have been in ministry long enough to remember a time when the ratio was more favorable, a time when every parish had a resident pastor and when many parishes had one or more associate pastors sharing the load and learning the ropes. Most priests of the Vatican II and pre–Vatican II ordination cohorts, whether active or retired, experience the current shortage of available priests as at least "somewhat" of a problem for them on a daily basis (see table 4.2). Post–Vatican II priests, who are in active ministry now and experiencing this shortage firsthand, yet who have been ordained long enough to remember a time when the perception of shortage was less acute, are even more likely than the older cohorts of priests to say that the shortage is at least "somewhat" of a problem to them on a day-to-day basis. By contrast, the most recently ordained cohort of priests, whose only experience of ministry is in a Church where all are stretched thin, are less likely than older cohorts to see this as a problem to them. Age and energy may be factors as well.

We asked priests to describe some of the challenges of having fewer priests available for ministry. A priest in his 30s contrasted his own situation with that of 1960s associate pastors surveyed by Joseph Fichter, SJ

Table 4.2
Importance of Selected Problems on a Day-to-Day Basis, by Ordination Cohort
(Percentage who say each issue is a
"somewhat" or "great" problem to them)

	Pre–Vatican II	Vatican II	Post–Vatican II	Millennial
Shortage of available priests	68%	66%	70%	59%
Unrealistic demands and expectations of laypeople	42	54	60	55
Difficulty of working with international priests	28	33	32	30
Conflict with parishioners or laity about issues	21	27	34	32
Difficulty of working with women	7	3	5	4

(1968). As we already described in chapter 2, many of those young priests were unhappy with the lack of responsibility in their ministry:

> Certainly, responsibility has its own crosses. Here I am, not even forty, and my goodness, who would have thought that I would be a pastor for ten years now? That's ridiculous! Who becomes a pastor when they're thirty? So there's some crosses in making men pastors at a young age too.

Said another, older, priest:

> We are going through a robust merger process. We are closing forty to fifty parishes within the next year. This is a big process and will provoke many hurt feelings for many years . . . The reality is, we have a third less priests than five years ago and in the next forty years we're going to be half of this, so it needs to be done. The challenges are: how do we get people to understand where we are coming from and the reality of the shortage of priests? I see the workload for the priest increasing. Most people only see us on Sunday.

Fewer priests and more Catholics also translate into more demands on a priest's time. More than half of priests say that the unrealistic demands and expectations of laypeople are at least "somewhat" of a problem to them on a day-to-day basis. Pre–Vatican II priests are less likely than younger priests to cite this as a serious problem for them. Likewise, older priests are less likely than younger priests to say that conflict with parishioners is a problem for them on a daily basis. However, about half of pre–Vatican II priests are retired from ministry and less likely to be experiencing these issues on a day-to-day basis.

One priest describes the challenges of lay expectations and workload this way:

> The work is growing while the number of priests is decreasing, so there is much more expectation as to what the priest must do in his parish, with the local community, and for the diocese. If a priest is not careful, I think it could be overwhelming, daunting, and lead to burn out rather quickly.

A priest who took over a parish that had been administered by a religious community had to try to explain to his parishioners why he could not provide the same level of pastoral services that they had come to expect when the parish had several religious priests in residence. He described his experience as follows:

> I am now there by myself so I had to cut back on a few things and I was met with a great deal of hostility simply because they don't realize that I'm all by myself. My predecessor had help.

Another explained his frustration like this:

> Ministry is becoming more and more sacramental. Priests just do sacraments. I don't do counseling any more. I'll talk to people for half an hour and refer them to someone. You know, when we were talking about spiritual reading, I mean you've got to be kidding! There is no time for that kind of stuff, nor leisure . . . It doesn't exist anymore.

Although it is perhaps less of a problem for them on a daily basis, conflicts with parishioners or laity about issues may become even more frequent as there are fewer priests ministering to more Catholics. In the days when multiple priests served in a parish, they could share responsibilities and even specialize in certain aspects of ministry. For example, the youngest associate was often assigned to supervise the youth group, while another might handle most couples' counseling and still another would be responsible for sacramental preparation. Parishioners, too, would regularly seek out a favorite confessor or a priest with whom they had a closer relationship for advice or a favor. Multiple priests ministering in a parish often meant that parishioners could seek out a friendly ear or "shop around" for a priest that would accommodate them. That is no longer possible in most parishes, where a single priest is the ultimate authority figure.[3] Conflicts with parishioners or laity on issues is a problem for one in three priests, with those ordained more recently and thus still in active ministry more likely to feel this way. One priest shared his frustration with conflicts caused by parishioners' heightened expectations:

> One of the challenges is the expectations of people. That seems to have changed a great deal. Especially in hurting situations like a funeral or even weddings, peoples' egos are caught up in these events. It is also hard to set boundaries and invite people to change in any fashion.

Another priest described a conflict with his parishioners over the use of parish funds. Although both sides sincerely believed they had the best interests of the parish at heart, the interaction was still stressful:

> The parish was purchasing some homes around the parish to build green space and a few parishioners disagreed with me on that. They came in and talked to me. It really bothered me because they were on the steward-ship committee. I respected and liked them and yet they couldn't see the importance of getting some green space around our property. And each of them lived on large lots, if not acres. They couldn't see the inconsis-tency: "Can't we have a little breathing room around here for our kids? Yet you can live on acreage and not have any trouble with that?" Those things are just part of the human condition.

Nevertheless, conflicts with parishioners or laity over issues are a fact of life, and a reality that one in three priests struggle with on a daily basis. This priest describes the psychological toll that such conflicts take on his life:

> I help out in a particular parish. It is the wealthiest and the most Repub-lican parish. And I struggle with my perception of their true Christian values whenever I dare to preach Catholic social teachings. I've had every-thing from people walking out, to standing up to argue. It's a real struggle for me as a priest. I'm not the pastor and I understand the pastor's perspec-tive. Maybe I am offending some of his biggest donors. But as a priest it's really disheartening and I had to kind of balk. It is not my parish but I have some strong feelings about the Church's social teachings and see this as really Jekyll and Hyde. These people are very loving. They bring

---

[3] According to CARA's *National Parish Inventory*, even ten years ago six in ten parishes had only one priest in residence (Gautier and Perl, 2000).

food to the poor. But boy if you talk about immigration reform and compassion for immigrants or any number of social teachings you get this radical reaction which is disheartening.

Attitudes Relating to International Priests

Many bishops have looked outside the United States for help in addressing the issue of too few priests for ministry. Perhaps as many as a fifth or more of all priests currently living in the United States were born elsewhere. In this study, 11 percent of responding priests were born outside the United States. However, we believe that this is probably an undercount of the actual percentage of foreign-born priests in the United States. A CARA study of dioceses conducted in 1999 found that 16 percent of priests identified by US dioceses were born outside the United States (Froehle and Gautier, 1999).

Three in ten priests in this study say that working with priests from other countries is a problem for them on a day-to-day basis (see table 4.1). The survey did not ask priests about their experience in working with international priests as associates or colleagues; most likely, the majority of priests do not work with another priest from outside the United States on a daily basis. Not surprisingly, international priests are less likely than US-born priests to indicate that working with international priests is a problem to them. Likewise, there is little difference among the ordination cohorts on this attitude, but individual priests often talk about problems they have experienced in working with international priests. Said one priest in a focus group:

> We have fifteen priests from India and several from Africa. That's definitely a short-term solution. We're discovering with international priests that after they come and they're here for a while, they go home and are half acculturated. They are not fully of us but they can't go home either.

Another priest, in a different setting, related his experience with the international priests in his diocese:

> It's good to have them and, of course, they have their part to play regarding diversity and the needs in the parish. Things come out [in conversations with parishioners, such as,] "They can't speak English; I can't understand them." [Another problem is that] they're not available for certain things. They become limited in what they are doing instead of more active, but that depends on the individual. We have an Indian priest. He slows down his homily, but some parishioners asked him to print out his homilies and he did. He's kind and gentle and has a following.

One priest was quite vocal about his suspicions concerning the motivations of international priests who come to the United States for ministry. He related the following:

> When I was a pastor I had several people living with me who were internationals. You begin to question the agenda. Why would any bishop from around the world let somebody go to America unless [he] didn't know what to do with him, like the "old lady in the shoe"? . . . I had a young guy living with me for a while who was very nice, young, good looking, charming. He played the language card. He didn't speak English very well at all; he got along on his smile and his charm; the people were falling all over him even though they couldn't understand a word he said. I couldn't understand a word he was saying . . . It came to a question of whether we should or shouldn't incardinate him. The person they wanted to talk to is me. I'm not saying he's a bad guy or he's a bad priest; I'm not saying he is immoral; I'm just saying I think he's got an agenda. I think he's pulling the wool over people's eyes with his language thing because he could choose to learn English but he doesn't want to. People give him things because he's cute and he smiles. So someone says to me, "They only come here for the stipend." I said that's manipulation. Well he's a warm body, he's ordained and we need him. So that's the solution to the vocation crisis. We just bring in people who may or may not be nice, may or may not be manipulative, may or may not be child molesters.

Seven in ten priests in this study said that it is at least "somewhat" important to them to have open discussion about collaborating with international priests working in the United States. One priest in a focus group suggested a need to learn from the international priests what it is that they feel they contribute to the Church in the United States by their ministry here:

> It is important to try to find out what they can contribute to us, especially the new arrivals. They are going through a very difficult time in terms of their enculturation. I'm not sure anybody is asking them seriously to reflect pastorally about what they can help us on.

Several priests described the difficulty of developing and maintaining a sense of presbyteral community with so many priests of differing nationalities. Said one priest who had formerly been a member of a religious order:

> I was a religious brother before I became a priest. When I was first ordained I used to look on the presbyterate the same way I looked on the community

to which I belonged. I saw all the other priests as my confreres. I feel that has broken down a lot over the course of being ordained. Some of it has to do with priests coming from other countries who just get plopped into the middle of diocesan life. We're just employees of the same company. That's the relationship I see now.

Another priest described the need to provide more consistent preparation for international priests who are coming to the United States for ministry. He recommends that dioceses could benefit from open discussion about how best to prepare international priests for ministry:

> There is not sufficient work on enculturation of foreign clergy. We don't get national programs. Dioceses are scrambling to figure that out. So that's a huge need not being answered—we are too quick to grab for solutions and bring in foreign clergy.

This priest raises the question about the trade-off for the diocese in bringing in international priests for ministry:

> There is a great challenge, I feel, in this situation. There will be a problem of adjustment: how the international priests can adjust from their point of view and from the point of view of the people, the beneficiaries . . . With this kind of adjustment, a diocese will have no way of depending on international help. To have programs that assist the international priests to be of greater service, effective service, will be a real problem initially. To overcome that, several programs have been put into place. They have started doing it. But it is a great challenge for the dioceses that depend on the international priests. And it is not going to go away soon.

While the diocese benefits from having more priests available for ministry, the challenge is to provide resources to assist the international priests (and the people they serve) to adjust to one another. The priest quoted above also cautions that depending on international priests could be only a short-term solution to the problem of too few priests for the pastoral ministry needs of the diocese. He implies that open discussion about these issues would be a good thing.

Trends in Attitudes Relating to Increased Collaboration

Another reality of parish life in the United States today is that pastors are less likely to live and work with other priests (associates, or parochial vicars), but instead tend to live alone. They work with a variety of trained lay ecclesial ministers and permanent deacons, who have assumed many of the responsibilities, such as religious education, sacramental preparation, youth ministry, and facilities management, which previously had been assigned to priests. For the most part, priests have adjusted well to this change and have welcomed the additional collaboration. Since 1993, between a quarter and a third of priests surveyed have agreed that it is "very important" to them to have open discussion about sharing their ministry (or collaborating in ministry) with permanent deacons.

As table 4.3 shows, support among priests for lay ecclesial ministry has increased steadily across each survey in this series. At the same time, their support for the third statement in the table has remained virtually unchanged. Two in three agree that priests should achieve greater status as competent professionals in the eyes of the Catholic community, but they do not express any more urgency about this topic than they did in either 1993 or 2001—even as diaconal and lay ecclesial ministry have grown in size and acceptance in parishes.

Table 4.3
Trends in Attitudes about the Priesthood and the Church Today
(Percentage who "somewhat" or "strongly" agree)

	1993	2001	2009
Parish life would be aided by an increase in full-time professional lay ecclesial ministers.	—	72%	81%
The Catholic Church needs to move faster in empowering laypersons in ministry.	70	73	77
It is urgent that priests achieve greater status as competent professionals in the eyes of the Catholic community.	65	67	68

Eight in ten priests agree that parish life would be aided by an increase in lay ecclesial ministry and most priests are open to the idea of laypeople assuming more responsibility for parish life. Many of the priests talking with us in focus groups shared a perception that collaboration is key to vital parish life. Some of their comments include the following:

> Clearly the church is more collaborative today. I have been at my parish nine years and the previous pastor was there for eight years. He had everything in place and I took the ball and ran with it. Our church really evolved over the two administrations. More people are getting more and more involved in more things and that's exciting to me. I just try to get out of their way.

You've got to have a good organization, good people working with you. I have a great secretary, a great choir director, and a great person who oversees the plans of the building. I can walk out and come back seven days later and know that everything was done right. You can lay off the pressure. I meet with them every day . . . I'm very happy with everything, but you've got to have people you trust. Lay it off . . . Delegate!

What I do is, I use lay people as much as I can. For instance, they can even help with communion services and things like that. So, I really feel that this idea that the priest or the deacon has to do everything, we are in a different age.

Some priests feel that the Church is not doing enough right now to encourage the laity to become more involved in parish life. They recognize that it takes time to create a culture of involvement among parishioners as well as time to form laypeople for ministry. The priest quoted below worries that there will be a gap in parish services unless more is done to prepare lay ministers:

I feel we need to do a lot more to get the community of the Church to take more of a sense of ownership . . . and to be more involved because this whole idea of the clergy doing everything, or even priests doing as much as we are doing now, is going to continue to change. We're simply not going to be able to offer people the same level or the same amount of parish services as what they were being offered twenty or thirty years ago when parishes that have one priest frequently had three.

One diocesan priest we interviewed for this project shared how he encouraged collaboration in his parish:

Part of how I see priesthood is to be one who gathers people. For years I gathered all sorts of people into the rectory for very informal dinners to get to know them better, to listen to them. And in that process sometimes somebody mentioned something they were very interested in or you just sensed some leadership ability. Then I invited them or called them to a deeper level of involvement. Since I've been here, about three years now . . . people have really taken leadership roles in adult education, peace and justice kinds of stuff, and a men's spirituality group. I have a parish council and a finance council . . . They care about it. Part of what I told them when I asked them to be on it is: Unless it's something about faith and morals, I want to hear your piece and I want you to hear my piece, but in the end we're going to work on a consensus model. And it works. It takes time, but people don't feel that they go to the meetings and then

Father does whatever the hell he wanted to. It's not my parish. They've been here long before I've been here and will be here probably long after I'm gone. So I've really tried to work at that.

This priest also explains how he tries to find leadership from within the parish and then work with them in a shared ministry:

> I think we need to find leadership from within the people . . . rather than imposing our will on them or telling them what is going to happen. . . . We need to collaborate with the laity rather than taking the whole burden on us that we have to minister to them. We need to bring in the new idea of collaboration and then work on that so you're not holding the burden yourself and it is theirs to share.

At the same time, this priest explains why collaboration can often be seen by priests as threatening, because it involves his relinquishing some control:

> I think [my greatest challenge as a priest] is connected with collaboration in some way. As good as it is, I have a little fear about it because we kind of lose our sense of where we are because of it. Maybe it's for the good but I'd have to be able to appreciate that a little bit more. Not to fear it but to accept it in a good way, when people are there to help you. For anything that doesn't have to be done by a priest, let somebody else do it or let them help you, whichever makes the most sense.

Other priests, in separate interviews, describe the challenge of collaboration as being able to recognize and resolve the conflicts that arise inevitably among people of goodwill who do not see eye to eye on an issue. They explain that conflicts must be managed tactfully rather than autocratically, so that collaboration will be maintained.

> Something I'm experiencing now in the current parish: There's a finance council here, which we're required to have. Under my predecessor, they met monthly and sometimes the finance council was calling the shots. I'm thinking, "No, you're simply advisory. I run things by you, but you don't control the money." My predecessor had this rule that any time he wanted to spend something more than two thousand dollars he ran it by the finance council to get their approval. I'm thinking, "No, that's not even the diocesan policy."

> On our finance council this year we have a new person who teaches finance at a university. So she wants to do everything according to the rulebook. Saying it that way sounds terrible, like we're not doing it by the book.

But she doesn't understand Church or parish. So she wanted an audit. . . .
A full audit would have been a very costly thing. People really discussed
it and looked at alternatives. We came up with, I think, a very good alternative that pleased everyone. We had what's called a procedural audit. It
gave people a new sense of confidence about the financial strength of the
parish, as well as the importance of the finance council. But initially I felt
insulted, like there was an implication I was doing something with the
money. But we talked all that out. The people didn't side with either me
or with this woman but tried to understand: What are the values at play
here? How do we work this out? I think everybody now feels very good
about it.

In general, then, priests see the need for sharing responsibility for
parish life with others. They recognize that laypeople have high expectations for parish life and that a single priest cannot possibly do it all alone.
When we asked priests how important it was to them to have open discussion about collaborating with others in ministry, about three in four
said it was at least "somewhat" important to have open discussion about
collaborating with lay ecclesial ministers and with deacons. However,
priests ordained before Vatican II were much more likely than the most
recent ordination cohort to feel that open discussion about these topics
was important (see table 4.4).

Table 4.4
Importance of Open Discussion in Selected Areas,
by Ordination Cohort
(Percentage who say open discussion on each topic is
"somewhat" or "very" important)

	Pre–Vatican II	Vatican II	Post–Vatican II	Millennial
Collaborating with lay eccle-sial ministers	83%	78%	76%	65%
Collaborating with deacons	81	72	72	64
Collaborating with interna-tional priests working in the United States	77	67	68	62
Working with lay administra-tors in c. 517.2 parishes	76	65	63	56

Likewise, about two in three priests said it was at least "somewhat" important to have open discussion about collaborating with international priests or about working with lay parish administrators.[4] Again, the most recent ordination cohort appears to be less concerned with open discussion about these topics as well.

One priest in a focus group described this orientation toward collaboration particularly well. He referenced St. Paul's experience of establishing new Christian communities in a time when the Church did not have sufficient presbyters to administer them:

> Maybe it would be good to go back to what they did in the New Testament. Paul couldn't be everywhere at the same time but undoubtedly, when he formed the Christian communities as he did, he left elders behind who were responsible for keeping things going. That was a collaborative style.

Trends in Attitudes about Working with Women

Eighty percent of lay ecclesial ministers are women (DeLambo, 2005:45). Women are half the Church and a vital part of parish life. Most priests seem to be comfortable working with women. Referring back to table 4.1, fewer than one in ten said that working with women was even "somewhat" of a problem for them on a day-to-day basis.

The following comment is from a religious priest whose current ministry is primarily administration for his order but who helps with preaching and other ministry in his spare time. He describes how he encourages and supports women in ministry roles in the schools where he helps out:

> I do a fair amount of helping out as a presider with women's communities, [including] four all-girls Catholic high schools, and obviously they need a priest presider. Sometimes I just can't meet all of their dates because I have other commitments and because that's not my primary ministry. When it's not a holy day of obligation or a solemnity we should just say, "Gee, this is an opportunity for competent lay preaching." Because it's not necessary or essential to have a Eucharistic celebration. . . . Certainly a lay woman can preside and preach and lead people in prayer. She's baptized, confirmed, and ready to go. What good modeling for those young women to see one of their teachers or principals or whoever it is, reflect

---

[4] There is a provision in the Code of Canon Law (revised 1983) for a bishop to entrust the pastoral care of a parish to a deacon or a layperson when there are too few priests in a diocese. These parishes are sometimes called 517.2 parishes, after the canon that references them. The title for laypeople who are entrusted with this responsibility varies by diocese but is most commonly called parish life coordinator or lay administrator.

on the Gospel and break it open in a way that gives them life. That's exciting to me. To invite my colleagues in ministry, who are lay women in the Church, to do that, to step up to the plate, it's exciting for me. And to see them take it and do such a great job, even better than I am, that's pretty exciting.

This same priest expresses a concern shared by many of his generation when he describes how his experiences with women in the Church shaped his formation for ministry and helped prepare him to work comfortably with women in ministry. He worries that the men currently being prepared for priestly ministry may have less exposure to women in their formation process than he did and may not be as comfortable working with women in ministry:

> A concern I have around priesthood and Church is the relationship with women in the Church. Every other member of the Church is a woman. I continue to be concerned as to how well we are integrating the gifts of women in the Church. I just think that we could do a greater job with that. Again, I'm really grateful to my religious community for the formation it gave me. I was in formation for eight years. I'm going to guess that for at least half of them I was supervised by a woman for my supervised ministry. So a woman had to give my evaluation. I had to report to her. She was the one who gave me feedback. That was a wonderfully formative experience for me. I think those types of experiences need to be more available in seminary preparation. . . . I think it's very, very important that priests and bishops have healthy regard for and relationships with women in the Church.

In fact, there are some indications that the attitudes of the more recently ordained cohort may be less accepting of collaborating with women in Church ministry. Eight in ten priests overall agree that the Church should allow women greater participation in all lay ministries; among priests of the millennial cohort, however, the proportion is two in three (see table 4.5).

The following passage is from a pastor in his 30s. He describes his frustration in trying to work with a laywoman, a religious sister, who he felt was excluding him from parish responsibilities that he believed were rightly his:

> When I came here, Sister was doing all of my job. So I did not renew Sister's contract. The previous pastor thought he needed a sister to help him. It wasn't the model that I wanted. Sister was trying to play priest, and that's a huge frustration to me. I wanted to do priestly things. Sisters

can do the sister things. And the lay people can exercise their part of the body. Every part of the body is important. When we run into problems is when sisters start taking over parts that don't belong to them. I want to meet the families I'm preparing for baptism. I'm not just going to come in and pour water over their heads. I want to meet them and prepare them, and that's not Sister's job. . . . Things are working out just nicely now because I've hired wonderful lay people to do many of the things in the parish. I don't need to print programs, put ashes and palms out, order daily meditation booklets. Why should I bother with all that? It's important and I need to make sure it's getting done. But I want to take my role as teacher in preparing for the Sacraments seriously, and that's what Sister was doing.

This young priest, a member of the millennial cohort, is full of energy and enthusiasm for his ministry. He doesn't have any problem delegating tasks to the laity, but he is concerned that the sister has taken over a pastoral role (preparing parents for the baptism of their child) that he feels is his responsibility. Members of the millennial cohort are more likely than the older priests to agree with the statement, "It is essential to uphold the distinction between priests and laity in the Church." Eight in ten priests of his cohort agree with that statement, compared to about two-thirds of priests in each of the three older cohorts (see table 4.5).

These priests of the millennial cohort do not appear to be concerned about their status; they are slightly *less* likely than older cohorts to agree that "it is urgent that priests achieve greater status as competent professionals in the eyes of the Catholic community." Neither do they appear to be overly concerned with power; more than half say they would be happy to attend primarily to the sacramental life and let the laity assume responsibility for most other functions. What they do feel strongly about is making a clear distinction between themselves and the laity. When asked about their level of agreement with the statement, "Ordination confers on the priest a new status or a permanent character which makes him essentially different from the laity within the Church," two-thirds of millennial cohort priests (64 percent) agree "strongly," compared to 48 percent of post–Vatican II priests, 36 percent of Vatican II priests, and 48 percent of pre–Vatican II priests (these percentages on level of agreement are not shown in the table).

These newer priests are also *less* likely than older cohorts to agree that parish life would be aided by an increase in full-time professional lay ecclesial ministers or that the Catholic Church needs to move faster in empowering laypersons in ministry. The data cannot tell us precisely how much of these differences in attitude are a function of fewer years

Table 4.5
Attitudes about the Priesthood and the Church Today,
by Ordination Cohort
(Percentage who "somewhat" or "strongly" agree)

	Pre–Vatican II	Vatican II	Post–Vatican II	Millennial
The Catholic Church should allow women greater participation in all lay ministries.	84%	89%	82%	65%
Parish life would be aided by an increase in full-time professional lay ecclesial ministers.	88	90	76	62
The Catholic Church needs to move faster in em-powering laypersons in ministry.	84	86	75	65
Ordination confers on the priest a new status or a permanent character which makes him essentially different from the laity within the Church.	75	61	77	88
It is essential to uphold the distinction between priests and laity in the Church.	66	58	67	79
I would be happy to attend primarily to the sacra-mental life and let the laity assume responsibility for most other functions.	66	68	61	55

in ministry (and therefore likely to change over time) and how much may be attributed to a real change in orientation among priests in their attitude toward laypeople in ministry. There is certainly a perception among many older priests that younger priests today do not share their enthusiasm for collaboration in ministry with laity, particularly with women. One priest expressed the sentiment this way in a focus group:

A lot of the guys who are recently ordained, especially the guys from other cultures, come in with a different sense. Collaborating with the laity—they're reluctant. That's a concern for people. They don't collaborate very well, [particularly] with women . . . Some come from cultures where the priest is kind of a hierarchical figure that the priest is not here in the United States.

Trends in Attitudes about Priesthood Itself

The data in table 4.5 suggest that priests ordained since 1992 (the millennial cohort) are significantly different from the priests ordained before them in their attitudes about collaboration, particularly collaboration with women and other laypersons. This finding is supported by anecdotes and by comments from other priests in interviews and focus groups. Hoge himself suggested, in previous writing from this series of studies on priestly life, that he observed an emerging difference in orientation toward ministry among priests (see the extended discussion of the "cultic model index" in chapter 2). But is there a shift in attitude among priests today about what it means to be a priest and, if so, what are the implications of that trend for collaboration in ministry?

The trend data in table 4.6 do not suggest a significant shift among priests in their fundamental attitudes about priesthood. Priests are only slightly more likely in 2009 than they were in 1970 to agree with the statement, "I feel that I am most a priest when I am saying Mass and hearing confessions." Likewise, seven in ten still agree that ordination confers a permanent character that makes a priest ontologically different from a layperson. And a majority still agrees that celibacy should be a matter of personal choice for diocesan priests. Just as in 1970, only about a third of priests today agree that this ontological difference between priests and laity is a barrier to the full realization of Christian community.

The attitude that really does distinguish priests today from their brother priests in earlier surveys is their sense of presbyteral unity. Priests in 2009 are significantly more likely than the priests in earlier surveys to agree with the statement, "What is lacking today is that closeness among priests which used to be present." This difference is statistically significant. Even as late as the 2001 survey, just about half of priests surveyed responded in the affirmative to this statement. By 2009, seven in ten felt that way.

Table 4.6
Trends in Attitudes about the Priesthood and the Church Today
(Percentage who "somewhat" or "strongly" agree)

	1970	1985	1993	2001	2009
I feel that I am most a priest when I am saying (celebrating) Mass and hearing confessions.	72%	62%	70%	73%	80%
Ordination confers on the priest a new status or a permanent character which makes him essentially different from the laity within the Church.	71	68	70	77	73
Celibacy should be a matter of personal choice for diocesan priests.	54	53	58	56	58
What is lacking today is that closeness among priests which used to be present.	52	45	52	55	70
The idea that the priest is a "man set apart" is a barrier to the full realization of true Christian community.	33	32	28	26	36

This concern about a lack of closeness among priests is related to a couple of other factors that perhaps can help explain some of the change in attitude. First, religious priests are less likely (61 percent) than diocesan priests (74 percent) to agree with the statement. Religious priests are more likely to live in community with other priests of their order and to share ministry with them. Diocesan priests are much more likely to live alone and to minister in isolation from other priests.

A second factor, however, is that priests in active ministry (70 percent) are *less* likely than retired priests (79 percent) to agree with the perception of a lack of closeness among priests. It may be that retired priests are reflecting nostalgically on a previous time when there were more priests to share the workload. Priests in active ministry today are just as fully engaged as priests were in 1970 in all the aspects of pastoral ministry that give meaning and purpose to their lives, although they are less likely than in years past to be sharing that ministry on a daily basis with other priests. Their collaborators in ministry today are laypeople and deacons, who take on many administrative functions and free up the priest to attend to the pastoral needs of the parish.

One priest described for us the way this collaboration worked in his parish:

> I think collaboration is a very important thing. . . . The wisdom of having someone take care of the business component of the parish on a day-to-day basis just makes all the sense in the world. When I was pastor, my parish was 4,200 families and I had a business manager. I was there. I signed things. I knew what was going on. I knew when things were coming up. For the most part, unless it was a major thing, like a roof or parking lot or something, I was briefed on it and gave the okay, but I didn't interact with it beyond that. I just find that to be essential. Without that I would never have gone out to do any ministry, running a place that size: 57 employees, 27 acres, with buildings all over the place. It was a full-time job just taking care of the temporal goods. . . . A business manager was essential for doing interviews and hiring people and those sorts of things. Certainly I was a part of that, but I didn't do it all.

This collaboration in the administrative aspects of parish life enables the priest to do what he feels called to do—pastoral ministry—and helps him to have more of a sense of common purpose with his brother priests. Another priest described his situation this way:

> In one of those large parishes I was in formerly there was a school, so you've got a whole school staff with a principal, a religious education director, and a youth director. You have to work with them, the parish council, the school board, and all those types of groups. Obviously the pastor is the final decision-maker but they're the ones who live there. They're going to be there after you're gone. And they know their business. . . . You've got office staff also, the bookkeepers and all that. But parish councils and finance councils and advisory boards are key.

Conclusion

Collaboration in ministry is vital for the Church. As the numbers of priests and religious decline and the number of Catholics continues to increase, this sharing in ministry has become the normative condition of priestly life. Priests, on the whole, are supportive of collaboration and see it as an asset to their priestly ministry, not as a liability. Although more recently ordained priests exhibit somewhat lower levels of acceptance for lay ministry, this may be more a function of their relative inexperience in pastoral ministry than a fundamental shift in attitude toward lay ministry itself.

These comments from one priest illustrate the sentiments of many others about the value of collaboration in ministry:

> I spent two years in a parish with three missions in [the South]: four churches, with three hundred Catholics. There were two of us there. I was the pastor. . . . With the missions, we were there on Sunday and maybe one other day. They weren't large churches, but the responsibility for upkeep fell to the lay people. If the place floods, somebody there is going to have to deal with it. . . . I mean you can get there within an hour in some cases, from one place to another. But if somebody's very sick or dies or another emergency happens, and you're not there to do it, somebody in the church has to respond to it. They were very good in these parishes about doing that. They knew that they were missions and they treated themselves as a community and ministered to one another. In some ways the priest was almost not necessary for the day-to-day ministry that went on.

Chapter 5

The Multicultural Reality of
Priestly Ministry Today

Multiculturalism brings a richness in terms of styles of prayer, devotional practices, and a deep sense of family. I find that extremely enriching for the overall parish community.

—Priest in a focus group

To speak of a multicultural church . . . is a redundancy. Is there any other kind of church in our Catholic tradition?

—Archbishop Wilton Gregory, Rome, January 9, 2008

It is no secret that both the Catholic Church in the United States and the priesthood itself are becoming increasingly multicultural. It is now commonplace, especially in the southern and southwestern dioceses of the United States, and in almost all large cities throughout the country, to find bilingual parishes where Mass is celebrated in both English and Spanish. The liturgy at many ordination ceremonies reflects this cultural and linguistic diversity with the first reading proclaimed perhaps in Spanish, the second reading in Vietnamese, and the gospel in English. If the estimate that CARA researcher Mark Gray (2010) makes is correct, there will be about 12,520 diocesan priests in active ministry by the year 2035, more than a third less than the numbers who were in active ministry in the year 2010. As the ratio of active diocesan priests per parish is projected to decline from 1.05 to 0.84 or even to 0.70 within that time frame, it is very probable that US bishops will continue to "import" priests from abroad (Gray, 2010). This means that besides needing to rely more heavily on the collaboration of laypeople, as explained in the previous chapter, priests in this country will come to depend even more on the assistance of international priests. This reality presents both abundant blessings and enormous challenges.

As table 5.1 demonstrates, the multicultural reality of the Church is a concern for priests today. Two-thirds of the participants in our study felt that it was at least "somewhat" or "very" important to have open discussion about ministry in ethnic or multicultural parishes or about multiculturalism and diversity in general. Almost seven out of ten considered it important to address the issue of collaboration with international priests working in the United States. Obviously, this complex topic demands careful attention and an effective pastoral response. Multiculturalism is not just an abstract concept; it is the reality of our Church today.

Table 5.1
Importance of Open Discussion in
Areas Related to Multicultural Issues

	"Somewhat" or "Very" important
Ministry in ethnic or multicultural parishes	66%
Multiculturalism and diversity	68
Collaborating with international priests working in the United States	69

Father Allan Figueroa Deck, SJ, the former executive director of the USCCB Secretariat of Cultural Diversity in the Church, stated that "immigration has always been at the heart of the American experience" and that "ethnic ministry has become the main ministry of our time" (Anderson, 2008). Referring to a 2008 Pew Forum survey,[1] Deck stressed that the new and emergent groups of immigrants are on track to becoming the majority of US Catholics within a short period of time.

Data gleaned from the report by the Subcommittee on Hispanic Affairs in the 2008 USCCB document *Embracing the Multicultural Face of God: Recognizing Cultural Diversity in the Church* support this claim. Hispanics/Latinos compose more than a third of all Catholics in the United

---

[1] "Religion in America: Non-Dogmatic, Diverse and Politically Relevant," Pew Forum on Religion & Public Life, last modified June 23, 2008, http://pewresearch.org/pubs/876/religion-america-part-two.

States today. They have been responsible for 71 percent of the growth of the Church in this country since 1960, and more than half of all US Catholics under the age of 25 are of Hispanic/Latino descent. As of July 2007, the estimated Hispanic/Latino population was 45.5 million and demographic projections predict a more than doubling within the next forty years, reaching 102.6 million by the year 2050.

As mentioned in chapter 1, despite such a large representation among the Catholic laity, only 15 percent of newly ordained priests in the United States are of Hispanic/Latino descent. In the older generations of priests, their percentage is even smaller. This was a concern that some participants mentioned during our focus group discussions. One priest stated quite pointedly, "The Hispanics are filling the pews but are not producing their own priests." Before delving into that specific challenge and some of the others that multiculturalism generates, it is worthwhile to listen to what some priests in our focus groups said when asked, What gifts does multicultural diversity bring to your ministry?

One priest who serves at a large inner-city parish that is host to many different ethnic groups enthusiastically related:

> This is what the Catholic Church really is. What's Catholic about us is the ability of these folks [recently arrived immigrants], coming from a variety of cultures and language groups, to come and to tell their stories. Hopefully, we can hear those stories and process them all. One night [at my parish] we sang "Silent Night" all together in a variety of languages. It had a real neat effect.

Another priest at the same focus group spoke about the joy that he has experienced within the multicultural setting of his parish:

> I have also been a part of a large multicultural community. What inspired me the most was being enriched by the inter-connectedness and the joy that is inherent in such settings. . . . I find it interesting that the spiritual direction work I have done with people of different cultural contexts has influenced and enriched my image of God.

At a different listening session, an older priest marveled at how much time the non-Anglos in his parish spend at church on any given Sunday:

> It seems that church is a big part of their life, like when they come to church it is not just from nine to ten o'clock and then I'm gone. I got my thing done. They make a morning, a day of it.

Finally, another priest gave a glowing summary of his own experience by stating that "there's a vitality and enthusiasm for life that different cultures bring to the Church."

During the same focus groups conducted around the country, priests were also asked to comment on how multicultural diversity has been a challenge to their ministry. A priest who is currently experiencing some of the tensions that are generated when different cultures come into contact spoke about how the communities in his parish seemingly do not want to have anything to do with each other:

> I live in a parish that is heavily Spanish and multicultural. The pastor is trying to improve his linguistic skills in Spanish and in dealing with their culture. I really don't believe, personally, that there is any desire on the part of the two communities in the parish to have anything to do with each other. They are quite happy being who they are. There's a 12:30 [Spanish] Mass and they have their Hispanic devotions, their Hispanic music, their Hispanic food. The pastor is trying to bring two communities together but they don't want to be together. They say, "We want our church to be Spanish . . . Not that we hate the Anglos, we just don't want anything to do with them and the Anglos feel the same way."

An elderly priest spoke about how trying to cater to all the needs and requests of the different ethnic groups can be very taxing on a parish priest:

> A pastor who is a good friend of mine said that the Holy Thursday Mass at his parish would not be very well attended because that is one of the few Masses they do bilingually. A lot of the Hispanics won't come because some of the Mass will be in English and the white people will go across town to the other church because it will be partly in Spanish. People went out of their way not to participate in the liturgy, which was purposely organized to bring them together. The pastor did two Good Friday services: one in Spanish and one in English. Talk about killing priests. . . . On a larger issue, a lady in my parish said, "Let them learn English; my grandmother had to learn English." So there is an attitude as well with the people who are there. . . . It's a difficult time in transition.

A priest from an inner-city parish focused on the economic hardships that his many immigrant parishioners face on a daily basis:

> One struggle that I've had is the economic neediness of the immigrants. They tend to be of lower socioeconomic status and are the first ones to be

> laid off, and many times they don't even have documents. And so when laws change it's harder for them to get jobs. Trying to respond to the human needs and the poverty is a challenge.

Similar to the earlier quote about the Hispanic community not producing their own vocations, a diocesan priest complained about a certain "just-one-way" mentality of taking from the community without giving back that obviously annoys him:

> The immigrant families are growing. We have more than two hundred baptisms per year but no vocations coming from the community. This "just-one-way" mentality makes it very difficult.

The range of commentaries above shows that the experience of multi-culturalism is definitely not monolithic. Some people see it as a major blessing and a sign of vitality, whereas others find it a challenge and a source of disunity. Much could be said about multicultural diversity among Catholic laity today but since this book focuses on priesthood, we will devote the rest of this chapter to the multicultural reality of the priests themselves.

Multicultural Priesthood Today

Before the launching of this study, the most current research on multi-culturalism in the priesthood in the United States was published in 2006 by the late Dean Hoge and Father Aniedi Okure, OP, in their book *International Priests in America: Challenges and Opportunities*. In their first chapter, they clearly demonstrated that during the more than two-hundred-year history of the Catholic Church in this country the existence of a large base of foreign-born priests has been the rule, and not the exception, as many people have mistakenly thought. "The Catholic Church in the United States has always had international priests serving its parishes, and in most of its history, it depended on them. Only in one short period, from about 1940 to 1960, did Americans produce enough homegrown priests. The rest of the time foreign priests were present in great numbers, and at times dominated the church" (Hoge and Okure, 2006:1).

Hoge and Okure (2006) highlighted various moments throughout the past two centuries to prove their point. For example, in 1791, at the first US Church synod, held in Baltimore, four out of five of the clergy present were foreign-born. At the second plenary council in 1866, again held in

Baltimore, two-thirds of the bishops in attendance were born outside the United States. Among the various nationalities (for example, French, German, and Italian) that came to serve, the Irish were by far the most numerous. They had the obvious advantage of being able to speak English. By the end of the 1800s, priests who had been born in Ireland ministered in almost every diocese across the nation. It is fascinating to see the parallels that exist between the criticisms leveled against Irish clerics of yesteryear and the ones aimed at foreign-born priests today. Not only did many people in the pews consider the Irish as "outsiders" and "hard to understand" but so did many of their brother priests.

When Father Andrew Greeley conducted the first of this series of studies in 1970, he found that roughly 10 percent of all priests serving in America at that time were foreign-born. Interestingly enough, that percentage corresponded to the same proportion of Catholic males in the general population who were also born outside the United States, according to data that Greeley and Peter Rossi had collected in 1966. A national survey of priests conducted by CARA in 2002 estimated that roughly 15 percent of all active diocesan and religious priests in parish ministry were born outside the United States. The percentage rose to 19 when considering only those ordained in the previous ten years. The trend is definitely moving upward.[2]

Returning to Greeley's 1970 study, he highlighted one major dispro-portion that existed between priests and the general population of Catholic males. He found that while 17 percent of US Catholic males in the general population were of Irish paternal ancestry, 34 percent of religious priests and 39 percent of diocesan priests claimed Irish heritage. Even more interesting, 49 percent of bishops in the country at that time were of Irish descent. "In other words, while only about one-sixth of the American population is Irish, more than one-third of the clergy is Irish, as is almost one-half of the hierarchy" (Greeley, 1972:28).

A question in the 2001 CARA priest poll asked white and Hispanic/Latino priests, "What country or part of the world did your ancestors

---

[2] It should be noted that foreign-born priests may be underrepresented among respon-dents to our survey. A CARA study in 1999 estimated that international priests represented 16 percent of all priests serving in the United States. Hoge and Okure (2006) also used this estimate. If we take into account the higher percentage of foreign-born among the newly ordained, that number should have climbed slightly during the last five years. However, in this sample, they represent only 11 percent of the respondents.

come from?" It is important to note that up to three responses were allowed so that someone could have said that he was a mixture of Irish, German, and Polish descent or some other combination. Perl and Froehle (2002) found that a large proportion of priests (44 percent) still reported Irish ancestry, significantly higher than all Catholic males (22 percent). They also found that priests were disproportionately likely to be of German descent (35 percent) in comparison to Catholic males on the whole (20 percent). The other group that stood out, but in reverse, were Mexicans, who represented at the time of their study 20 percent of the national Catholic male population but less than 1 percent of the priests.

Although Irish ancestry is still prevalent among US priests today, the number of native Irish priests has become a mere shadow of what it used to be. The wave of Irish clergy coming to the United States ended in the early 1980s, when the vocation crisis hit Ireland. The majority of Irish priests working here today arrived many years ago; many of them are now retired. When people in the pews think of an international priest today, they almost automatically think of someone from Africa, India, the Philippines, or Latin America, but not from Ireland. Those days are gone.

As stated previously, during one period, from the mid-1940s through the mid-1960s, the United States produced enough of its own vocations to be able to staff its own parishes and even send some of its sons abroad as missionaries. After Vatican II, however, everything changed. Droves of priests left ministry in order to marry, fewer young men entered major seminary, almost all minor seminaries closed, and the well-documented clerical decline was set in motion. By the 1980s, US bishops had begun to look overseas once again to remedy this perceived shortage.

As an elderly priest in a focus group stated, "The African priests really saved us. We have about fifteen to twenty of them. We would have closed more parishes without the African priests." In a similar vein, a pastor of a large parish spoke in glowing terms about his Vietnamese associate, saying, "There's just the two of us. He takes care of the 250 Vietnamese families with a Mass in Vietnamese every Sunday afternoon. . . . For Holy Week last year, everybody came together. Our prayer of the faithful was read in different languages." After such a successful experience, the pastor felt energized to organize a parish-wide picnic. He felt that the presence of his Vietnamese associate was the key to the smooth integration of the two communities. Other priests were not as positive in their comments about the foreign-born priests, saying that many of them do not speak English clearly enough. Others feel that by importing these men, the bishops are not addressing the real problem of a lack of home-grown vocations.

The rest of this chapter will focus on these international priests (who come mainly from Africa, Asia, and Latin America) and how they compare to the US-born priests and other foreign-born priests from Europe (predominantly Ireland) and Canada.

Country of Origin of Priests Serving in the United States Today

Of the 933 participants identifying their country of origin, 826 were born in the United States, 44 in Europe, 6 in Canada, 30 in Asia or the Pacific Islands, 17 in Central and South America, and 10 in Africa. For the remainder of this chapter, and for the subsequent analyses, we divide the participants in the study into three categories: those born in the United States (826), those born in Europe or Canada (50), and those born everywhere else (57) whom we will call "other international" priests. The actual home countries of these 57 other international priests are Argentina, Brazil, Colombia, Cuba, Ghana, India, Mexico, Nicaragua, Oceania, Peru, the Philippines, South Africa, Sri Lanka, Syria, Uganda, and Vietnam.

Age Differences

As table 5.2 shows, the first statistically significant difference we found when analyzing these three groups hinged on their average ages. Priests in this study who were born in the United States are 64 years old, on average, as are those born in Europe or Canada. Those born elsewhere average 52 years old, more than a full decade younger than their confreres. This difference corroborates the finding of Hoge and Okure (2006), who reported that the average age of international priests in 2004 was 47, ten years less than US-born priests.

Table 5.2
Average Age of Priests, by Place of Birth

	All Priests	Priests in Active Ministry
Born in the United States	64	60
Born in Europe or Canada	64	58
Other international	52	52

Table 5.3
Background Characteristics, by Place of Birth
(Percentage in each category)

	Born in US	European or Canadian	Other International
Age group			
39 or younger	3%	6%	14%
40–49	11	18	35
50–59	21	8	24
60–69	30	28	14
70–79	24	28	11
80 or older	11	12	2
Ordination cohort			
Pre–Vatican II (ordained before 1964)	26%	28%	7%
Vatican II (ordained 1964–77)	35	39	19
Post–Vatican II (ordained 1978–91)	24	13	23
Millennial (ordained 1992 to present)	15	20	51
Ministry status			
In active ministry	77%	76%	98%
Semiretired (receiving at least partial retirement)	8	2	2
Retired (receiving full retirement benefits)	15	22	0

Another way to look at the age difference is by grouping the priests into decades by birth. Table 5.3 shows that while only 14 percent of those priests born in the United States and 24 percent of those born in Europe or Canada are less than 50 years old, almost half of the other international priests belong to that age category. If we analyze ordination cohorts, a similar pattern logically emerges. Half of the priests from Africa, Asia, and Latin America belong to the millennial cohort compared to only 15 percent of US-born and 20 percent of Europeans and Canadians. Given their lower average age, it comes as no surprise that the overwhelming majority (98 percent) of the other international priests are in active ministry compared with only about three-quarters of the other priests. The bottom section of table 5.3 shows the exact breakdown by ministry status.

Parish Ministry

As mentioned in chapter 1, most priests today are assigned to a parish as their primary ministry. Since, as the data in table 5.3 revealed, priests born in the United States, Europe, and Canada are more likely than the other international priests to be older and retired, table 5.4 shows assignments taking into account only priests who are currently in active ministry.

Table 5.4
Parish Ministry, by Place of Birth (among Active Priests Only)
(Percentage in each category)

	Born in US	European or Canadian	Other International
Are you currently assigned to a parish?			
Yes, one parish (with or without a mission church)	62%	80%	76%
Yes, more than one parish (e.g., clustered parishes)	12	9	15
No, but I help out in a parish	14	3	4
No, not engaged in parish ministry at this time	12	9	6

Even with this active ministry filter in place, the difference in assignments between the US-born priests and the other international priests is noticeable. What is curious about this particular analysis is that it represents one of the few times when European and Canadian priests are more similar to their other international confreres than they are to the Americans. While three out of four priests born in the United States are assigned to at least one parish, nine out of ten of both groups of foreign-born priests fall into the same category. This difference could be explained in part by the fact that US priests are two to three times more likely to be assigned to full-time diocesan administrative posts and to educational apostolates (analysis not shown here) than are either set of international priests. In that same analysis, we discover that while only 5 percent of US-born priests are assigned as associate pastors (also known as parochial vicars), 12 percent of the Europeans and Canadians and 24 percent of the other international priests occupy that role. In general, however, as has already been noted, the role of associate pastor is becoming less common as more (and younger) priests are filling empty pastorates.

Sense of Disconnectedness among Priests

Partly due to the importation of priests from around the world and to the fact that an ever increasing number of priests are living on their own as solo pastors, it is not surprising that some of the participants in our focus groups complained about not knowing many of their brother priests. During the "golden era" of homegrown vocations in the United States, most of the priests in a diocese attended the same seminary and so had a common point of reference. That personal historical bond has all but disappeared. Some priests told us that they don't even know the names of their brother priests in their dioceses. A young US-born priest described the problem in this way:

> At the Chrism Mass this year a priest from Africa came up to me and said: "Father, this is so strange. I look around the room and do not know who half of these priests are." I didn't have the heart to tell him that neither did I, and I began to feel the same way. I was ordained only thirteen years ago and I could look around during the Chrism Mass back then and know the names of just about everyone in the room. There is an increasing lack of ability to do that now. When you go to sit at a table at a priest gathering, all the Poles are at one table, then the Filipinos sit together, and the white people sit together. It seems like the solution is just to call Poland and order priests and they send a half dozen. I think that we are not looking at the long term view and that we are just taking a quick fix, we are just plugging holes.

Another priest said that he no longer feels that the priests in his diocese are his confreres. He said, "We are just employees of the same company. That's the relationship I see now." He attributed this change of mentality to the high influx of international priests in his diocese. He did not blame the foreign-born priests for creating the problem. In fact he felt badly for them, seeing them as men who have been "plopped down into the middle of our diocese."

Ideological Differences

The sense of disconnectedness among priests today is due not only to the distinct and distant geographies where they were raised as children and young adults but also to the ideological differences generated by the cultural milieus in their homelands. These differences are evident in table 5.5, where, using the "cultic model index" developed by Hoge and colleagues (2006), we observe some important ideological differences in attitudes concerning priesthood. As explained in chapter 2, Hoge's index ranks survey respondents, in part, according to how strongly they feel a priest ought to be a "man set apart." Only 7 percent of the other international priests are in the lowest ("progressive" or "liberal") quartile of the scale, whereas 25 percent of the US-born priests and 29 percent of the Europeans and Canadians are in the same quartile. On the other end of the same spectrum, 37 percent of the other international priests are in the highest ("traditionalist" or "conservative") quartile of the scale compared to 22 percent of the US-born and 18 percent of the Europeans and Canadians.

Table 5.5
Cultic Model Index, by Place of Birth
(Percentage in each category)

	Born in US	European or Canadian	Other International
Lowest quartile (ideologically "progressive")	25%	29%	7%
Second quartile	32	14	28
Third quartile	21	39	28
Highest quartile (ideologically "traditionalist")	22	18	37

Attitudes toward the role of women in the church are also sometimes used as a kind of ideological litmus test between "progressives" and "traditionalists." In an analysis not shown here, only 24 percent of the other international priests strongly agreed with the statement that "the Catholic Church should allow women greater participation in all lay ministries," compared to 52 percent of the US-born, Canadians, and Europeans. From that analysis and the one shown in table 5.5, some would say that priests from Africa, Asia, and Latin America are more "conservative" than their North American and European counterparts. Of course, part of this difference can be attributed (as mentioned in chapter 2) to a more "traditionalist" tendency among recently ordained priests. But other international priests are still relatively traditionalist even after controlling ordination cohort.

Differing Confidence Levels

Since these three groups of priests come from such diverse backgrounds, we thought it would be worthwhile to examine differences in their levels of confidence in various ecclesiastical entities. We asked them how much confidence they have in the decision making and leadership of the USCCB, the NFPC, their diocesan bishops, the presbyteral councils in their dioceses, and their diocesan pastoral councils. If they belonged to religious communities, we also asked about their confidence in the Conference of Major Superiors of Men and the leaders of their religious institutes. We found statistically significant differences in only three of the seven categories. As shown in table 5.6, a full quarter of the other international priests expressed a "great deal" of confidence in the USCCB, compared to only 8 percent of those born in the United States. At the low end of the spectrum, we found that 17 percent of US priests reported "very little" confidence in the USCCB, compared to only 1 percent among the two groups of international priests. It is hard to find an explanation for this difference. Could it be that international priests felt compelled to give the "socially desirable" (and safe) answer, or have they simply had a better experience with the bishops' conference? Why such a lack of confidence among those born in this country? Since we did not ask any follow-up questions in this area of the survey, any further comments would be based on speculation.

Although the differences are not as stark, priests from these three geographical regions also differ significantly in their level of confidence in the decision making and leadership of the NFPC. (As was stated in the introduction, it was the NFPC who commissioned CARA to conduct this survey.) The second section of table 5.6 shows that other international priests are the ones most likely to report "very little" confidence in the NFPC. What is also interesting in table 5.6 is the fact that 13 percent of the Europeans and Canadians express a "great deal" of confidence in the NFPC, compared to only 4 percent of US-born priests and 6 percent of the other international priests. Once again, without specific follow-up questions to this question, we can only wonder about the reasons for such differences.

Table 5.6
Confidence in the Decision Making and Leadership of
Selected Ecclesiastical Entities, by Place of Birth
(Percentage in each category)

	Born in US	European or Canadian	Other International
How much confidence do you have in . . . the USCCB?			
A great deal	8%	18%	25%
Quite a lot	27	20	21
Some	45	45	43
Very little	17	1	1
How much confidence do you have in . . . the NFPC?			
A great deal	4%	13%	6%
Quite a lot	21	26	18
Some	45	28	35
Very little	30	34	41
How much confidence do you have in . . . the diocesan pastoral council?			
A great deal	3%	14%	10%
Quite a lot	16	21	29
Some	42	39	44
Very little	40	27	17

Finally, regarding the confidence priests feel toward their own local diocesan pastoral councils, we found a pattern very similar to their attitude toward the USCCB. Four out of ten US-born priests say that they have "very little" confidence in their own diocesan pastoral councils. Only one of four Europeans or Canadians feels the same way. Even fewer other international priests (one out of six) express the same level of distrust. Perhaps future research could address these somewhat puzzling differences to find out if they exist in reality or are simply the product of the social conditioning of international priests (especially those from Africa, Asia, and Latin America) who seem hesitant to criticize authority figures or who may fear expulsion if they verbalize any kind of disapproval.

Differing Levels of Support

Besides finding out how much confidence these priests have in the above mentioned organizations, we asked them (in thirteen separate questions) how much support they receive from their brother priests, their presbyteral councils, their bishops, the Vatican, their families, and their nonpriest friends. We also asked how much support they derive from the people to whom they minister and with whom they minister, as well as from the USCCB and the NFPC. For professed religious we added three questions concerning the support they experience from their local religious communities, the leaders of their religious institutes, and the Conference of Major Superiors of Men.

We found statistically significant differences (table 5.7) in only three of the thirteen categories: (1) level of support from brother priests, (2) support from the Vatican, and (3) support from nonpriest friends. Since we had learned during the focus groups that the families of most international priests still live in their home countries, we expected that those priests would report the least support. To the contrary, 67 percent of the other international priests reported strong support from their families, compared to the 59 percent reported by US-born priests.

Support from Brother Priests

It is evident from the first section of table 5.7 that the other international priests do not always feel welcomed and supported by their brother priests in this country. Twelve percent say that they receive little or no support from brother priests, compared to only 4 percent of Americans and 6 percent of Europeans or Canadians.

In one of the focus groups, a diocesan priest from India, who is now serving as an extern, illustrated his experience in this way:

> My experience is that most priests are welcoming, even though some are not. Some do not like to speak to us, especially not to Indians. I have also seen that in regard to the Nigerians. I felt like that. But our [local US-born] bishop is a fantastic bishop. He knows us personally. He calls us by name and he knows everything about us. I really appreciate that.

In the same focus group, a priest from South America relayed a different, more positive experience by stating, "I am very proud to say that 99 percent of the local American clergy are very welcoming to me as an international priest."

Table 5.7
Support Experienced from Selected Sources, by Place of Birth
(Percentage in each category)

	Born in US	European or Canadian	Other International
How much support do you experience from brother priests?			
Strong support	39%	33%	26%
Somewhat strong support	38	33	33
Mixed or inconsistent support	20	29	28
Little or no support	4	6	12
How much support do you experience from the Vatican?			
Strong support	10%	23%	26%
Somewhat strong support	21	18	31
Mixed or inconsistent support	29	25	26
Little or no support	39	35	18
How much support do you experience from nonpriest friends?			
Strong support	62%	60%	47%
Somewhat strong support	32	23	40
Mixed or inconsistent support	5	13	11
Little or no support	1	4	2

An Indian priest who belongs to a religious order said he thinks some of the difference in experience among international priests is due to the quality of the pretransfer orientation that they receive in their homeland. He felt that his religious order, which has forty-five international priests currently working in the United States, provided a very useful orientation program for them:

> Nothing was a shock for me when I came here. We were taught that when we go to a new place you have to understand that some people may not really welcome you, but the majority will welcome you. And even that is the same with the clergy. Therefore, it was not a shock for me because I attended an orientation course. But a person who comes without that, it could be a great problem. . . . I have my own religious order in the United States so I don't feel a big problem.

Support from the Vatican

The middle section of table 5.7 shows that international priests report more support from the Vatican than do US-born priests. International priests are less than half as likely as US-born priests (18 percent compared to 39 percent) to express that they experience little or no support from the Vatican. Perhaps the responses to this question are actually more reflective of the ideological differences highlighted in table 5.5. As stated there, other international priests tend to express more "traditionalist" or "conservative" attitudes than their US counterparts as do the priests of the millennial cohort when compared to those of previous generations.

Support from Nonpriest Friends

Returning to their more quotidian realities, the third section of table 5.7 demonstrates that US-born priests report stronger support from nonpriest friends (62 percent) than do international priests (47 percent). Perhaps some of this difference can be attributed to a language barrier. International priests may have a harder time making friends because English is probably their second language. An older American priest in a focus group spoke with great admiration about a Korean priest who worked with him a few years ago. He explained that "this priest sat at his computer two hours a day to learn English. He had a program that he practiced. I applauded him." Notwithstanding that example of studious determination, other priests in the same focus group stated that not all foreign-born priests are so deeply motivated or disciplined.

Besides the language barrier that may impede international priests from developing deeper and more supportive friendships with nonpriests, some expressed a certain amount of rejection that they experienced from the very people whom they had come to serve. A priest from the southwestern part of the United States shared his own "mixed-bag" experience:

> With regard to the laypeople, most people are welcoming but some are not. I had an experience when I was celebrating Mass. One person came to me afterward (and I was only here six months), and said, "You know, we are suffering because of you. And we cannot understand your accent. And we have to suffer because we do not have priests. So, we are suffering." Then he left. Some people are really worried about international priests. But most are very cooperative, very welcoming, very supportive. Some say: "Father, you are doing very good. You are improving. You are learning a lot of things." And they are encouraging us.

Another international priest at the same focus group made light of his experience by saying, "In general the people are welcoming. They are very warm, especially in the summer. But there are also a few in whom you can sense some discriminatory attitude."

Difficulty of Working with International Priests

Not surprisingly, as was mentioned in the previous chapter on collaboration in ministry, foreign-born priests are less likely than US-born priests to indicate that working with international priests is a problem to them. Two-thirds of international priests said that it posed "no problem at all," compared to one-third of the US-born priests who responded in the same way. The Europeans and Canadians struck a middle ground, with just under half (47 percent) indicating that working with other international priests was not difficult for them.

Importance of Open Discussion on Multiculturalism

We return now to the first set of statistics that we reported at the beginning of this chapter (see table 5.1), in which at least two-thirds of the priests in this survey felt that it was either "somewhat" or "very" important to have open discussions on the three topics of (1) ministry in ethnic or multicultural parishes, (2) multiculturalism and diversity, and (3) collaboration with international priests.

In analyzing the responses according to the three groupings of priests that we have employed throughout this chapter, we discovered that there were no statistically significant differences among the groups in their responses to the need for more discussion on the topic of collaboration with international priests. All were similar in their agreement that this is at least "somewhat" important. The groups differ in attitude about the importance of discussion on the topics of multicultural parishes and multiculturalism in general. Since both topics are so similar and the responses were almost identical, table 5.8 presents only the question concerning multiculturalism and diversity. It is clear from this analysis that international priests consider multiculturalism to be a more important topic than do the US-born priests.

Training in Ministry within a Multicultural Setting

Half of the priests from Africa, Asia, and Latin America consider it "very important" to openly discuss multiculturalism; likewise, they are the ones who would appreciate having more opportunities to receive training in this field. Table 5.9 shows that they are three times more likely than US-born priests (59 percent versus 18 percent) to say that they would find it helpful to receive more training in this regard.

Table 5.8
Importance of Open Discussion on
Multiculturalism and Diversity, by Place of Birth
(Percentage in each category)

	Born in US	European or Canadian	Other International
Very important	33%	44%	50%
Somewhat important	36	24	23
Only a little important	24	20	18
Not at all important	9	11	5
I don't want it discussed	1	0	0

Table 5.9
Helpfulness of Opportunity for Training in
Ministry within a Multicultural Setting, by Place of Birth
(Percentage in each category)

	Born in US	European or Canadian	Other International
Very helpful	18%	36%	59%
Somewhat helpful	39	40	21
Not very helpful	33	24	11
Not at all helpful	11	0	9

Conclusion

Throughout this chapter we have focused attention on both the positive and negative aspects of multicultural ministry. We have acknowledged the strengths it can offer and the challenges it can pose. We have seen how some people have embraced it with joy and enthusiasm while others have endured it with frustration. For the foreseeable future, whether one likes it or not, the Roman Catholic Church in the United States will continue to grow in this multicultural dimension, both in terms of laity and of priesthood. As stated at the beginning, such change will bring with it abundant blessings and enormous challenges.

We close this chapter with a hope-filled quote from the homily that Pope Benedict XVI delivered in Washington, DC, on April 17, 2008. In our increasingly multicultural Church, served by an increasingly multicultural presbyterate, this is a call to unity and to action:

> Two hundred years later, the Church in America can rightfully praise the accomplishment of past generations in bringing together widely differing immigrant groups within the unity of the Catholic faith and in a common commitment to the spread of the Gospel. At the same time, conscious of its rich diversity, the Catholic community in this country has come to appreciate ever more fully the importance of each individual and group offering its own particular gifts to the whole. The Church in the United States is now called to look to the future, firmly grounded in the faith passed on by previous generations, and ready to meet new challenges— challenges no less demanding than those faced by your forebears—with the hope born of God's love, poured into our hearts by the Holy Spirit.

Chapter 6

Effects of the Sexual Abuse Scandal

The anger I have is that the malfeasance of the diocesan administration has *deeply* harmed individuals, the victims. The scandal was an earthquake in the life of the Church and we will be trying to rebuild this city for generations. There's a constant dark cloud over the life of the Church, and it didn't *need* to be there.

—A priest explaining why he publicly criticized his bishop

Sunday, January 6, 2002, was something of a slow news day nationally. On Saturday, a teenager had killed himself by flying a small airplane into a Tampa office building. Absent any evidence that the act might be linked to terrorism, however, coverage of the event was now second-page material. There were reports of minor successes in the pursuit of al-Qaeda leaders in Pakistan and possible al-Qaeda-linked terrorists in Africa. Op-ed columnists speculated darkly whether Saddam Hussein would be the next target of the US military. Despite these mostly unremarkable news stories, January 6 is a date some priests we interviewed could name off the top of their heads, much as some people can immediately name the date John F. Kennedy was assassinated or the Twin Towers were destroyed.

That Sunday an article appeared on the front page of the *Boston Globe*. Titled "Church Allowed Abuse by Priest for Years," it detailed the case of John Geoghan, a former priest of the Archdiocese of Boston. Geoghan was about to face a criminal trial for molesting a single boy, but well over one hundred other people had accused him of sexually abusing them when they were children. Investigating over many months, the *Globe* had gathered documents showing that Geoghan's superiors transferred him among six different parishes, mostly after they were aware of appalling accusations against him. By itself the publication of this one article was nowhere near as momentous or memorable as an assassination or a terrorist attack but looking back, it was "the beginning." Four days later, *Globe* staffers signaled that they viewed the story as quite important, following up with an editorial and seven articles related variously to Geoghan, an apology from Archbishop Bernard Cardinal Law, and broader implications for the Catholic Church's handling of misconduct by its priests. On the same day, the *New York Times* picked up the story, running a brief article about Geoghan and the archdiocese's pledge to reform the way it responded to accusations of clergy abuse.

Still, interest in the case might well have died out in the following weeks. News reports about sexual abuse of minors by Catholic priests, and the seeming indifference of their bishops or superiors, were hardly unprecedented. Numerous clergy sexual predators had previously received national coverage, going back to a case in Louisiana in the mid-1980s. During 1992 and 1993 a very large number of accusations against priests had become public (John Jay College Research Team, 2011), and the news media had given the abuse problem a fair amount of scrutiny that, in retrospect, might have progressed until it reached the magnitude of explosion soon to be seen in 2002. But for various reasons the media's attention had waned. In mid-January 2002, however, something happened in Boston that kept the story alive and eventually triggered critical mass. A superior court judge decided that previously private archdiocesan documents related to the Geoghan case should be made public, and, on January 18, the judge denied a final attempt by the archdiocese to delay this order. The *Globe* suddenly had access to a trove of paperwork that not only revealed more about the Geoghan case but also referenced dozens of other Boston priests accused of abusing minors. On the last day of January the reporters published a chilling overview of the problem in the archdiocese, revealing that at least seventy archdiocesan priests had been accused of abusing minors during the previous four to five decades (Globe Spotlight Team, 2002). Though few of these cases were as horrific as the Geoghan one, the scope of the problem far exceeded what most people imagined. Yet it turned out to be the tip of the iceberg. The *Globe* hammered away, publishing articles on the scandal nearly every day during February.

A turning point came that month when other newspapers around the country began scrutinizing cases of sexual abuse in their local areas. As the firestorm from Boston swept across the country, the staggering breadth of the problem gradually came to light. Eventually it would become clear that at least one priest in virtually every diocese in the United States had been credibly accused of sexual abuse at some time in the past (Goodstein, 2003). Nor was the problem limited to dioceses; horrific stories emerged of abuse within some religious communities of men (e.g., Associated Press, 2007). Catholics who were already aware of the sexual abuse issue now learned that the lessons of the early 1990s had gone unheeded by some bishops and superiors. In many places, a priest who had formerly offended remained in parish ministry, although perhaps in a different parish. Parishioners typically were not informed about the reasons for the change in personnel and remained oblivious to the situation up to the very day when their priest was suddenly removed from ministry. As press coverage gave courage to victims who had not previously come forward, dioceses and orders learned for the first time of the crimes of many other priests.

This state of affairs stretched out for months. The New York Times Company had purchased the *Boston Globe* in 1993. The *Times*, which had not been in the forefront of early 1990s coverage of the abuse issue, now tore into the story ferociously. A scandal-related article appeared on the front page of the *Times* nearly every week for nine straight months. For their part, some bishops and religious superiors allowed the story to drag out by not immediately releasing all the facts available to them. A priest describes how the scandal commenced in his diocese:

> We had a convocation of the priests in the diocese just after stuff broke, and Bishop [Name] assured us that it was over. There were no more names coming out. This was on a Thursday. That following Monday there were several new names on the front page of the [local paper]. So we weren't very trusting at that point.

The initial emotions experienced by priests as the scandal unfolded in 2002 are probably similar in many ways to those felt among ordinary Catholics at that time: horror, disbelief, sadness, and anger. In the case of priests, these emotions were often amplified by personally knowing some of the men accused of abuse:

> Obviously, I was tremendously saddened to learn the extent of the abuse. I had deep sorrow that so many young people had been abused, and that they had been abused by people who had been committed, or were supposed to be committed, to their well-being and growth and development— and were, on the contrary, contributing to their potential downfall. That was just disheartening on so many levels.

Even now, eight years later, it's kind of hard to summarize or put it into words, but I just remember it being like a tsunami that hit, or an earthquake. It went all year. It preoccupied each day. You'd open the paper and ask, "Who else?"

Oh, it was just heartbreaking. It was horrifying. People suffered, so I was sad. I was angry too that some people did what they did because other people looked the other way. That made me very, very angry.

I felt great pain. It was terribly hurtful. Some of our guys were wrapped up in that. I had kind of grown up with [members of my order] in high school. . . . It's like losing a family member, like the death of a loved one, even. One accused priest in my order had been my confessor and spiritual director. There was a lot of pain hearing what was being said about him and others.

I felt very angry and pretty much disgusted about what I was hearing and seeing. It was a kind of betrayal of who we were. But mostly it was anger at the [diocesan] administration, that they let this go to the extent that it did. . . . It was in the newspaper every day and the more that came out, the more angry we all got—or at least I got any way. I really felt badly for the victims, terribly. I had no sympathy for the guys, especially the really bad ones, the serial pedophiles and the serial sexual abusers.

An outside observer of the Church might suppose most priests were fully aware of the depth of the sexual abuse problem prior to 2002. However, those we spoke with—at least those who were not in positions of Church leadership—often told us that although they had known of previous cases of clergy sexual abuse, they remained unaware of the full scope of the problem. A priest from a diocese where a great number of cases came to light in 2002 recalls,

I was aware of the stuff in Louisiana through *National Catholic Reporter* articles. I was also aware of stuff in Newfoundland.[1] In my ministry I have dealt with maybe twelve to fifteen men and women who were victims of sexual abuse as children, some of them abused by priests, but none who grew up in my diocese. A lot of that was before 2002, so I was not unaware that this was a problem out there. What I was unaware of, however, was that it was such a problem in my diocese. In fact, I think I had only known of one case here, where a priest had abused a teenage boy, and I didn't know the priest's name.

[1] In 1988, there were revelations of abuse at Mount Cashel, an orphanage operated by the Christian Brothers in St. John's, Newfoundland.

A priest from a different diocese shares similar thoughts:

> I had a sense as a newly ordained priest [in the 1970s] that there were probably priests who were acting in a homosexual manner towards young men, high school kids of sixteen, seventeen, eighteen. I had no first-hand knowledge of it; it was only by hearsay. I was unaware of anyone at all who would have touched a child. But then, of course, when it all started to break in 2002, I became aware that this is a real problem. If I had become aware of a priest abusing a child—regardless of what the diocese would have done—I would have reported it. I think that might have been true for most priests, if it was actual pedophilia. That's such a horrendous deed that I couldn't imagine a priest being aware of that happening and not saying something or doing something.

A priest who was a seminarian in 2002 remembers the following:

> You would hear about it [sexual abuse committed by priests] every once in a while on the news. In the mid-1990s, a number of years before I was even in formation, there was a case of a priest in our diocese who was brought up on charges and taken out of ministry. He made a pass at, maybe, a seventeen-year-old young man. It hit the papers an awful lot. It happened in a parish in the next town over from where I was living. So as an issue, as something that did happen once in a while, I was aware of it. . . . I had an acquaintance, a fellow who was a year behind me in the seminary. He was very well informed about things, better informed than I was. He said he had spoken with people that he knew in the Archdiocese of Boston about this scandal that was about to surface. This was maybe less than two months before the scandal really broke in early 2002. He said, "When this breaks, it's going to be hellish." Sure enough, it was.

A small number of priests told us that, in fact, they did not know about the sexual abuse problem at all prior to 2002. The sense of shock expressed by these priests when the scandal broke will probably resonate with many lay Catholics:

> I never knew anything about this. I was still on the younger side and had no idea this stuff was going on.

> I had no idea. Like laypeople, I think, I learned about it when I opened the newspaper one morning in 2002 and found that a seminary classmate of mine was one of the primary abusers. In our time in the seminary [the late 50s and early 60s] we were very conscious of the drinking problem, and that was really the emphasis: watch out for the drinking. Never did I have the inkling there was any kind of a sexual problem.

Of course, as recognizable as the initial emotional reactions among priests might be, the perspectives and experiences of clergy regarding the scandal are in many ways unique relative to those of lay Catholics. In this chapter we examine how the scandal has affected priests—not the abusers themselves but the ordinary priests who remain in ministry and in good standing in the Church. We will present some survey data, but most of the material in this chapter draws on the words of priests themselves. Many of the priests who are quoted here participated in one of the three focus groups or were selected randomly from among respondents to the survey. However, we intentionally interviewed additional priests with particular backgrounds. For example, we sought out priests in dioceses that were particularly affected by the scandal, priests involved in ministry with young people, and priests who were in formation at the time the scandal broke.

Interactions with Catholic Laity

One way the sexual abuse issue touches average priests is that, as leaders and representatives of the Church, other Catholics often go to them with their questions about the scandal, their pain, and their desire for reassurance. On rarer occasions some lay Catholics direct their anger about the scandal and Church leadership toward the priests nearest them. However, with a few exceptions—particularly priests in parishes where abuse previously took place—most pastors told us that they have received a great deal of affirmation and support from their parishioners and have not found themselves the targets of hostility. This attitude is consistent with findings from surveys conducted at the height of the scandal; most pastors remained in high esteem among their own parishioners. For example, in a poll of Boston-area Catholics conducted by the *Globe* in April 2002, just 18 percent said they viewed Cardinal Law favorably, but 75 percent nevertheless viewed their local parish priest favorably (Paulson, 2002).

> From people in the parish, I haven't felt hatred, or "We don't like priests," or anything like that. This year [2010] people were asking me about the scandal and the Pope. So on Good Shepherd Sunday I addressed it in a sermon. Otherwise, I've really been unaffected by the scandal.

> One of the things that really struck me as a [resident] priest in the parish was that, when all of the headlines were hitting, how much the people identify not with the bishop or the diocese. They identify with the pastor. They identify with the parish. They weren't as shaken as I expected them

to be. They've related to their baptisms, their weddings. . . . I thought there was a remarkable strength of relationship between people in the pew at that parish and their parish priests.

As the scandal broke in 2002, many ordinary priests had the unenviable task of apologizing for the actions of those above them in the Church hierarchy, of answering questions, and of assuring Catholics, sometimes in the face of understandable skepticism, that their children would not face danger in the future. A religious order priest remembers this:

I was principal of a Catholic high school when all this was going on in 2002 and was very concerned about what this meant to those young people. I remember visiting every religion classroom to speak to the students, to apologize to them, to explain what happened, to explain that safeguards were being put in place to prevent, as far as possible, this happening again . . . to really let them know from a priest they interacted with on a daily basis that the Church is still a safe place for them. I remember feeling really responsible, quite frankly, for assuring those young people in my charge that they still had a safe place to call home, to celebrate the sacraments, to pray.

A priest in a diocese that was strongly affected by the scandal felt compelled to address the issue with his parishioners:

To my knowledge no priest abused a child in my parish. What was alarming for people was so many of them had either grown up in one of the parishes where these guys had been assigned or, for example, their sister was raising her family now in one of those parishes. Everybody knew somebody who was in a parish, or close to a parish, where one of these guys had been assigned, and of course these priests had been moved around a lot. For the first two weekends after it broke I preached only a two-minute homily at all the Masses. Then I had an open mic session and let people ask whatever they wanted to ask. They asked questions like: Did I know this was going on? How could this have happened and nothing was done about it? I tried to respond as best I could. I'm *really* glad I did that because I think it's what people needed. That may not have been the best thing to do liturgically, but I just felt I would be able to reach literally hundreds more people that way than if I had said, "On Wednesday night we're going to have a time for you to come and ask questions." To this day people still reference that and say how important that was for them. . . . Beginning back then and to this day, every single Sunday in the prayers of the faithful in my parish we have an intercession: "For those who have been abused and betrayed by the Church, and for the restoration of confidence in the Church, let us pray to the Lord."

A priest describes taking over a parish where the previous pastor had just been removed due to abuse that had taken place elsewhere, in other words, not at that particular parish:

> The bishop called, I think, on a Monday and asked if I would come out here by Wednesday. The impression I got from the diocese was that half the parish was on one side of the parking lot facing the other half and brickbats were being thrown and names being called and all this sort of stuff. It wasn't quite that way. . . . The first Sunday we basically talked about why I was here. Each night the following week I had an open house for anybody who had any questions or concerns, but I said, "I'm not on the inside of any of this." We had maybe eighty people the first night and then it went down by thirds each night of the week. The last two nights couples who had come to earlier meetings came and said, "We've heard everything you had to say. We just wanted to come by to support you." I think the healing for most people happened because, as far as we could tell, there was no abuse here.

The challenge was even greater for priests who had to pick up the pieces where abuse of minors had previously occurred. In such circumstances, priests were not apologizing for something far removed but for harm experienced by members of the immediate parish community. Though some of those priests experienced support from parishioners, many also faced a more intensely focused anger than that experienced by a typical pastor. Below are recollections of two priests who have served in parishes where abuse previously took place:

> I'm in a parish where a number of the cases that we had in the diocese occurred. I've talked to parishioners, some of whom have just simply stopped going to church because they're so angry and upset. Others are just devastated by the fact that a priest who they thought was such a wonderful person has now been publicized as somebody who is an abuser. These people are really hurting. I've experienced it in my own family. I have a brother who still goes to church but he's no longer supporting the church financially. He's a very good Catholic. And one of my sisters-in-law, there's just no talking to her about it. I just kind of avoid the topic because she's just so angry and so upset. Interestingly enough, a lot of the anger I've experienced is not just against the individual predator priest but against the diocese and against the Church in general for not having done something about this sooner. I haven't experienced anger directed at me personally, but I've taken on the role, when I've talked with people, to apologize in the name of the Church and to hopefully help them get through their anger. Some of that has been successful. Some of it not so; the hurt is just very deeply rooted.

> At the next parish over the pastor was accused and removed in 2003. I got
> the call that I was going to be the administrator of his parish. All the al-
> legations against him were substantiated and he is on prayer and penance,
> self-admitted. It was really tough moving in to take his place, being that
> I didn't know any of this stuff. There was really nothing in place at the
> time for handling this kind of situation, but I personally called a physician
> friend of mine. I got a social worker. I said, "We need to have a parish
> meeting." The church was full and people were *really* pissed off. People
> were saying to me, "You're the neighboring pastor. You should have
> known." Well, we're diocesan priests. We don't necessarily have that kind
> of connection. You might work now and then with the guy next door on
> a combined penance service, those kinds of things. But other than
> that. . . .

In a national telephone poll conducted by CARA in spring 2003, 9 percent of lay Catholics reported that they had known someone who had
been sexually abused by a priest. We do not have a comparable estimate
for priests, but the proportion seems likely to be higher. Over time, priests
typically serve in many different parishes or ministries, where they interact with many lay Catholics. Among priests who were in ministry for a
long time prior to 2002, and particularly among those in dioceses where
the problem was extensive, the odds of having personally known a victim
are, it seems safe to say, not trivial. Reaching out to victims of abuse or
their families is among the greatest challenges experienced by priests in
the aftermath of the scandal. One priest recalls:

> The parish where I was first assigned forty years ago later had an abusive
> priest there. I mixed with the families more in my first parish. There were
> people that I'd celebrate birthdays and holidays with. I was going through
> the paper with the list of victims and it's like, "I *know* that kid." So I called
> his parents. His mother answered, and there was suspicion: "Why are you
> calling?" "Well, because I called to apologize." "Did the bishop tell you
> to call?" "No, the bishop would be pissed off if he knew I was calling. It's
> just that I'm sorry this happened." It ended up well. She and I talked for
> a while. Two days later her husband called and said, "We want to thank
> you for calling us. You're the first person that's apologized." I think once
> it got into a legal framework, the hierarchy couldn't say what people
> wanted them to. The lawyers would say, "Don't you dare apologize."

The Response of the Hierarchy and the Charter

In 1984 a priest of the Diocese of Lafayette, Louisiana, was impris-
oned for molesting dozens of children during the 1970s and early 1980s.

Gilbert Gauthe's arrest and eventual trial was covered by Louisiana news media, and the facts, as they came out, contained horrors that would later become an all-too-familiar litany in the worst clergy sexual abuse cases. Gauthe's victims had been taking their stories to the diocese for a full decade, but the gravity of the violations committed against them and the severity of the psychological harm they experienced were seemingly not grasped by diocesan officials. Financial settlements were eventually negotiated by lawyers representing some of the victims; however, victims and their families often felt they had been treated coldly and without compassion. The diocese never alerted police about Gauthe's crimes. Instead he was moved by two bishops from parish to parish, ministry to ministry, preying on new children at practically every stop. The bishops apparently placed faith in the ability of psychological treatment to cure Gauthe, though such hopes soon proved baseless given his recidivism. Jason Berry, a Catholic journalist covering the story locally for *The Times of Acadiana*, wrote an article about it for the lay-directed newspaper *National Catholic Reporter* (*NCR*). The article appeared on June 7, 1985. Accompanying it were articles prepared by the *NCR* staff on other cases of clerical abuse they had discovered since Berry first approached them about the story. This report was the earliest instance of national-level news coverage of the clergy sexual abuse issue. The *NCR* coverage attracted interest among a few secular news outlets—including *Time* magazine, the *Washington Post*, the *New York Times*, and CBS—each of which also began investigating the issue.

A Lafayette priest recalls effects of the publicity on him and other priests of the diocese. He also recounts a story demonstrating how far the notoriety of Lafayette spread:

> There was a feeling of embarrassment for the Church but also for myself as a representative of the Church, because it became so vitriolic. The media just really went after everything. Initially there was a sense, even, of paranoia among the priests of, "What are people going to think of *me*? How do I react to people if they ask me about this?" However, I can't recall any direct question to me about it from the laity. I think they were probably just as embarrassed as we were. . . .
>
> Maybe three or four years after it broke open, I was visiting Rome with a parish group. We were standing out in front of the Basilica of St. Mary Major, if I'm not mistaken. I had a clerical collar on. There was a monsignor or prelate who was stationed there. I think he was English. He was in full regalia. When he saw me he came up to me with an attitude of, "I'm an important person here" and introduced himself as a canon of the

basilica or something or other. I said, "It's nice to meet you. I'm Father [Name]. I'm from the diocese of Lafayette." His response was, "Oh, you're from that God-forsaken place." This city bus passed by and of course the passengers saw him standing out there in all of his regalia. They started hooting and hollering and making all sorts of derogatory comments—or so I assumed because I don't speak Italian very well, but it was obvious they were targeting him. I remember looking at him and saying, "Well it seems like we're not the only ones having problems."

Little did he realize how prophetic that statement would prove to be.

In 1985 two priests, Tom Doyle and Michael Peterson, along with lawyer Ray Mouton, took it upon themselves to prepare a report on the abuse issue for the National Conference of Catholic Bishops (NCCB)[2] (Berry, 1992). Each of the three men had become familiar with the problem through his ministry or work. The report stressed the severity of the situation, observing that recidivism among pedophiles was commonplace and that financial liability for the Church could be massive if steps were not taken to get a handle on the problem.[3] Just as important, the report represented an early attempt to advocate for a coordinated national-level response and for the bishops to dictate guidelines for dealing with the problem. It recommended creation of an NCCB committee to deal with the problem and an intervention team to help dioceses when cases arose. The authors called for pastoral outreach and openness with victims. They emphasized the need for extensive treatment and supervision of offending priests returned to ministry. The report was presented at a meeting of the NCCB, but the aftermath remains a matter of controversy. No committee was created and no guidelines for dealing with cases of clerical sexual abuse were publicly adopted by the bishops. The authors themselves became highly critical of the seeming lack of response to the report (Berry, 1992; Fox, 2002). Several people in positions of Church leadership assure us that behind-the-scenes efforts were made in the late 1980s by some of the bishops' advisors to improve the handling of sexual abuse (see also Euart, 2010). Also in the late 1980s, some US Church leaders and experts in canon law began urging the Vatican to make it easier to laicize[4] abusive priests, though little progress resulted (Berry and Renner,

---

[2] On July 1, 2001, the NCCB and the USCC were combined to form the United States Conference of Catholic Bishops (USCCB).

[3] The text of the report is available in Doyle et al. (2006).

[4] "Laicize" means to remove a man from the clerical state. This action is something only the pope can do. A bishop can remove a priest in his diocese from ministry or

2004:64–67). Despite these efforts, lack of action apparent to many observers on the outside would later help make the case for a more tangible response by the bishops.

Starting late in 1991 and continuing through 1992, a number of events coincided to cause a surge of media interest in the clergy sexual abuse issue. James Porter, a former priest of the Diocese of Fall River, Massachusetts, was arrested. He had allegedly abused over a hundred children and young teens during the 1960s and early 1970s (Butterfield, 1992). Following revelations of several abuse cases in the Archdiocese of Chicago, Archbishop Joseph Cardinal Bernardin appointed a special commission to study the problem. At the recommendation of that commission, he later established a board composed primarily of lay Catholics to investigate all future charges of abuse and to advise him whether to remove accused priests from ministry[5] (Steinfels, 1992a). Also during 1992 Berry published the book *Lead Us Not into Temptation*. After covering the Gauthe case, he had spent the ensuing years investigating cases of clergy abuse across the country. The book laid bare the consistently inadequate responses of local Church leaders in dealing with such cases. By the time Berry finished his investigation, he estimated that criminal or civil court cases had been brought against four hundred priests nationwide during the prior decade (Steinfels, 1992b). In a foreword to the book, Andrew Greeley wrote that the magnitude of the problem was probably even greater than what the book portrayed.

In June 1992 the NCCB responded by establishing an Ad Hoc Committee on Sexual Abuse and by publicly endorsing a set of guidelines for dioceses responding to allegations of abuse by priests. The guidelines did not constitute a formal "policy" or set of "regulations." The Catholic Church gives individual bishops a great deal of autonomy in handling

---

forbid him from functioning as a priest (i.e., forbid him from celebrating the sacraments or acting in any outward capacity as a priest). But he remains a priest unless the Vatican laicizes him. Formal procedures (designed in part to safeguard the rights of individual priests against the power of their superiors) made laicization a cumbersome process, even in extreme cases such as priests guilty of sexual abuse. Complicating attempts to streamline the process, John Paul II was generally trying to reduce the number of laicizations worldwide and reemphasize the permanent nature of holy orders.

[5] In a strange coincidence in 1993, a man filed suit against Bernardin and another priest for allegedly abusing him as an adolescent in the 1970s. Later, the man withdrew the accusation against Bernardin, saying that it was based on a "recovered memory" and that he could not be sure of its reliability (Woodward, 1994). This incident may have been one reason that early-1990s press coverage of the sexual abuse issue lost steam before reaching 2002 levels of intensity (Berry and Renner, 2004:117–19, 140–41).

affairs in their own dioceses, and the creation of mandatory, enforceable rules would have had to come from the Vatican, not the NCCB. Nevertheless the guidelines represented an important advance. Among other things, they called for bishops to reach out pastorally to victims and their families, report accusations to civil authorities as required by local law, and promptly remove credibly accused priests from ministry in order to evaluate them. The NCCB encouraged dioceses to establish their own formal policies incorporating these guidelines. Many dioceses took these recommendations seriously. A priest describes the policy his diocese put in place at that time, emphasizing care for the victims:

> Our formal protocol first started in the early 1990s when we did what the NCCB wanted everybody to do, which was to have a written policy in place. . . . Part of that protocol was that if you ever heard an accusation, no matter whether you thought it was credible or not, you had to inform the bishop, the office of priest personnel, or the chancery office. . . . Another of the rules was that anybody who made an accusation would get help, particularly counseling. We didn't care whether the accusation was true or not. That's the only way you can be fair and show that you're not doing this because you want to convince them not to go against the priest. We didn't want that. We wanted victims to feel free to say what the facts were. Also people who came forth would be advised, "We don't care if you sue the diocese or not. If you have a legal claim, you have a perfect right to sue the diocese. You have a right to go to the police if a criminal act has been committed. That's all your decision. But, no matter what, you will always get help, if you want it." Some people would not accept help because they were either angry at the Church or they felt they didn't need it because the abuse occurred twenty or twenty-five years in the past. Then there were several meetings with all the priests of the diocese in which all this was carefully explained. They were told what would happen to an accused priest, depending on the situation. Even if the accusation appeared likely to be false, a priest would be asked to stay away from his parish for a while until it was proved to be not credible.

Revelations of 2002—especially that many known abusers remained in parish ministry—made it easy to doubt that all dioceses took the NCCB recommendations seriously. Moreover, some dioceses that developed their own policies during the 1990s later came under criticism for being lax or careless in following them. There was no process by which any higher Church authorities ensured such policies were enforced. A priest who was formerly a leader in his religious order describes his early familiarity with the abuse problem but also his surprise at learning in 2002 of the way it had been handled in the diocese where he lived:

> I was provincial [in the mid-1980s.] We were just starting to be very alert to this because of all that had happened in Lafayette. . . . I got to know Bishop [Name] fairly well. . . . When this whole abuse thing became public I was truly shocked, I mean shocked, to find out that in the 90s he was still reassigning people. I would not have expected that, knowing him as I got to know him. But it clearly happened, so that was very distressing. It's a huge tragedy, above all a tragedy for the victims.

The priest of the Diocese of Lafayette who was quoted earlier experienced a similar reaction of disbelief:

> I distinctly remember thinking, "I can't believe in this day and age, after what we went through, this is still going on." I had assumed that it had been addressed to some extent at the USCCB. It just confounded me that any bishop would still allow something like that to go on and not address it.

In retrospect, a central problem was how to evaluate whether a priest who had been removed from ministry could safely return to ministry and, if so, to what kind. In 1992 Cardinal Bernardin had pledged not to place previous abusers back into parishes and, if they were returned to ministry at all, to insure they would not be assigned to ministry involving minors (Steinfels, 1992b). Other, presumably well-intentioned, bishops believed that some priests who had committed "minor" transgressions (if any can be called such) against older teenagers could repent and be trusted to control themselves in the future. A decade later, however, lack of a risk-free way to make this type of evaluation set the stage for a much more stringent and systematic approach to the abuse problem by Church leaders.

In June 2002, as the scandal raged nationwide, the bishops convened in Dallas for a regular biannual meeting. They had already received tentative approval from Rome for a true national policy. At the meeting they drafted a document titled Charter for the Protection of Children and Young People. Often referred to simply as "the Charter," it reaffirmed guidelines from 1992 but pledged to go considerably further. It called for each diocese to establish a majority-lay review board, like that in Chicago, to examine all allegations of sexual abuse and advise the bishop on their credibility. It dictated that a priest be removed from ecclesiastical ministry during the review board investigation of accusations against him. And if "a single act" of abuse is then "established" against a priest, he must be permanently removed from all ministries, even those where there could be no contact with minors. This provision has been labeled "zero tolerance." It applied retroactively. In other words, any active priest who had ever committed abuse in the past now had to be removed from ministry. Finally, the Charter explicitly addressed laicization, dictating that "if warranted," a priest not only be removed from ministry but "be dismissed from the clerical state." The bishops met again in November 2002 and codified the new procedures in a second document titled the Essential Norms,[6] which carried the force of Church law in the United States after it was formally approved by the Vatican the following month.

Most priests with whom we spoke recognize the necessity of the Charter and Essential Norms, both as a means of stemming the crisis in 2002 and of ensuring the ongoing protection of children in the Church:

> We have to have those Norms in place. No question. I think we've done a great job at raising awareness of the issue with all the trainings[7] and everything else that's come out of that. . . . The diocesan administration takes every accusation very seriously. They *have* to.

> Children are certainly much safer now than they were before. The Church, at least in my diocese, is being much more responsible about this kind of thing . . . and always errs on the side of safety.

A priest whose order's charism centers on ministry to young people says,

> There was a readjustment period [after the Charter was put in place]. . . . But I soon realized we have to go to the extreme to protect children and make sure it doesn't ever happen again. . . . It's good that we have zero tolerance for anything involving the abuse of children.

Nevertheless the Charter[8] and the way that bishops have implemented it remain controversial. That's probably understating it; some priests are

---

[6] The full title is Essential Norms for Diocesan/Eparchial Policies Dealing with Allegations of Sexual Abuse of Minors by Priests or Deacons. For the text of both the Charter and Essential Norms, see USCCB (2005).

[7] The Charter requires dioceses to hold training sessions for all employees and volunteers who come into contact with minors and also to perform criminal background checks on those people.

[8] For convenience, we generally use the term "the Charter" in the discussion that follows (which is the conversational phrasing most priests themselves use), while recognizing that the Essential Norms document is at least equally important.

very angry. Most do not necessarily air their feelings publicly, however. They are well aware that criticism of the Charter could be misconstrued as being unconcerned about the importance of rooting out abuse in the Church—and as caring more about themselves (collectively as priests) than about the victims. There are few topics we discussed with priests about which they were more nervous and more concerned that we protect their anonymity.

The greatest source of resentment about the Charter is zero tolerance, particularly the zealousness with which some bishops have moved to laicize nearly all priests in their dioceses who are guilty of abuse. No priest we spoke with advocated returning a man guilty of sexual abuse to ministry where he might have contact with a minor. But some question whether laicization should be a first resort for diocesan priests who have abused older teenagers. Many priests prefer the approach taken by religious orders. Rather than laicize a man who has committed abuse, an order may restrict him to a communal residence, allowing him to leave the premises only in the company of another member of the community.[9] This restricted lifestyle, without public ministry but still with the identity of a priest, is sometimes referred to as being on "prayer and penance." Sometimes diocesan priests are also placed on prayer and penance, though usually as a way station on the road to laicization rather than the permanent state more typical in religious communities. Below, three priests critique zero tolerance and, in some cases, suggest nuanced alternatives:

> I would consider few of the cases in my diocese to be pure pedophile cases. Most of them were cases of priests and teenagers. Only a few of the cases that I can recall had anything to do with pre-pubescence. I know a true pedophile, at least at this point in time, is incurable. Of course, I'm in total agreement because of my background in counseling. But if you're dealing with somebody who had a homosexual relationship or attraction to young men, especially those in their later teens, I think you're dealing with homosexuality and—I'm not justifying anything here—a whole different approach is possible. I think if people have homosexual tendencies and they are attracted to younger men, they have choices. Could the person

---

[9] In 2002, bishops and religious superiors who had previously placed known abusers only in ministries not involving minors sometimes came under criticism because there was no way to be certain the priests, free to move about on their own, were never in circumstances where they might encounter young people.

be encouraged through spiritual discipline, to possibly control his homo-sexual urges, to live out his celibate commitment? Of course, the abuse precludes any further ordinary public priestly ministry. But is laicization the only option for diocesan priests? The approach of religious communi-ties to the situation seems to me to be more just and merciful.

There's no longer any *degree* of abuse. I know of a case where a priest propositioned a seventeen-year-old. Under the Charter, his diocese is asking him to seek laicization. Nothing happened. *Could* it have happened? Of course, if the young man had said yes, it definitely would have hap-pened. Was it wrong? Of course, it was wrong. But is there any chance for this priest, who I see now as having real arrested development and immaturity? Is there a way to rehabilitate him? Does he have to just leave the priesthood immediately?

Zero tolerance is irrational. . . . The bishops should have stated the prin-ciples very clearly and said: The first thing is always going to be to protect victims. . . . Secondly, we're not going to abide any priest in the priest-hood who's a danger to children. The permanence of the priesthood means nothing in comparison to protecting children for the future. But we're not going to treat the guy who was in an alcoholic stupor and was homosexual and had an event with a seventeen-year-old—I don't condone any of these things—the same as somebody who has abused twenty people and who clearly has a sickness and is an ongoing danger. . . . To make believe there is no difference, that's all done for publicity. Zero tolerance: that means the guy who made a mistake but really doesn't have a sickness, now he's gone forever.

Priests critical of the Charter generally concede that there is tremen-dous pressure on Church leaders today to demonstrate that they are doing everything in their power to address the abuse problem. They are also aware of the difficulties of the past that led the bishops to institute zero tolerance. The priest quoted immediately above acknowledges,

I understand asking, "Is this priest a danger to children *in the future*?" is a hard judgment to make. Let me tell you, annulments are a lot easier deci-sion to make, to arrive at moral certitude by hindsight. . . . To make a decision about the future, it's not so easy. It's open to a lot of errors.

Beyond zero tolerance, priests critical of the Charter see it as a symbol of a generally aggressive posture some bishops have taken toward priests in an attempt to insulate themselves from criticism for being soft on sexual abuse:

I'm disappointed in how the bishops reacted to the scandal. Their response was: "It's a priest problem. Let's get rid of them and everything will go back to normal." It was a complete selling-out of the priests. The only thing they wanted to accomplish was to cover themselves. They could have admitted the mistakes they made in their approach to dealing with this problem. But they took a defensive position for themselves and an offensive position against the priests. Some of the most notorious bishops, for example Cardinal Law, he would have been better off if he saw the light and recognized his own mismanagement and arrogance. He only saw the light after intense scrutiny and a [letter calling for his resignation] from his priests.

More specifically, some priests lament a lack of support for those who have been accused of abuse—particularly during the period after the accusation has been made but before it has been substantiated by civil authorities or the diocese's own review board. It might appear easy to dismiss such complaints as reflecting greater concern for perpetrators than victims of the scandal, but a surprisingly high number of men we spoke with say they personally know an accused priest whom they believe to be innocent. In the 2002 *Los Angeles Times* survey of priests, only 34 percent of respondents rated the Charter's fairness to priests accused of abuse as "good" or "excellent." Forty-five percent rated it as "fair" or "poor" (Stammer, 2002). We tend to think that such attitudes can best be understood as a recognition that at least a few priests accused of abuse are innocent, accompanied by a strong desire to protect the rights of those priests.[10] Below, two priests we interviewed discuss the stance of bishops toward those accused of abuse:

[10] The 2002 *Los Angeles Times* survey of priests asked, "Thinking now of the recent allegations of sexual misconduct by priests, do you think that most, many, some, or only a few of the allegations are true?" Just 19 percent of priests responded "most," with 42 percent responding "many," 28 percent "some," and 7 percent "only a few" (Los Angeles Times Poll, 2002). Greeley (2004:101) takes these findings (among others) as evidence that a "state of denial" about the scandal that was characteristic of the 1980s and '90s is persisting in the priesthood. As alarming as the *Times* findings were, we aren't sure that such a severe conclusion is warranted today. The sexual abuse issue was discussed extensively in all three focus groups and in more than twenty individual interviews, among priests who spanned the ideological spectrum. Whatever the situation in 2002, very few priests we spoke with said anything to indicate that they believe most allegations of abuse to be false or a fabrication of the media. As one priest told us, "You'd have to be living in a cave in Afghanistan to think that most of these accusations aren't true."

There's a lot of mistrust of the diocese among the priests. We feel they don't have our back. If an allegation were made against me, I would be removed immediately, but they don't know what to do with a priest once he's removed. They give you a full salary but there's really nothing in place for support until the case is resolved. We've had a few guys returned to ministry [after being cleared by the review board] but they're usually returned as a real broken person.

In the Dallas Charter, all consequences fall on priests. Nothing is in there for bishops.[11] Diocesan priests are on their own. My brothers [in my order] always will be there for me. I know of a bishop, I don't want to say who, who said to his priests, "Our relationship is that of a CEO and an employee. If you are accused, you are on your own." That's pretty harsh. A hard line had to be drawn, but it hasn't been drawn in the right place.

Another priest criticizes bishops who refuse to pay the expenses of canon lawyers representing men whose cases are being heard by review boards or tribunals:

I find it frustrating that bishops, without even thinking, will pay thousands upon thousands of dollars for their civil lawyers to represent them in court. But when it comes to canon lawyers, which would be a minor—you can put that in bold print—*minor* expense to have priests properly represented in the canonical process, those bishops say, "No." That blows my mind. I will always appreciate what my own bishop did. From the moment when this first blew up in our face, he said, "Absolutely we will pay for that." . . . It's profoundly frustrating when I hear from canon lawyers, priests and laity, who have to be begging, pleading, and cajoling bishops to pay their bills.

A focus group participant held a position that allowed him to become familiar with cases of accused priests in several dioceses during the early 2000s. He claimed that one bishop was paying his priests not to fight the process of removal from ministry or laicization:

Some of the cases I handled were guys from [diocese names]. The treatment was abysmal. It was awful. They were given no recourse whatsoever. In one of the cases that I handled the ordinary opened his wallet and asked,

---

Thus, while false allegations are very much a concern to priests, we do not think that such concerns have blinded most of them to the real horrors of the scandal.

[11] Priests are correct when they complain that the Charter does not apply to the bishops. Under Church law, bishops do not have the power to create rules that are binding on themselves. Only the Holy See has jurisdiction over the bishops.

"How much is it going to be to make this go away? Just get lost forever."
It was unbelievable. That was the major reaction from the Dallas Charter.

Still another priest cites the following example, one in which a bishop
has remained unsupportive of his priests even after accusations against
them have been found not credible by his own review board:

> When a priest is accused, and until they do the investigation obviously,
> they remove the priest from ministry. One of the problems we're having
> with zero tolerance—and this is happening in a neighboring diocese, not
> my own—even after a priest has been cleared, the bishop is not putting
> him back in ministry. . . . It happened to one of my classmates. He was
> exonerated but couldn't return to any kind of ministry. He couldn't even
> publicly identify as a priest. Unfortunately due to other things he died two
> years ago, but at least the bishop allowed him to be buried as a priest. That
> bishop doesn't care. Once you've been removed, you're removed. At least
> in my particular diocese, if a guy has been cleared, the bishop restores
> him to ministry and he makes sure it's put in our diocesan paper that,
> "Father So-and-so has been cleared, everything's fine, and I am putting
> him back in ministry." He publicizes it so people know the priest has been
> cleared.

The survey asked priests how the implementation of the Charter and
Essential Norms has affected their own ministry. Table 6.1 shows that a
plurality of priests, 41 percent, say there has been no effect on their
ministry.

Table 6.1
Reported Effects of the Charter and
Essential Norms on Priests' Ministry

	All	Diocesan	Religious
What has been the effect of the implementation of the Charter for the Protection of Children and Young People/Essential Norms on your own priestly ministry?			
Hindered greatly	6%	7%	4%
Hindered slightly	24	28	15
Had no effect	41	36	51
Helped slightly	18	17	20
Helped greatly	11	11	9

Note: Diocesan priests were asked about the Charter, and religious priests were asked about the
Essential Norms.

Below is a comment from a diocesan priest who says the Charter has had no effect on his ministry:

> We had the [name of offender] case here in 1987 or 88 or so. Then there were policies put into place shortly thereafter. [The diocese followed what] the bishops' conference had in the 1990s, all those things that were voluntary at that point but based upon what some dioceses had learned. The Charter hasn't helped or hindered me so much because we had those policies. . . . It made it a little bit more stringent or demanding, but it didn't have much of an effect except that there were a few guys who were removed.

In interviews and focus groups, priests who say the Charter has helped their ministry and those who say it has hindered their ministry often talk about the same issue—the scrutiny that is now placed on priests in their ministry with young people. Some feel that the stringency and hyperalertness that accompany a zero tolerance Church culture draw undue suspicion upon ordinary interactions between priests and young people. In contrast, other priests feel that diocesan policies associated with the Charter help assure that they will not be wrongly accused exactly because the policies regulate interactions with young people:

> On the hindering side, one of the things priest friends of mine have said, and to some extent I agree with them, is that we find ourselves sometimes looking over our shoulder. . . . Like if we're walking through the school, before we allow a kid to come up and hug us or something like that, we think, "All right, who's looking? Is there somebody interpreting this in the wrong way because Johnny put his arms around my waist and hugged me?" Our children happen to be very affectionate to the teachers, to the faculty, and to the priests.

> I never have a boy or girl in the rectory. They cannot come through the door without their parent. I won't touch a child unless in front of church with mother and father and I high-five a kid.

> We built a church and the confessional has glass doors.

Some priests on both sides of the help-or-hinder divide specifically mention the fact that their own bishop has instituted a diocesan policy that clergy are not to be alone with a child.[12]

---

[12] Such policies are not formally required by the Charter but are closely associated with it in the minds of some priests.

My family tradition has always been that I would take my nieces and nephews out on their birthdays. I'd procrastinate buying them presents but then to make up for it say, "Come on. We're going to the toy store, and you pick out what you want." Then the Charter comes out. "Oh good. I cannot be alone even with my own relatives under a certain age."

A priest in a focus group discusses a similar requirement in his diocese about being alone with children:

In our diocese, you can't be alone with a kid. Good or bad, I feel a lot of things are to protect the priests. There are challenges, like a time with my youth group when a kid had no ride home. Do I take him home and be a good priest and violate the Charter? These are the questions we have to answer. Where do I show compassion and love as a father figure? But also, are we risking our own reputation?

Public Interactions and Publicity Surrounding the Scandal

If priests are now more self-conscious in their ministry with children, they tend to be even more nervous about interactions with strangers or the public. Few priests told us they have experienced naked hostility on the street, but many feel considerably more wary since 2002. A common example of a time when priests say they feel this way is while visiting patients in a hospital. This is an occasion when they typically wear their clerical collar and when they are bound to encounter many people who are not Catholic. Below are quotes from three priests regarding public interactions in the wake of the scandal:

I feel a difference when I go to the hospital now, if I'm in my collar, when I'm walking down those corridors. Sometimes I feel like an invisible man. There are people who won't even establish eye contact with me. You know, others are very gracious, but I've noticed a difference in that kind of setting. . . . I'm much more careful, not that I've ever done anything inappropriate, but you have to be so careful.

The scandal put everybody on eggshells. There were a number of priests who, in my diocese, were ashamed to wear the collar. My history is that the first time the bishop met me in a collar, he swore under his breath and said, "By God, you *do* own a suit." Anyway, I started to wear the collar a little more often, purposely. One Sunday afternoon I was walking down the street in my blacks. A family was walking with a child, who all the sudden decided he would rather walk with me than with his parents. I remember purposely walking slower to get him back closer to his parents than he was to me.

There was one incident the same year. When school registration started, we had a family that was not Catholic but wanted their daughter in the school. They said they had no problem with either the tuition or religious education. Within several weeks they began to make noise that they didn't put their child in there to be treated like a pagan and to be converted. They weren't paying tuition. The mother came over to the office one day to talk to the business manager. The school secretary sent the daughter over to meet up with her mother to drive her home. Her mother was waiting for her in the parking lot. When the girl came in I reached behind her to pull the door. I brushed her shoulder, and her eyes got as big as pie pans. I thought, "In the next thirty seconds my whole vocation could be shot to hell. I've got maybe about ten or fifteen seconds before she says what happened to her mother." I said, "Your mom's downstairs. Call for her." She went downstairs. I got the secretaries, the bookkeepers, and the business manager together right after and I said, "This is what happened: a girl came to the door to look for her mom. I reached behind her to pull the door. I brushed her shoulder. If anybody calls you to court, you've got it verbatim." We had a parish council meeting that night. I told the parish council what happened that afternoon. Nothing ever came of it, but it was like watching your life flash in front of your eyes.

For the most part, nothing has been personally directed towards me except for one occasion. I was doing a wedding. If I don't know a family very well, I often won't go to the reception. But this was a wedding where I kind of knew the couple, and I was trying to go to as many receptions as I could because I was a new priest and trying to show people that priests are people. Sometimes I would dance with the aunt or the grandmother or other people in the wedding party. At this reception I just had the perception that people that I *didn't* know were really staring at me with suspicion as I was dancing—so much so that I actually left the wedding reception very soon after I started feeling that. I just felt like I was *so* uncomfortable and so out of place and so judged. That was the only time that I really felt that.

Note that these kinds of experiences and feelings are not universal. A number of other priests told us that they have not experienced any negativity in relation to the scandal, nor have they felt particularly nervous about being public:

I wear my collar when I have a particular reason to that day, like when I have a funeral or wake. When I did have it on, I never met any of the hostility that some guys did. But I'm in a small town. Everybody knows me. I may have felt different if I was stationed some place in [the city] and was constantly walking by people who had no idea who I was. Being in a small town, it doesn't matter what you wear, they know who you are. They know where your car is parked. They know where you had dinner last night. [Laughs.] So, that wasn't a concern for me.

When we asked priests in interviews and focus groups about the biggest problems or challenges in their lives, it was only rarely that the sexual abuse scandal was one of the things that immediately came to their minds. In the few instances a priest mentioned the scandal in this context, it was typically in reference to the public image of the Church or the priesthood. As one priest briefly puts it,

> Another problem in my life is the Church getting a bad rap with some of these child molestation cases that occurred.

As some of the first quotes in this chapter indicate, enduring the onslaught of press coverage during 2002 was obviously very difficult for many priests—particularly for those in dioceses relatively hard-hit by the scandal. A few told us they simply stopped reading newspapers and watching the news at that time. Even now media attention to the issue has not disappeared. During a 2011 interview, a priest in a diocese deeply affected by the scandal reacts—with evident weariness in his voice—to ongoing coverage of the scandal in his diocese:

> Damn, today's [local newspaper] had another story beating us up. It just goes constantly and we never get a break, it seems.

Nevertheless, we did not encounter a great deal of anger toward the press among rank-and-file priests—at least not in the sense that they believe facts have been fabricated or systematically distorted out of vindictiveness toward Catholicism. Certainly some feel the intensity of the coverage has gone overboard, given the many other problems in the country and the world, but priests are generally not consumed by bitterness. Among those most critical of the press are individuals who, while in administrative positions prior to 2002, worked with priests accused of abuse. We provide two examples in the next chapter. The following quotes are what two "typical" priests (not in administrative positions) shared when asked how they feel about the news media:

> I'm very happy with the media. They're calling us to accountability. They *should* call us to accountability, and if that helps to put us back on track, *good*. We need that. It *is* scandalous. The news media is right about that. And, yeah, the media is not perfect. . . . But it's good that they're bringing this out because we need to bring it to light so that it can be healed.

First and foremost we have to step back as Catholics and really look at the fact that it's the media that's brought this to our attention and has really, I think, helped us. We need to get over the fact that we're somehow a victim of the media. Had the media not been so piranha-like, many of these issues were not going to be faced. On the other hand, to have witnessed a media frenzy like we have seen, I certainly would think that the media has to step back and analyze itself. . . . When you see that sort of attention and you have a whole section of the pool of reporters dedicated just to research this, I think it's a bit out of hand.

Frustrations that priests shared regarding external criticism of the Church and the priesthood were often not directed at the press so much as at other media outlets or other groups in society:

There was a suit against the Boy Scouts several months ago. The paper questioned a Scout official. He said, "We're not the Catholic Church." It was absolutely gratuitous. It's like, "Why in the hell did you say that?" The last thing I watch at night is Jay Leno, and if there's anything out there where you can connect a priest with a young boy, then he'll make a joke about it.[13] Give us a break sooner or later. Will you let this damn thing drop?

Attitudes toward Bishops and the Church Hierarchy

Priests feel much the same sense of outrage as lay Catholics do about the harm that clergy sexual abuse has caused to victims and about the culpability of the hierarchy in failing to respond to the problem. However, many priests also express a concern that laypeople do not—that they, the ordinary priests, have been placed in a position where they must defend or apologize for the Church when they are not the ones responsible for the scandal. As we saw in chapter 3, it is already challenging enough for some priests to represent the Catholic position on controversial issues. Now priests face the prospect of upholding Church teachings before laypeople who are all the more resistant, given the moral failings of the

---

[13] Not long before this interview, the following Leno joke had received a fair amount of media attention: "Oh, and a Catholic priest in Connecticut has been charged with stealing $1.3 million in church money and using the money for male escorts. Of course, his parish is very upset about this—except the altar boys. They're going, 'huh, dodged a bullet on that one.' Yeah, he spent $1.3 million on male escorts and, of course, the other priests were very confused. They said: 'Why buy the escort when the altar boys are free?' "

Church's own leaders. For some priests, this exacerbates existing frustrations with the hierarchy:

> I find the institutionalism of the Church to be hard for people where it intersects with their lives and the reality of everyday living. It is a challenge trying to explain the Vatican stand on several issues, particularly with the pedophile scandal.

> If there is anything that I am terribly embarrassed by [regarding the scandal,] it is the lack of contrition of the hierarchy. I am terribly ashamed. We're supposed to acknowledge our culpability and our sinfulness and be forgiven. But it has been placed on the guy in the trenches because they've passed people around and don't want to take and acknowledge the blame for that. What kind of example is that for the people, who are told that they need to go to confession?

> I'm getting angry because, as a priest, I am expected to be supportive of the Church. I feel like the bishops have put us in an indefensible position. The bishops are the ones who did so much of this covering up. They left priests out on a limb. The way we choose bishops in the Church has to be changed. I'm sick and tired of someone being made a bishop because he was such a good secretary. Let someone who is a good pastor be a bishop. We have to stop letting ordinaries hand-pick their auxiliaries. We have to stop ordinaries having too much say in who's going to be a coadjutor.

> I wrote a bulletin article about how, recently, the Vatican seemingly connected the penalty for pedophilia with the penalty for the ordination of a woman.[14] Whatever was intended, it was outrageous. And people here were very angry. A woman in the parish had an article in the newspaper called, "Excommunicate Me, Please." The response of people [who defend the Vatican] usually is, "Well, you have to understand how Rome works." And what I said in this article is, "No, Rome has to understand *us*. We're the faithful, the Church. They're not." . . . They don't *listen* to what people are concerned about, like the role of women in the Church.

Such feelings are less common among priests with more traditional theological beliefs. One expressed his confidence that laypeople who are faithful to the Church have not been shaken by the scandal:

> My opinion is that the ones it has hurt most of all are those that I would call the fence-sitters, Catholics who are, for want of a better word, corrupted by the society in which we live, the media and stuff like that. That's really hurt. Catholics who are—this is the way I feel—full of faith, who

[14] For background, see Reuters (2010).

are at Mass every Sunday, got over it because they had the brains to know
that everybody is a sinner in one way or another and they didn't have the
priests and bishops too high on the stand. . . . I don't think I lost any
Sunday regulars on account of the scandal.

When it comes to the scandal, lay Catholics have consistently been
more critical toward the bishops as a whole than toward their own bishop.
For example, in a January 2003 CARA telephone poll only 23 percent
of self-identified US Catholics gave a rating of "good" or "excellent" to
the job "Catholic bishops as a whole have done handling accusations of
sexual abuse by priests" (Gray and Perl, 2005). In comparison, 40 percent
gave a "good" or "excellent" rating to their "local bishop or cardinal" in
that regard. Comparable survey evidence for priests is not available, but
interviews suggest they share the same tendency as laypeople to be more
forgiving toward their own bishop—perhaps more so—because priests,
at least in smaller dioceses, personally know their own bishop and can
sympathize with him as an individual. A priest in a diocese that was
relatively hard-hit by the scandal says of his bishop:

> Some of the bishops have gotten beat up pretty mercilessly. Some guys
> needed to be beat up. I guess what I'm saying is guys like Cardinal Law
> needed to be hammered on. But our guy who was here during the height
> of our diocese's scandal, Bishop [Name], doggone, I know him and I know
> he's a man of his time. He and some of the bishops like him did the best
> they knew how to do given the time that they were coming from. When I
> was going through my most difficult periods of ministry, he was tremen-
> dously helpful. He really encouraged me. Bishop [Name] came to visit
> one of the guys I lived with who's now retired. I thought, "How wonder-
> ful." The scandal tore him up, just tore him up tremendously. He aged a
> lot in those days. Without the help of [his chancellor] to go through the
> minefield of legal challenges and media stuff I think he would have been
> overwhelmed by it.

A priest who was appointed to his diocese's review board[15] in 2002 describes an incident that elevated his opinion of his bishop:

> One of the things that came out in the press was a document, a memo
> from the bishop about a sexual abuse case. Well, there's no way of viewing
> it but in a negative way concerning the bishop and what he did. The key

---

[15] Although the majority of members of a review board are required to be laypeople,
the Essential Norms dictates that "at least one member should be a priest who is an experienced and respected pastor of the diocese/eparchy."

point the media wanted to keep showing is that this was a cover-up the whole time. In the memo, the bishop made reference to financial settlements and the need for keeping the case from becoming public. In the middle of one of our early review board meetings this document was brought up, and it was an uncomfortable situation. The bishop listened while laypeople on the board spoke.

After they finished, he responded with the context of when the memo was written. The parents of a young victim called and told him what happened. The bishop said, "Why don't you come in and talk to me and we'll see how we can help your son." The family showed up to meet the bishop with a lawyer. As soon as they sat down, the lawyer started saying, "Here is what we want." He was caught off guard and felt that he got ambushed. He was angry, frustrated. So after that meeting, mindful of what had just taken place, he wrote the memo. But when you take the memo out of that context, which the media did, it looked like his concern wasn't so much for the victim but for the money.

He explained himself the best he could, but I could tell that sitting there and listening to what those board members said—it stung him. But he not only stayed for the rest of that meeting, he continued to show up for every meeting. That's when the bishop's stock went up higher.

This is not to say that every priest will defend his bishop's actions. We interviewed a few diocesan priests who, soon after the scandal broke, openly spoke out against their bishop's handling of sexual abuse cases. Some did so publicly and others only in their parishes. These priests all report receiving great support from Catholic laity after they spoke out. One says, "I got *incredible* support in my parish. I got phone calls and e-mails from lots of people in my town, not just Catholics, saying, 'Thank you for doing that.' " However the priests report mixed experiences regarding repercussions from diocesan administration. Below, one of them speaks at length about why he chose to criticize his bishop in public and the consequences for himself. He begins by explaining why he was moved to speak out:

> I was in the midst of an assignment where things were just going so incredibly well. I felt like it was such a privilege to be a priest and that I was so embraced by my parish. Priesthood felt like it was in some ways everything I dreamed it would be. Then when this happened, probably the most startling thing was the anger that parishioners expressed—not towards me personally but towards the Church in general: "Aha, see? I knew it all along that these guys were really not what they say they are." So I had a sense that the credibility of the Church as I had known it was sort of disappearing.

I had a tremendous amount of belief in the leadership of the Church and the potential to deal with this. I kept expecting Bishop [Name] to say, "We now understand the serious, evil nature of this and the long-term effects on victims. I made mistakes and didn't really recognize the gravity of this problem and want to do something about it now." At some point I thought it would switch from the hiding and covering-up to really dealing with the situation. But then it just kept getting worse and worse. Each time a new story came out, the diocese kept pushing it away. It was embarrassing, almost. The confidence and belief that I had before had eroded. I couldn't imagine that the confidence or belief in the leadership by anybody else could stand up anymore.

To me, criticizing the bishop was a very clear decision about right and wrong. I was so convinced that the credibility of the Church had been so damaged that everybody would see that this was the right thing to do. I didn't really think too much about repercussions for me from the diocese. I was early into the priesthood. I was very idealistic about it.

Sometime later this priest was passed over for a position in a Catholic organization for which he had applied and interviewed. He feels that the rejection was a consequence of his having spoken out against his bishop:

The interview had gone incredibly well and there was a lot of enthusiasm for me. And then quite suddenly, in the middle of the hiring process, everything changed. It was like going from one end of the spectrum to the other. Suddenly the person in charge didn't even want to speak with me. I heard from the diocesan personnel director that I wasn't going to be getting the position. One of the people who works at [the organization] later said they were told I was too liberal. There haven't been any other things that have marked me as a liberal. In fact, I'm a pretty middle-of-the-road guy. But apparently somebody in the diocese thinks that I'm not really somebody who can be trusted.

Another diocesan priest describes how he renounced his bishop during a homily at his parish:

I publicly disavowed the bishop. I asked for his resignation before my parishioners here. I used a symbolic act. In ordination we put our hands into the hands of the bishop and promise obedience. I told my people at all the Masses one weekend that, "I remove my hands from the hands of the bishop until a worthy successor is brought in." I had expected at that time to get called in the next day and be, you know, thrown out. [Laughs.] But nothing happened. As far as I know, it was not reported to the diocese. . . . Eventually, we did have a new bishop. I was meeting with him about something else. I knelt before the bishop, told him what I did, and asked to put my hands into his hands and make the promise of obedience again. Then taking my hands into his, he said the words, "Do you promise obedience to me and my successors?" and I answered, "I do."

During 2010, when focus groups and most of the interviews took place, the sexual abuse problem in Europe was receiving a great deal of press coverage here in the United States. Pope Benedict XVI himself fell under scrutiny for events that previously happened under his watch as an archbishop in Germany and for previous actions as prefect of the Congregation for the Doctrine of the Faith. Because of this coverage, priests spent a fair amount of time reflecting on the scandal in Europe and the Vatican. Most of the discussion falls beyond the scope of this chapter, but it is worth noting some of the attitudes that priests shared regarding Church leadership in Europe. We heard much criticism of European bishops. In fact, one priest wished that the press would be *more* critical of them. And several priests talked disparagingly of "Rome's" or "the Vatican's" response to the scandal (some quotes to that effect have appeared earlier in this chapter). However, when speaking about the pope, priests were generally not as harsh as we expected. Even some relatively liberal priests, who are disinclined to praise Benedict's theological stances, feel he has made efforts to improve the handling of the sexual abuse problem in the Church worldwide. Below is one such opinion:

> The Church did not handle the issue well, particularly the Vatican did not handle it well. Frankly I think Benedict's doing better. . . . John Paul was terrible on this issue, terrible. I do think Benedict is trying to do the right thing. I think he's had a breakthrough from meeting with some of the victims and is trying to feel his way toward dealing with this more aggressively, in the way it should be dealt with.

Morale, Priestly Fraternity, and Support in Dioceses Strongly Affected by the Scandal

As chapter 2 emphasized, priests are generally very happy with their lives and ministry. There is no overarching morale problem in the priesthood. However, as we have already noted, the year 2002 and the years immediately following it were a trying time for many priests. Below, a diocesan priest describes how, even today, the scandal and his anger at the bishops sometimes gets him down:

There are days that it literally gets me to the point that it is difficult to function. There was one day I finished with Mass in the morning and I said to my secretary, "I'm going upstairs. Don't call me unless the house is on fire." I went upstairs in my room and spent about three and a half hours feeling angry and depressed. It got to the point where it actually paralyzed me for the day. . . . The *New York Times* is making mince meat out of us because we handed it to them on a silver platter. I find that hurtful, and I just go through the motions on some days.

The priest quoted above does not belong to a diocese that was particularly hard-hit by the scandal. In fact, his bishop has a public reputation as having done a stellar job responding to the problem. Imagine, then, what it has been like for priests in dioceses where the explosion of 2002 was much larger and where local media were saturated with the issue for months on end. Father James Burns and colleagues examined priests in the Northeast—the geographic region where the scandal has been most intense—and found an incidence of psychological trauma and burnout of 17 percent, a rate approximately double that of comparison groups of Protestant clergy and of Catholic priests in the Southwest (Burns, 2008, 2010). A priest who is himself not from Boston but has close ties there says of that archdiocese,

A lot of folks didn't go out in public with a collar on unless they were doing ministry because they'd get funny looks. . . . And the morale was terrible. By 2005 it was just awful. Everybody was just down in the dumps.

Several priests spoke with us about how they coped with the somewhat unique stresses of being in a hard-hit diocese during the intense years of 2002 and immediately after. A common theme in their reflections is the importance of priests supporting one another to deal with emotions such as anger and discouragement. One priest feels that has not happened enough in his own diocese:

We hunkered down into our bunkers and we tended to isolate. "Just leave me alone. Let me run my parish." We figured if we stay away from the diocese, that's a better thing. Most of us enjoy parish ministry. We enjoy the people. We find life there. So it's not all a bad story. Unfortunately, we're not Congregationalists. We need to be together.

Three men from hard-hit dioceses recall how they were able to weather the hard times through the camaraderie and fraternity they shared with other priests:

A year after the scandal broke a counselor who worked with the diocesan family ministries office offered to have some sessions with priests because some of us were really bubbling with anger. We did that. We had several sessions together. That was helpful, just to vent, to feel that we weren't alone, that everybody was going through this. There are some things you could say to the group that you just didn't want to talk about with a family.

I did get involved with a group of priests who were supporting each other. There was sort of a closing of the ranks and pulling together. We had Saturday night dinners where eight or ten guys would gather, which was something that hadn't happened before and hasn't really happened since. There was just this need to be together, and not even necessarily talking about what was going on with the scandal the whole time, although that was definitely part of the conversation. But just being together and knowing that few people understood the way that we did what it was like to be in our shoes.

It was gut-wrenching, heart-wrenching working with these cases [of priests who had committed abuse] in the tribunal. You just sit there and are *disgusted* by the whole thing and saddened by the sickness of the criminal mind. Who would do this to a young person? It was painful, to the point of tears at times. We had to support each other. I had a good priest friend who was also involved in the tribunal. We would have to process almost every day, just kind of sit there and talk it out with each other. It wasn't necessarily something that we could process on a daily basis with anybody else. But at least we had each other and we talked it through. If I hadn't had that, I don't know what would have happened because it just overwhelms you. It's so profoundly sad and depressing. It can draw you into that darkness and you can just stay there.

Is there a dark side to priestly fraternity? Some have argued that there was an unwritten code of silence in the priesthood over the years that allowed the scandal to fester—one that extended beyond Church leaders and led ordinary priests to overlook or minimize the crimes of their brothers (e.g., Greeley, 2004:104–5). We cannot adequately answer this question ourselves, but we will share the thoughts of two priests from hard-hit dioceses who reflected with us on it. Asked if he feels there is some degree of collective responsibility for the scandal in the priesthood, a member of the millennial ordination cohort says,

I would agree that that could be possible. Some guys that had been in the culture for a long time may have contributed in the sense that there were pastors who knew that a guy was doing this, but they didn't know how to deal with it. All they wanted to do was be rid of the problem from their little corner of the woods. I don't think anybody at that time would have felt like they had any power to change the situation—that it was up to the diocese and the leadership to actually do something about these things. As long as the guy was moved out of their parish, they felt like it was being dealt with. I think that's why the anger goes to the leadership so much because they were the ones trusted to actually deal with it.

An older priest brings up the subject while discussing priestly fraternity:

> There are priests who aren't particularly friends of mine, but I would get up at four o'clock in the morning to go help them out—and maybe in less than morally high situations. "You've got your ass in a sling and I'll come bail you out. But by God the next morning we're both going to talk to the bishop." . . . I think there *is* a brotherhood of priests. I'm not sure if it was a cover-up brotherhood. I would hate to think that it was. I think it *should* be a challenging brotherhood.

Causes of the Clergy Sexual Abuse Problem

Debate rages within the Church over why the clergy sexual abuse problem has been so vast in the United States and, as is increasingly apparent, much of Europe. To a large degree the debate has devolved into a left-right culture wars clash over whether the problem can be attributed primarily to the celibacy requirement or to homosexuality within the priesthood. Answering the question itself lies beyond the scope of this chapter,[16] but we wish to briefly mention the reactions of priests on the topic. Perhaps our most important impression is simply that the debate is not foremost in priests' minds when it comes to the scandal. When asked in focus groups and interviews to reflect on the sexual abuse issue, priests were much more likely to volunteer their feelings about the Charter, their anger at Church leadership, their caution when interacting with young people, or their experiences talking about the problem with parishioners. Priests almost never raised the issue of celibacy in relation to the scandal unless we specifically asked them about it. When we did, the most common reaction was skepticism that celibacy and abuse are closely linked. Asked if he believes celibacy plays a role in causing sexual abuse in the Church, a priest with experience in counseling responds,

---

[16] This issue has recently been addressed in great depth by researchers with expertise we lack (John Jay College Research Team, 2011).

It would be nice to simply say, "No." There are certain individuals for whom, because they only relate to children in an inappropriate way, their flight to celibacy was obviously unhealthy. For the majority of individuals with this problem, however, it is not an issue of celibacy. That is pretty clear in the research. Eighty percent of offenders in the United States are white heterosexual married males. If I raised the question, "What is it about being heterosexual and being married that makes you more prone to offending a child?" I think people would understand the absurdity of the question. It's the same as asking, "What is it about being celibate that makes you offend a child?" It's illogical.

Priests are somewhat more likely to volunteer thoughts on homosexuality in relation to clerical sexual abuse. Their attitudes generally break down the way that one would expect, with more traditional priests apt to believe that homosexuality has contributed to the problem, or is at least closely associated with it, and more liberal priests vigorously denying that this is true. One priest identifying himself as gay says:

> One of the things that I didn't like about any of this, that's still going on, is that you'll talk to laypeople, and they'll say, "This is happening because we have all these gay priests. If we get rid of all the gay priests, we won't have this problem." And I've said, "But the studies have shown that's not true, that the majority of pedophiles happen to be heterosexual." But even though you show them the statistics, they don't believe it. Even many of our bishops are still saying it. This is not only in our country but in the other countries as well.

A few more quotes that touch on homosexuality and the scandal appear in chapter 8, in the context of advice to young men considering the priesthood.

Conclusion

In many ways, the emotional reactions of priests when the scandal broke in 2002 probably resemble those of lay Catholics. Priests felt horror and sadness for victims, anger at diocesan and religious order administrators, and shock at the scope of the problem. Many felt particularly acute shock—and pain—at revelations that fellow priests they personally knew were guilty of abuse. Most priests are not preoccupied by such emotions today, although pain lingers for some of them, particularly in dioceses that were hard-hit by the scandal. In such dioceses there were typically more priests removed from ministry (and therefore a greater likelihood of personally knowing at least one of them) and far more intense local press coverage, which in some dioceses continues to the present day.

Most priests we spoke with understand the need for the Charter and believe that young people are better protected because of it. They support the removal of priests who have committed abuse from any further ministry that involves contact with minors. Far less support exists for automatic laicization of all diocesan priests guilty of abuse. Many priests prefer that dioceses follow the lead of religious orders and place some of these men in "prayer and penance," with restrictions on their mobility but also with affirmation of their identity as priests. Moved by the recognition that some men accused of sexual abuse are innocent, many priests also feel it is important that support be offered during the review process to those who have been accused and that exonerated priests be allowed to return to their previous ministry.

A plurality of priests responding to the survey say the Charter and Essential Norms have neither hindered nor helped their own ministry. A common complaint among the three-tenths of priests who say the Charter and Essential Norms have been a hindrance is that zero tolerance exacerbates the challenge of interacting with young people without drawing undue suspicion upon themselves. Others feel that guidelines associated with the Charter, besides having helped restore the confidence of their parishioners in the Church, actually work to protect priests from unwarranted accusations.

With the exception of some priests in parishes where abuse previously took place, the great majority of pastors we spoke with report that they received tremendous personal affirmation from their parishioners when the scandal broke. Priests in hard-hit dioceses often turned to each other for support in the aftermath of the scandal because what they were experiencing was so difficult for those outside the priesthood to fully understand. But many of those priests also emphasize the importance of support from the laity in getting through. Asked if there is anything he would want to say to lay Catholics regarding the scandal, one priest shares the following story:

> When it broke I remember going outside walking the dog one night around the church. A car with four young men pulled up. One rolled down a window and threw a beer can at me and said, "There's one of those fags." I was devastated. I went into the rectory alone and kind of cried to my dog, thinking, "I don't want to do this." From there on I began to think, "Everybody's watching me." I stopped wearing my collar. I'd wear it for

Sunday Mass and funerals, but other than that, I wasn't wearing my collar anywhere. It just felt like everybody was looking, everybody was snickering.

One day, several months after the stuff broke, I was standing at the door shaking hands at the end of Mass. A woman came up to me. She said, "Can I talk to you?" She seemed angry. My feeling was, "Oh, here we go again." The parish I was in had an abuser, a previous priest. There were a lot of people talking about it. I was just so beat that my stomach dropped. But she said, "Father, when you walk down that aisle, you pick your head up and you look at us. You haven't done that for months. We love you. We care about you. You *look* at us when you walk out." I thought, "Wow." I didn't even realize that I had my head down. I was still kind of embarrassed to be a priest. . . . What I would hope is that people can see their priests as human beings, just like the rest, who need support.

Chapter 7 continues the discussion of the sexual abuse scandal. It presents the personal stories of nine priests who have been touched by the scandal in significant ways.

Chapter 7

The Sexual Abuse Scandal
and the Stories of Nine Priests

> I think the pain that the structure's going through is deserved. So I don't
> have much sympathy for the pain of the structure of the Church. I feel a
> lot of pain for victims.
>
> —*Father Eric*

The previous chapter discussed effects of the sexual abuse issue on
priests in general. This chapter develops some of the same themes but
does so in a different way. It presents in greater depth the stories of a few
individual priests whose lives and ministries have been affected by the
scandal in very significant ways. These stories are told mostly in the
priests' own words, with limited analysis or exposition from us. Though
their experiences are certainly far from typical of the "average" priest,
we hope that the extended accounts presented here will help show how
real priests have had to deal, in one way or another, with the challenges
of the sexual abuse problem.

Using personal contacts, we sought priests with a variety of experiences and also a diversity of viewpoints for this chapter. We have not
tried to verify every specific fact presented here, but for all the priests
we do have independent confirmation that their general stories are true.
In a few cases we have changed or obscured minor factual details to help
shield the identities of priests. All names of people and parishes in this
chapter are pseudonyms.

Father Al: A Pastor at "Ground Zero"

For many years Father Al has served as pastor of the same parish,
which he describes as "the Ground Zero of the pedophile crisis of my
diocese." However, when Father Al arrived in the parish, he was unaware

of what had happened there in the past. He soon became concerned about behavior around young people by a priest in residence in the parish, and he had that priest removed from the rectory. Credible allegations of sexual abuse of young people were also later made against Father Al's predecessor and other priests who had previously served in the parish. Parents of some of the victims remained in the parish, but for many years, the abuse was not widely known among other parishioners. In 2002 everything became public, and Father Al had to deal with parishioner anger.

> I was assigned here in the 1980s. There was another priest in residence in the parish who was involved in diocesan-level ministry when I arrived. I was very uncomfortable with his presence and his behaviors with boys. I tried to indicate to the bishop that this was not a very good situation, but the bishop wasn't open at the time to hearing anything different. In hindsight I would have tried harder to have him removed from ministry. But I did succeed in having him transferred out within a few months.

As the years passed, Father Al began to learn of a very troubling past in the parish and of the pain carried by some of his parishioners whose children had been violated:

> I found out about abuse committed by priests prior to my arrival through diocesan information in a piecemeal kind of manner. I reached out to parents of some of the victims, those who were known to me and still in the parish. The parents of those who were victimized were very angry, very hurt, and very disillusioned with the Church. They felt very deeply that a sacred trust had been violated.
>
> The abuse in the parish prior to my becoming pastor became public in 2002 with the Dallas Charter and zero tolerance. It was a horror show, quite frankly, when it all broke. From the release of diocesan records of prior settlements, and with subsequent settlements, it became evident that four priests who had been assigned to the parish here in the 1970s had serious, credible allegations against them. The settlements probably totaled many millions of dollars. The fact that abuse had taken place in the parish wasn't surprising to some of the parishioners after the fact. They had often been troubled that they knew something was going on but couldn't put their finger on it. Although they were not surprised, they were very concerned and angry that the facts were not made known when the abuse was happening rather than years afterward.

Father Al responded to these revelations by holding listening sessions that allowed parishioners to share their feelings:

In 2003, when the crisis hit a high point here in the US, I held a number of open forums with the parishioners. The first was a forum with the bishop. He came along quite reluctantly. Probably seventy or eighty people attended that forum. It was very difficult for the bishop. People were very angry. But I remember him saying at one point, "The buck stops with me. I assume responsibility for what has happened on my watch." I think that was a very truth-giving moment. It was a rather difficult situation, but it was a good thing that we did it.

Then we had a number of sessions with parents of victims, which I sat in on with the bishop. They were very painful but, again, very cathartic. I conducted subsequent forums with parishioners myself. As long as people wanted to come to forums, I had them. The forums had a healing dimension to them, that people were able to speak their minds and get whatever facts were becoming available. At the end we offered a public healing session in the parish. The bishop participated in that. We invited parishioners and anyone else who felt a need to be present. I felt that it provided a sense of closure. Those who didn't come felt they were invited, and those who came felt that we'd been able to put a period at the end of this entire disaster.

A priest here in the 1970s made attempts to abuse a young man who was later the president of our parish council. We had a special celebration at the parish and I asked him, as president of the council, to share something on the journey of the parish and its ministries. He shared his personal experience of the attempted victimization. The bishop was present and I'd alerted the bishop that he had wanted to do this. There were mixed reviews of his having done it, but I felt he did it in a fairly good way. I think it was therapeutic for him.

Father Al discusses how he was affected personally by being pastor of this parish in the aftermath of when the abuse took place:

It was very stressful. I never knew how it was all going to end. There were times I thought maybe I should just get myself transferred to another parish and let somebody else come and deal with the situation. But I stayed with it and I'm glad I did.

One of my sources of support was a close priest friend who had done research on the clergy sexual abuse problem. His advice was to be forthright with the facts as they became available. I found that very helpful. The parishioners have a very deep appreciation, I think, for the fact that I hung in there and tried to deal with the situation transparently. It was a very purifying process and I feel that the parish has grown in a positive way through the crisis because we dealt with it as openly and frankly as we could. There is a good level of trust that has been built back up.

This experience has given me a greater sense of reverence for young people and for children in particular. We, as Church, must recognize the first principle of Catholic social teaching: the basic human dignity of each person, made in the image and likeness of God. We must have reverence for the weakest and the most vulnerable of those amongst us. Unfortunately as a Church—institutionally, and I think clericalism has had a lot to do with the abuse crisis—those who are most vulnerable in the entire abuse crisis were seen as somewhat expendable. They were voiceless. We protected ourselves and denied our basic core teaching of the dignity of the human person. It overrides every other concern, including the institutional image of the Church.

Publicity in 2010 about the clergy sexual abuse problem in Europe opened old wounds for some of Father Al's parishioners:

I held two forums again recently because of the crisis at the universal level of the Church—the curia and Vatican level. The forums also addressed parishioner concerns about a local issue. I had about thirty people show up for the first forum and twenty for the second. A question that came from one parishioner was: "How come the Vatican has not taken a page from how we in the United States have responded to the crisis?" I said, "Well, it takes a long time for the word to get from the bottom of our institutional system to the top." It was rather evident to this parishioner that in the Vatican some denial is still going on. But I myself think Benedict has probably been more forthright with it than he's being given credit for.

During this time I had a letter from another parishioner. He said, "I'm not only leaving the parish, but I'm leaving the Church because of the ongoing crisis and especially the lack of credibility around the Vatican response." He indicated what he liked about the Church in his letter—that he liked the Eucharist, the sacraments, the traditions, and devotions. So I called him up and invited him in. I said: "Andy, I don't have a lot of difficulty agreeing with some of the observations in your letter. But it seems to me you're going to throw the baby out with the bath water. How are you going to deal with the absence of Eucharist in your life? With all that is positive in your experience of Church, how are you going to replace that? Jesus didn't make very good choices when He chose the twelve. One betrayed Him. Another denied Him. And all the others cut and ran. And yet Jesus came back to them and said, "This is who I'm working with." The Church is no more or no less credible than Jesus was to the people of His time. And so, Andy, I think you need to give some pause, reflection, and thought to what you want to do."

Well, I got another letter from him two weeks later. "You know what?" he said, "I'm staying. What you shared with me makes sense."

Father Bob: Returned to Ministry after a Long Ordeal

In planning this chapter, we hoped to relate the story of a priest who was accused of sexual abuse but was later returned to ministry after the accusation was found to be unsubstantiated. This proved to be more challenging than we had envisioned. Over the course of several months we used personal networks to approach several priests who had been through such an experience. However, when asked if they would be willing to be interviewed, all of them immediately or eventually declined. Usually the priests identified one of two reasons for their reluctance to talk with us. For many, being accused of child abuse was highly traumatic, and they were now trying to put the experience behind them. And often priests had been advised by lawyers to never speak to anybody about their cases, even after exoneration. Less commonly, there had sometimes been so much publicity surrounding their accusations that priests felt it would be difficult for us to shield their identities.

Finally we were introduced to Father Bob. In 2002 he was accused of having sexually abused a young person many years previously. His diocese removed him from ministry while the accusation was investigated. Many months later the diocese deemed the allegation to be unsubstantiated, so he returned to a warm reception at his parish. Perhaps because no civil suit or criminal charges ever emerged from the accusation, Father Bob readily agreed to talk with us about what he had gone through. Additionally he feels press coverage of his return to his parish was favorable and that there is widespread belief in the community where he lives that he is indeed innocent.

In Father Bob's view, the most important part of his experience is the great support and encouragement he received from his parishioners during the ordeal—though he is quick to say that this may differ from experiences of other priests who have been accused but ultimately exonerated. By contrast, he remains angry at the diocese over the way it handled the episode. He feels the accusation against him was so dubious on its face that it did not warrant his removal from ministry. In our view, his story exemplifies some of the almost inevitable consequences of a post-scandal and post-Charter era in which diocesan leaders, under extreme scrutiny from the press and legal authorities, feel they must take every accusation of abuse very seriously. Another notable aspect of this story is the length of time it took for the diocese to review his case. Abuse victims have sometimes felt frustrated with the time it takes for dioceses to investigate the priests who have harmed them and then permanently remove those priests from ministry. This was particularly true in the years immediately following the 2002 deluge, when dioceses were swamped with cases. The length of the review process has also been a frustration for some priests who have been accused but wait with the expectation that they will be cleared.

Father Bob begins his story by describing how he learned that he had been accused. Note that to help preserve his anonymity, excerpts below omit important details about the accusation itself:

> I came into the rectory. The secretary said, "Father Walsh wants you to call him right away." I knew who Walsh was. He was the priest in the diocese who had the thankless job of informing priests of accusations against them. My first reaction was, "I'm in trouble." All of us priests in the diocese were waiting for shoes to drop on us. The atmosphere was so charged. When I made the phone call, he told me that the bishop wanted to see me and that they had an accusation against me. The accusation was that many years ago I supposedly raped a young man. I had no recollection of the man. I said, "You just ruined my life." It was terrible. I called a lay friend of mine. I said, "I've got to talk with you." We met and cried together for a while. Then I went back to the rectory. It's a wonder I didn't break my arm because I took a fist and, boy, did I pound the wall. I just kept saying, "I didn't do it. I didn't do it. I didn't do it."
>
> I saw the bishop and Father Walsh the next morning. They said I had to leave the rectory by three o'clock that afternoon. All I would be able to do as a priest was to say Mass privately. I said, "This will ruin my reputation. It's going to ruin my priesthood. It's all over for me." When we finished the conversation the bishop said to me, "Now, Father, we haven't abandoned you." I said, "You already have. Goodbye." They had told me not to tell the parishioners. They were going to send somebody to the Saturday afternoon Mass and that person would tell the parishioners. Unfortunately, whatever was going on in the diocese, the right hand didn't tell the left hand what it was doing. That afternoon the diocese announced my removal to the press. That night all the television stations were down at the parish bombarding the people. It's not a nice thing to see your picture on television. I felt devastated, completely alone.
>
> About a week after that, I was interviewed by a lay man with a criminal justice background who was working for the diocese. He came to the hotel where I was living and spent about forty-five minutes interviewing me. He asked, "Did you do it?" and that sort of thing. He was with me. He said, "I've got to do this, Father, because they asked me to do it. But I don't want to do it." He was very respectful, a good Catholic.
>
> I would call the chancery every day saying, "What's going on?" They would never return my calls. I had retained a lawyer, just to protect myself. And he was also ignored completely by the diocese. In fact, the diocese

finally sent him a letter saying, "Don't contact us anymore," so I was completely in the dark about the progress of their investigation. The institution considered me a pariah.

Father Bob discusses how he coped with being on leave and the contrasting levels of support that he received from other priests and from the laity:

> Over the years I had not taken many vacations, so I treated the first three months on leave as a vacation. After that it became a day-by-day struggle to get through. I kind of went into a cocoon and just shut myself off from everything. Even before this I didn't have many priest friends, so I didn't have much contact from other priests. A couple of times guys from a group of priests in the diocese called me on the phone.
>
> What kept me going was the fact that the parishioners banded together. They circled the wagons around me. If I didn't have their support I probably would have left priesthood. All the way through those months they did not waver as to my innocence. If I sent you all the material that I received from the parishioners, you could write a whole book. There wasn't a day in the time that I was out of ministry that I did not get at least one card of support. It was overwhelming. They held a prayer vigil every Sunday night. When the diocese came down to try to explain to them what was going on, they practically drove them out. They were very angry. The parishioners were screaming at the bishop and the other priests who showed up representing the diocese.
>
> In fact, it became a town thing. It was not only parish support, but the secular community supported me too. They were equally outraged. They put yellow ribbons around every tree and pole they could find in the town. Signs went up on lawns: "We support Father Bob." When I would go shopping in the local stores, people who knew who I was would always come up to me and offer encouragement. Their negative comments were always against the administration of the diocese, not me.
>
> One of the helps for me was that the day after I was dismissed a parishioner contacted me and presented me with a copy of Cardinal Joseph Bernardin's book, *The Gift of Peace*. The first part details his experience of being falsely accused and I adopted his mantra, "The truth will set you free."

Eventually, the diocesan investigation progressed. After a good deal of time, the allegation was found to be unsubstantiated, but not before Father Bob was put through an intense evaluation:

About a month or two after being put on leave I got called in to the chancery. I expected them to tell me everything was okay: "The accusation was baseless and ridiculous. Go back to work." When I got in there they said, "We want you to go to this institute [out of state] to be psychologically assessed. I said, *"What?"* They said, "We know in cases such as this there is repressed memory." They were accusing me of repressing it. I had two hours to make a decision whether to go. If I didn't go right then, they'd put my case on the back burner. There would be no progress until I went and there wouldn't be another opening for two months. So I went to this institute for a week. I was interviewed by psychiatrists, psychologists, drug addiction counselors, spiritual directors, and doctors. I took every psychological test that was ever created. [Laughs.] The ultimate was a test of my sexual tendencies. When I finally went to be informed of their evaluation, the head psychologist looked at me and said, "What the hell are *you* doing here?" The test showed that I had no homosexual tendencies, no pedophilia tendencies, or anything like that. They cleared me completely.

One day many months later I got a phone call from the chancery telling me the bishop would like to see me and asking if I would wait ten days. So I said to the guy, "Should I be cautiously optimistic?" And he said, "Oh please, just give the bishop ten days." But the fact that he told me to renew my apartment lease for only one month gave me the impression that I was on my way back. The day I met with the bishop, he said, "You can go home." He also said, "I'm sorry for what we put you through."

I was walking on air. The parishioners had a celebration for me. Did they ever! For Mass, it was a full church. Then over in the parish center they had "welcome back" signs and all kinds of goodies. The newspapers and television stations came, so I had to give an interview. Now I know what it's like for those people on television when they have a lot of cameras in front of them. Oh, I know just what they're going through. It's a sea of people and lights. So my leaving the parish got on the news, but then they put on the news my coming back.

Asked if any priests called to congratulate him on being restored to ministry, Father Bob recalls,

No, but as I said, I didn't have many priest friends, so I did not expect any to call me. Guys were afraid to be with one another because you didn't know who was going to get accused next. My coming back was still in the middle of the mess because the real bad guys were still in court and their cases were still being covered by the press. You didn't want to be around a priest if you didn't know him. There was one priest that was off the job for a few years just because he was associated with a couple of guys who were accused.

Finally, Father Bob reflects on the extent to which he has been able to place the experience of being accused behind him:

> When I came back and during the last eight years I just put myself back into the job. Otherwise I wouldn't get anything done. But every time I see something in the paper about the scandal it comes back again. The emotions do come back, but then, I don't let them run me. I've got more important things to do. When I retire, hopefully, it'll be completely behind me.
>
> When all is said and done, the spiritual significance of my experience is that when you lose everything that matters to you in life, identification with the person of Jesus becomes the central point of living—in this circumstance, identifying with the suffering Jesus and then with the resurrected Jesus.

Father Chris: Member of a Diocesan Review Board

Father Chris's bishop appointed him to the diocesan review board when it was formed in 2002. One reason he was appointed is that Father Chris has a degree in counseling and has ministerial experience counseling both victims and perpetrators of abuse. Under the requirements of the Dallas Charter and Essential Norms, the board is made up largely of laypeople, most of whom are professionals in fields such as law, criminal justice, social work, and psychology. The board also includes a few members of women's religious orders. Father Chris, during the several years he spent on the board, was the sole member of the clergy with a vote. Although the bishop, chancellor, and vicar general are typically present at the board's meetings, their role is to provide information and consultation for the board members' deliberations.

At first, all the allegations investigated by the board were against priests who were either deceased or who were by this time no longer in ministry. Not until about two years after its inception did the board first take up an allegation brought against a priest still active in ministry. Since then, there have been several other such cases. Father Chris describes how the board proceeded:

> I was never personally involved in the direct interview of the victims, gathering the facts. In the committee, we generally farmed that out to two or three laypeople who would talk directly with the victim and gather

the information. That would be brought back to the committee and then the question was: Is this credible? If so, we would advise the bishop. The bishop, having suspended the priest during the investigation, would then proceed to make that suspension permanent. That was difficult because these were priests who were either active in ministry or recently retired. I personally knew at least three of the priests whose cases we reviewed.

Below, Father Chris discusses his experiences on the board and these three cases—one of which involved a pastor he worked under as an associate and another of which involved a personal friend:

I found reviewing the active cases very hard because you know the men and you know their goodness, and now their sin. In one case the fellow had been my pastor and I admired the man. I still do. I recognize that this was something he had done years ago in his early priesthood, and I believe he probably never did it again. But nevertheless the victim rightly came forward and made a credible accusation. I believe the accusation and public knowledge of it eventually destroyed the priest. He literally had to go into a nursing facility, and eventually he began to lose his mind in terms of being in touch with reality. I would visit him. He briefly knew who I was. Then he was back into our history, when I was his associate. He might have ended up with dementia anyhow, but I just think it really devastated the man. He wasn't that old. I think he died very sadly.

It was very difficult for me also because of the way the diocese handled the death of that priest. . . . There was no notice of his funeral Mass. His family was there, obviously. But it was kind of kept quiet. It was at a heated moment with the sexual abuse issue in the news here. They were attempting to avoid pickets and that type of thing. Even we other priests didn't have the chance to get to his funeral. Granted, the man did something wrong. I'm not denying that. But in any of these cases, while you own the fact that they've committed a terrible deed, that's not the whole of the person. It just didn't seem to me that there was much room for grace, or reconciliation, or mercy. I thought it could have been a regular funeral Mass for a priest. Then you could have talked about how, like all of us, we're weak and we're sinful, but we're also good people. But that didn't happen, at least on an official level.

I did feel good that the parish that he had been a pastor in, and where I had been his associate, had a separate memorial Mass for him. The people knew him as a very good pastor, and a number of us priests went to that. A good number of lay people showed up for that, and his family showed up for it. There was a genuine acknowledgement of his humanity but also his gifts, despite his weakness and sin.

In another case the priest exercised his right to come before the board and present his side of it. I felt very badly because I knew the guy. He had been behind me in formation. It wasn't, in my mind and in many people's minds, a really serious breach. I mean there was no sexual contact. It did not involve genital activity, let's put it that way. But it was nevertheless within the definition of abuse. I just felt very badly, as he was trying to save his reputation and his name. It was a hard call on the part of the board. But the evidence was—again if you took the broad definition of abuse—that it fell into that category. So that fellow was relieved of his priesthood.

We did have one case where we had to review an accusation and we were able to exonerate the priest. I was a personal friend of his. The priest was temporarily suspended according to the Charter by the bishop while he was under investigation. The investigation was conducted and we found that the accusation was not credible. And so that priest was restored to ministry. I was glad of that. The accusation had been in the newspaper, but also we made a point of making sure it was in the newspaper that he had been exonerated. There was a gathering of priests, a typical diocesan gathering, and the bishop very pointedly welcomed him back. We all gave applause. So he had the support of all of us, and I think he knew that.

I myself, even though I was his friend, was unable to call him during the suspension, even to give him a word of comfort, because I was on the board. I did not want to create the appearance of a conflict of interest. I didn't want it to turn out that—if I were asked had I talked to him about this thing—I would be excluded from any vote. . . . . I didn't want to jeopardize that. I didn't want to have to recuse myself from the process. . . . . His exoneration was a highlight of my time on the board.

Father Chris reflects on his overall experience on the board and summarizes his feelings about the sexual abuse scandal generally:

I was glad I was on the board. It was at times painful. But I was glad that I was able to at least put my two cents into the process. I guess like most priests I feel sad that the abuse happened, because of the victims, and because of the damage done to the image of the priesthood itself. I'm grateful that, for the American Church, it's now in a sense past, at least in terms of the heat of it anyhow. Maybe legal and financial repercussions are still going on, but there are few fresh cases that are coming up. I feel badly for the Church in Ireland and the Church in Germany because they're just going through it now. I believe—and I say this not as some sort of piety—I really do believe that we will come out stronger. And I think that now there's growing recognition, especially in Europe, that abuse is not a "priest" problem so much as it is a Church problem. . . . . And there's recognition of the whole role that bishops have in terms of being responsible. In the end, with God, we'll work through it. We'll be able to bring good even out of this horrendous evil.

Father Doug: Chancery Official and Pastor

Father Doug is a diocesan priest who has experienced the sexual abuse problem from both the administrative and pastoral sides. For many years he worked in the chancery of his diocese. While holding diocesan administrative positions, he dealt with several cases of priests accused of abuse. Later, when the scandal broke publicly in 2002, Father Doug's bishop asked him to lead a parish where the previous pastor had been accused of abuse. It was several years before turmoil related to parishioners' hurt and anger over the abuse issue subsided. Father Doug found himself a target of that anger among some members of the parish because of his own background as a diocesan official.

Below, Father Doug relates the experience of first learning about abuse cases in his diocese in the 1980s and the sense of unreality that accompanied it:

> I was very young when I began in chancery administration. I started in the tribunal in the early 1970s and in the chancery office in the mid-70s. . . . It was a total shock to me when I first came across an abuse case. I just never even imagined that anything of this magnitude could ever happen. People must think, "Well, priests knew about this all the time." I certainly did not, prior to the early 1980s. And I was in a position where you could hear a lot more than most priests. I mean I would see anything. The first time I did hear an accusation I didn't believe it. I'm sure you've read things about this, how people, when someone in their own family is accused of sexual abuse, will not believe it. They'll defend the person or deny any evidence that other people might take as strong evidence. I certainly had that reaction. And I think a lot of priests did in the beginning. "How could a priest ever do such things?" Even after accepting that clerical sexual abuse was a real problem, I never imagined that it would be on the scale that has come out.

Father Doug discusses his involvement in responding to some of the early cases that arose in his diocese:

> I worked closely with other priests, including one who dealt a lot with the victims and really helped them. I dealt more with the accused priests, determining whether or not they could function again. In my diocesan

work I don't think I ever encountered a case that was strictly pedophilia, that is, a case in which the victim was a pre-pubescent child. They were almost all teenage boys. One or two might have been teenage girls but most of the abuse was related to homosexuality, and along with that, arrested psycho-sexual development and sometimes other addictions, quite often alcoholism. That's why the diocese often sent accused priests for therapy and relied on the assurance of psychiatrists that, with continuing therapy and support, they could continue to function without being a danger to young people.

I remember one case we had, and it was a terrible thing. This priest was a real predator of teenage boys. I was one of the people who made sure that he never ministered again. This came out in the 90s. But the abuse itself had occurred in the late 70s or so. At first we had information from one victim, but the accusation was vague. It wasn't very clear how serious the situation was, and the priest was sent for counseling. Then a second victim came forward and I interviewed him myself. His allegations made it clear that this was a serious situation and that the priest had to be removed from ministry completely. The victim and some people support-ing him said they knew other people victimized by this priest. They wanted us to make a full-blown public declaration against the priest at the parishes where he had worked, to encourage people to come forward. I didn't think that was a good approach. Rather than go through a public thing I thought it would be better to go on a one-on-one basis. I asked them to share the names of the other victims or, if they couldn't share them because of confidentiality, to encourage the victims to contact us directly. We would want, first of all, to help them and secondly to understand better what was really happening at the time of the abuse.

Well that really didn't turn out to be necessary. I and Father [Name] met with the accused priest. The amazing thing was that he admitted everything. We certainly got enough details on what had happened. He admitted that there were many young people that he had abused over the years in different circumstances. By "many" I mean twenty to thirty. Here, I'd been dealing with this problem for a while now and I was still shocked. Oh my God, I just couldn't believe this could go on. He was truly a psycho-path. He was not even aware what kind of impact this was having on the people he was talking to. So at this point we went to the bishop and told him there was no way that this priest could ever, ever function anywhere or even be recognized as a priest. I knew that we had to use every means at our disposal, canonical and otherwise, to get him out of the priest-hood—this was all before the USCCB's Charter and Essential Norms. However, some of the victims became angry with the diocese because we didn't handle the case of this particular priest exactly as they wanted.

During my time in administration another priest was arrested. People— both laity and priests—came to me at that time and asked, "Are you going to arrange for him to be bailed out of jail?" I said, "Absolutely not. I'm not going to use diocesan money to bail out a priest who's been legitimately arrested." Then people wrote letters to the diocesan newspaper about this, attacking me for not bailing him out. They were saying, "He's in the hands of the Church. The Church has got to take care of him." Other people wrote and said, "Are you kidding? I don't want my donations used for that kind of thing." Oh! You can't believe what was going on at that time. In that particular case, another priest got some private individuals to put up money for the priest's bail. Eventually, the accused priest was convicted and served time. The ironic thing for me was that, later on, others challenged me as being too "soft" on these things. I'm the guy who left a priest in jail!

Father Doug discusses the negative reactions in the local media and among laity in the diocese in 2002 after the sexual abuse issue received national attention:

That reaction was the most frustrating part about it, I have to tell you. The most hurtful aspect of what I and other priests experienced was the fact that people did not seem to know that the diocese had been acting responsibly about these matters. And if anything, they turned the facts upside-down and made it look as if we hadn't been doing the effective things that we were doing to address the problems that were brought to our attention. Some people attacked our integrity. Maybe it's a point of pride—and every pride has to be taken away from you—but in all my years, even though I've disagreed with a lot of people, nobody had ever questioned my integrity until this whole explosion occurred.

Actually I myself was not caught up in too much media coverage. One of the priests I worked with received much more attention and the reason was that he had been dealing directly with victims. I hadn't. But the media was very unfair about the whole thing. Instead of our diocese being looked upon as a sort of exception—that we had dealt immediately and very professionally with any accusations and helped victims—we were pilloried along with everyone else in the country. In fact, when people took the time to learn the facts, they found that we were exemplary. When the National Review Board sent around its people to our diocese, they studied everything very thoroughly and they were amazed by all this publicity. They came into our diocese thinking it was going to be a huge problem. And they said, "What were they all talking about?" And we said, "We can tell you what they were talking about. They were talking not about facts but about their own prejudgments, based on the publicity generated about other dioceses; they just lumped everyone all together."

The bishop had to address vacancies in parishes due to the scandal, and he asked Father Doug to return to parish ministry, which Father Doug did. The parish where he became pastor, as it happened, was one of those where the priest described above as "a predator" had served. But that was not the only trouble facing the parish:

> Besides the fact that there was this history of this very bad priest who had abused teenagers for some time, in the 1970s, accusations were made against the pastor who was there just before me. Now this priest had a medical issue. Unfortunately he created a real problem in the parish because he didn't tell people he was being accused. He should have told them, "I have a medical problem, *and* an accusation has been made against me which I deny. My doctor has told me I just can't handle all this and live, so I'm resigning." Instead he just talked about his health and told only half the truth—even though he *knew* that the allegations were going to come out. But sometimes it's hard for people to face up and say what they have to at the right moment. At any rate, two weeks after he left the parish, the accusation came out in the paper. This caused a great deal of turmoil in the parish. People were attacking the bishop. They were going crazy. The bishop said to me, "You've got to take over one of my parishes." He gave me a choice of parishes and I was probably overly optimistic. I was already getting knocked around a little bit. I thought, "Well, why not, I might as well go to the parish in crisis. Maybe, based on my knowledge of the facts and the procedures, I can be in a position to explain things rationally and help people deal with these sensitive issues." I didn't realize just what a challenge it was going to be.

There was resentment among some parishioners toward Father Doug because of his prior administrative involvement with sexual abuse cases in the diocese. For a time, it simmered quietly. But after he had been at the parish for about a year, it came to a head when Father Doug faced a protest movement from some parishioners who were upset and wanted a change:

> I was being attacked in the parish because I was formerly a diocesan official, and some parishioners saw that as a way to attack the bishop. This wasn't helped by the fact that pastors can sometimes promote the idea that the diocese is something to be kept at arms-length, an attitude that was ingrained in some of my parishioners. Also, I was a different kind of

person, maybe a little bit more straight-laced in regard to how a parish is run. A small group in the parish wanted a different kind of pastor. Eventually there were real protests. They told me they wanted me to resign. I said, "I'm not going to resign." That started a real year of hell. They had a public meeting and brought in a couple of sex abuse victims, including the victim I told you about before, the man who had wanted me to publicize about the multiple offender in all his former parishes. I felt that this victim was being used by these other people. Many parishioners attended the gathering. Some people defended me. It was a raucous meeting. Meanwhile, I arranged a prayer service in the church, which many parishioners came to. I said, "We're not going to talk about anything. People have a right to say what they want, how they want. We're just going to pray here for the peace of our parish."

I then wrote a letter to the parish answering accusations they were making about how I had handled sex abuse cases, which were all false. They really didn't understand how things worked. I sent the letter to every single parishioner. Most people were happy with that. Then the group had another meeting because they didn't like the fact that I countered them. It was a terrible time. I remained very quiet, very steadfast. I knew you couldn't fight the media on this. There's no way. You're not going to change people's hearts through the media. You have to do it just by being their pastor, being patient. You can never lose faith in God. I have to tell you that the Psalms that I prayed in the Breviary every day never meant more to me when I read them. "My God, You are my protector."

Relatives of that same victim started coming to my Masses and standing up while I was preaching. They wouldn't say anything; they just stood quietly in protest. This went on for a good nine months. I stopped putting the names of which priest was saying the Mass in the bulletin to avoid such disruption as much as possible. Undercover police were there because they were concerned about such behavior. Ironically, such actions were so off-putting that many people rallied to protect and support me. In addition, those who were still against my presence in the parish didn't want to be identified with such silent but upsetting disruptions of the liturgy, but they were caught in a dilemma. No one would believe that they were not associated with such behavior. In other words, when emotions are running high, the facts don't matter, only perceptions matter.

Father Doug describes how the situation eventually calmed and resolved itself. He also talks about his feelings looking back on his experience in the parish:

Finally the victim himself called me up because he feared that because of the trouble in my parish, his family was facing retaliation from the diocese (another fear that was completely unfounded). I was really nervous about this meeting. I said, "Come and talk with me. But I want it one-on-one. I'm not going to talk with anybody else there." He came to my office and I had taken precautions. I had the blinds down so that nobody could look in. I thought it was going to be a media thing. It wasn't. He was a very sincere person. He wasn't accusatory, not at all. It was a very pastoral meeting with him. I asked if he needed help. He said he was doing fine. To be honest with you, I actually enjoyed the conversation. It was one of the best conversations I had that entire year. I said to him, "Any time you're in town, come and see me." Do you know that was the last time that any of his relatives ever appeared at my church? He took care of it. Isn't this amazing? The victim of that worst offender resolved a lot of this because we talked about it rationally.

During the next year everything seemed to calm down. Some of those who were disgruntled left. The parish held listening sessions during Lent to let people talk about what they were feeling, how things were going in the parish. It actually turned out very good for parish life. We went through some tough times together. We were all the better for it, to be honest with you. Life at the parish became really enjoyable. I think that some healing took place. It was important to provide accurate information and to get these feelings out in the open and share them. Actually, during all the turmoil, I had received an enormous amount of support. I had a file like this. [Shows how large with his hands.] Among all these letters to me there were only two or three negative ones. Nearly every one of them was a supportive letter, people affirming me. I responded to each one personally, including the negative ones, thanking them for sharing their honest feelings with me. I kept them all, but, even after things calmed down, I found it too painful to go back and read them. It was so hurtful to remember that time. I finally got rid of them.

Father Eric: Priest and Victim

As a child Father Eric suffered sexual abuse at the hands of a priest in his parish. He graciously shared his story with us. In the early part of his life and priesthood, he rarely talked about the abuse with anybody. Eventually, through therapy, he began to address the consequences of the abuse in a more direct way and found some healing. Being more open about the abuse in recent years, to the point that he has mentioned it in homilies, has given other victims of abuse the opportunity to approach him and share their own stories. Father Eric was also involved in an effort of a victims' support group to arrange a healing service at a church in his diocese.

My abuse happened in the late 1950s when I was ten to eleven years old. My home parish was right across the street from a retreat house run by [a religious order.] A lot of their priests would come over and say Masses at the parish. I was a server. My abuse happened in the sacristy after Mass. Generally there were always two of us serving Mass, and this priest who belonged to the order would isolate one of us by asking him to stay a few minutes longer to help put away vestments and things like that. I would get cornered in the sacristy, which he could lock so that no one else could come in. The abuse would go on for ten to twenty minutes. My parents would be waiting in the car outside patiently. The amount of time didn't seem to faze them because this happened so frequently. This went on for about a year and then just stopped as suddenly as it started. I never said anything at the time, not to my parents, not to anyone. I didn't understand what was happening. I knew something was wrong, but I couldn't even name that. I was too young.

The abuse created a number of long-term issues for Father Eric:

Sexually, it confused me completely. This was the 1950s. Mom and Dad were Depression kids and it wasn't the kind of home environment where parents would say, "Oh, let's have a conversation about sex." Sexual under-standing of self has been a struggle for my entire life. It really is rooted in all the confusion of what was happening at that time. I think I'm natu-rally kind of an introverted personality type, but this probably led me to be even more so. I tend to be very analytical about my affective life. It takes me quite a while to be in touch with the meaning of what I feel.

I still have a very sharp suspicion of anybody in authority. I've told this to every bishop I've ever served under so they would know. I don't trust structures very much, and ironically here I am, a Catholic priest pastor who, for most people, *epitomizes* the structure. And I'm always on guard about who's the next person that might turn on me. For victims, there's a leeriness about trusting people, about extending yourself in relationships that could potentially be very helpful to you.

For many years Father Eric rarely talked with anybody about the abuse, and tried to believe that it was behind him. He describes some of the few times he disclosed his story. He also talks about an event in his parish that led him to seek professional help in dealing with after-effects of the abuse:

I just buried the whole thing. I sat on that and kept it quiet for years. I'm much more comfortable talking about this now, but fifteen years ago I couldn't even mention it. I disclosed it, once, to a counselor who was working in the seminary when I was starting there in the early 1970s. That was the only time I talked about it in formation. It was one session. He recommended further counseling and I said, "No." I figured, "I disclosed it. It's over." I just kind of put the lid on it again. Then in the 1980s I disclosed to a pastor that I was stationed with. He was very patient and kind in listening to me. I don't know that he could fully understand the impact of it all, but he was very gentle with me. I didn't talk to any priest about the abuse before that. That was a good twelve years after I was ordained.

Several years later Cardinal Bernardin was accused. The accusation was withdrawn and he had a healing encounter with his accuser. I wrote him and I told him what had happened to me. He wrote back the tenderest letter I've ever received. He thanked me for the words of encouragement to him. He was the first person in the Church to apologize for what had happened to me. That was the first time I'd ever made any peace with anybody in a position of authority, who I always expect to be, by nature, devious and not trustworthy.

In the mid-1990s there was a murder of a six-year-old member of the parish where I was pastor. He was killed by a teenager who was a next-door-neighbor and also in the parish. I went into a rage against the teenager. I just lost it. It got to the point where I really thought I was going to have a complete breakdown. That's when I linked with a therapist and started about five years of therapy with her. I said to the therapist that my rage at this kid was a thousand times larger than the event. I knew something wasn't fitting. She said, "You never really learned what a feeling or an emotion was." My anger had gotten so submerged. That was a breakthrough for me. She was a godsend. Those years of counseling were really when everything began to heal for me.

As part of that whole recovery cycle, I went to the religious order. I wanted, as part of my therapy, to say, "This man did this. You need to know this. I hope he doesn't have any access to children." And I wanted an apology. That was all I wanted. I was met by the provincial, the vice-provincial, and a battery of lawyers. I never got the apology. And they never disclosed to me whether they knew of other victims of that priest or not. I presumed that other kids had been victimized, though I had never heard anything.

I did find out at that meeting that the priest had died the year before. He was buried at the order's nursing and retirement home. I said, "I want to go there to visit his grave." They did do that for me. They called ahead to the staff at the retirement home and said that I had known this priest and, ironically, he had been a friend. But I didn't care what they were saying; it got me in there. That's where it really kind of changed for me, in that I began to hear other stories about this man: how he had been treasurer of the community and saved the community from some financial distress. A lot of people liked him. He had an outreach to poor people. It kind of put a human face on my tormentor, as I called him. I was able to go to his grave site and make peace with at least that part of my history.

Soon after he began therapy, an abusive priest was appointed as an associate to the parish where Father Eric was pastor. It later led to a decision by Father Eric to leave his diocese for a new one:

I had been pastor of my parish by myself for about a year. Then the diocese assigned an associate, a priest I didn't know. He had his peculiarities, but he seemed like a typical kind of priest. Two years into the assignment I went off on an eight day retreat. Coming back I was picked up at the airport by somebody who worked in the parish. He told me that the associate had literally had a psychological breakdown that week and kept mumbling to people, "I've got a court case this week, and my whole future's in that court case." That's all the associate kept saying. He was already gone from the parish when I got back from the retreat.

I called the personnel director that very night. I said, "My associate is gone. People are telling me he's been saying for the last week that he's got this court case coming up." I got dead silence on the other side of the line. I said, "Is there something here I need to know that you haven't told me?" He said, "Well, I can't talk about that. It's confidential." I said, "This is not going to fly with me. If there's something about my associate that's going to become public, I need to know. Either I come down to your house now at 1:00 a.m. and we hash this out in person or you spit it up right now." So he said, "All I can tell you is that there's a court case that has to do with accusations against him by three teenage boys, and I can't say any more than that."

It didn't take a rocket scientist to see what the hell was going on. When the associate arrived he had asked me if he could start a boys' basketball league, which I thought was kind of strange because we didn't have a school. He had been removed from his previous parish because of those accusations against him and the bishop and diocesan officials were keeping me in the dark. And the personnel director *knew* that I had begun therapy for my own abuse. He knew that this would be a problem for me. . . . I later found out that my associate did abuse somebody in my parish while I was pastor. I knew the pattern, and that's exactly what I dreaded. It was terrible, horrendous. Frankly that's why I left that diocese. I couldn't trust them.

During the course of the ministry he was assigned to in the early years of his priesthood, Father Eric met and developed a good relationship with the bishop of another diocese. In the late 1990s, Father Eric's mother passed away, giving him the opportunity to leave his original diocese and be incardinated into the diocese of that bishop. In 2002, less than three years later, the sexual abuse issue erupted nationwide and Father Eric's new diocese was among those that were relatively hard-hit. By this time, having gone through therapy, he was more open in talking about the abuse he suffered. He sometimes mentioned it in homilies, and his story was known to some people in the diocese. Below, Father Eric relates how he became involved with a victims' support group and how he later helped them organize a healing service for themselves and other abuse victims of the diocese:

> When things broke here I tried to convince Bishop Anderson to be more proactive and up-front in responding to the problem. One day I literally begged him to go on a pilgrimage for healing to every parish that had had a priest who had abused children. I could never budge him to do that. I like Anderson a lot. He's a fine person, but I think he really lacked the capacity to fully understand a victim. I think bishops operate out of the thinking that with a little therapy you get over it and can get on with life. They don't understand the long-term effects. The people in diocesan ministry that have understood me as a victim are the clinical psychologists and social workers, those types of people. Some priests and even [a lay diocesan official], who I consider a friend, just do not quite understand how recovery functions for a victim.
>
> There was a victim's group that, for months, had been meeting on their own at Nativity Church in the diocese as a kind of a support group for themselves. One of the members of the group had heard about my own story and invited me to come and sit in on one of their sessions. I did that, and I went back over and over again, just hearing their stories. So I became connected to the group.
>
> In ongoing conversations within the group, some of them would raise the idea, "Maybe we should have a gathering here for people that have left the Church." After I got the group to trust me enough, I said, "Let's put together a healing service for all of you together here at Nativity. Let's open it to the public and invite anyone who wants to come. And let's pray to God that it can be one of many that will follow." They jumped on that. It took me two months to convince Bishop Anderson to attend this healing service. I said, "Meet with them and just listen to them. You don't have to say a damn word. Just go and listen." At first he couldn't do it, but eventually I got him to agree. So I worked with the group and with the diocesan worship office to put together our own service. Part of the service was a blessing—because we couldn't re-consecrate a church—of those

areas of Nativity Church where abuse had happened. It kind of hit my own experience because one of those places was the sacristy. But there was just that one service. The bishop didn't feel comfortable with any more.

Father Eric also has had the opportunity to listen to victims of sexual abuse who have approached him on a one-on-one basis.

> Every time I've disclosed my story in a homily, just mentioning the fact that I've been abused, three or four people will come to me after Mass or call me on the phone and tell me similar stories—not necessarily people who have been abused by a priest, sometimes by a family member. The way I've been ministering to those people is just listening. I think the most important need for victims is that they simply cannot tell their story to anyone. It's very risky to disclose the story. Lots of us have had the experience, when we have attempted to do it, that people have kind of turned their back; it's either too much for them to handle or they don't know how to respond. I give victims some space to be able to tell their story to somebody that they know understands it and receives it without judgment. And I acknowledge their pain. I know in my own recovery that was the hardest part, being able to express my pain and being able to put myself in a vulnerable position where a person could say, "You've got to get over it. Have a stiff upper lip." I never say anything like that.
>
> I've always worked from the position of: This story, as painful as it is, is also sacred. The healing presence of God is in the disclosure of the story. I try, by presence, to say, "I'm here with you and God's here with us."

Recently Father Eric learned of another victim of his abuser, to date the only other victim he knows of:

> A year ago I got a phone call from a grade school classmate. I saw his name, which was David, on caller ID. Our families had been close as children, but I thought, "What in the world would this guy be calling me for? We have not communicated since my mother's funeral a dozen years ago." He had gotten my home phone number from the diocese. He said, "I have a question to ask you." I said, "Okay, what's going on?" He said, "Do you remember—" and he named the priest that had abused me. I tell you, I started crying like a baby. And of course, he's crying at the other end. He didn't have to say any more. Then he mentioned two other boys in the group of half a dozen of us that ran around together who he suspected had also been abused. He asked me if I had ever heard anything about them, and I said, "No."
>
> The only other person besides me he had disclosed to was his mother. I said, "You've never been to a counselor?" He hadn't. Of course I didn't

know anybody from his state but I eventually came up with a priest counselor in his diocese who was recommended to me by a professional. But
to my knowledge he never went. David's now drifted out of contact again.
He doesn't reply to my e-mail or phone messages, which is a pattern with
victims. After disclosure you feel you've risked so much and become so
vulnerable that you tend to withdraw.

Father Frank: Friend to Multiple Abusers

Three of Father Frank's priest friends were removed from ministry
soon after the scandal broke in his diocese. Prior to that time, he only
knew that one of them had committed sexual abuse against minors, a
man he believed was in recovery. Revelations about the pasts of the other
two priests came as a shock to him. He reflected with us on his friendships with those three priests and his attempts to maintain ties with them
since their removal from ministry. Father Frank has also made efforts to
reach out to victims of the scandal in his diocese.

Below, Father Frank talks about his friendship with the first of the
three priest friends who were removed from ministry. A significant part
of this story is that the friend once served as an associate pastor in a
parish that Father Frank's family belonged to when he was a child. However, the two were not there at the same time because his family moved
to a different parish shortly before the priest was appointed associate.
They did not meet until much later in life.

> One of the friends was a number of years older than me. He had served
> at a parish where I had been as a kid before he came in as an associate. I
> also served at that parish as an associate when I was first ordained. We
> met in a support group. I was a young priest and he was one of the guys
> I looked up to. He gave me a lot of encouragement. I knew him as a good
> guy in a lot of ways, one who did some really good work. But he also hurt
> a lot of kids. He was accused of multiple offenses. His victims were actual
> children. He's one I probably would say is a real pedophile.
>
> When he was accused in 2002, part of me was asking, "Is this another
> media exposé where they're trying to attack the Church and be sensa-
> tional?" But when it was reported that certain victims had publicly come
> forward, oh geez, I knew some of them by name. I knew some of their
> parents too. In fact, one victim's parents were friends with my parents. I
> just felt sick. I heard stories that some of the parents had approached the
> pastor and he went to the bishop but wasn't believed at that time. And in
> this parish I could have been among his victims if I hadn't moved after
> the fourth grade.

He will be in prison, I think, for the rest of his life. We've kept in touch. I've written him. I saw him a few weeks ago, in fact. I was out to the prison for Saturday morning Mass. In prison he's found a niche for ministry. He's in charge of RCIA there. Although he's been laicized, he's still considered a priest by the inmates. He's called "Father" there by some of the guys. I think he feels a lot of remorse. He's told me he went to a bishop that we had many years ago and said, "Maybe I shouldn't be a priest. I have these urges and I just can't seem to control them." The bishop kind of poo-poo'd it. He was an old guy and said, "Oh no. You're a good priest, Father. Take the pledge and you can stop." So I think he was in touch at some level with the wrongness of his actions. But anyway the abuse continued.

Another of the friends had been with me in a more recent priest support group. He was a little bit younger than I am. He did some things that were wrong and hurt people. I think his victims were early adolescents, twelve or thirteen-year-olds, rather than real young children. Some were servers, like the stereotype. He was involved with drugs and alcohol and I think it contributed to his acting out. I knew about his past, but he was dealing with that. He had gotten help and was involved in a recovery group. It seemed like he was learning and growing. I thought he was kind of reha-bilitated and I tried to reach out to him.

He was back out in public ministry. Then after the scandal broke he was accused by somebody else, alleging he had abused him many years before. My friend claims those last charges against him were false, that somebody saw that they could get on the bandwagon and get a settlement. It was his word against theirs, and his word didn't really carry a lot of weight. Anyway he was convicted and he also spent time in prison. So he's bitter and angry. I think he has taken responsibility for the cases where he did abuse but he feels like he's been used in that last case. He also feels like he's done a lot of work in trying to reform, to change. And now that he's out of prison I think he feels a certain amount of abandonment by the diocese—and fear. "Here I am. What do I do?" What does a priest sex offender do for the rest of his life? Being a sex offender is worse than being just a convicted felon. I mean, what kind of job can you get? It's a real struggle. We have dinner occasionally. I try to be a support to him.

With the third priest friend it was a different situation. I think he was a real victim of the one-strike-and-you're-out policy. He was a pastor at a parish that was very peace and justice oriented, very inclusive and very socially conscious. He had done some great work there for about the last ten years. But he had had an incident when he was in his early years of ministry. I don't know for sure, but I think he had gotten involved with a teenager. He went through therapy, made amends to his victim, and was not, at least from all appearances, a repeat offender. But because of the Charter he was suspended right after that Bishops' meeting in Dallas. We kept in touch for about one year, then he really didn't want to. I tried to call him on his birthday or other occasions, and he just didn't respond.

After the scandal broke, Father Frank made several efforts to reach out to victims of the scandal and their families, beginning with people he knew in the parish he had spent time in as a child:

I talked with a couple of the victims from that parish. And I wrote and later talked to the mother who was friends with my parents and who I've known all my life. I tried to reach out that way. In that letter I tried to convey my deep sadness and concern: "I'm so sorry that you suffered through this. I just feel sorry, and if there's any way I can be there for you, I want to be." There's not much else I could say. I sure didn't have any magic answers. But she was grateful to hear from me.

I also went to two initial meetings of a chapter of Voice of the Faithful that was formed here in the diocese. I heard some stories from victims who spoke at the meetings. I heard a lot of pain. One of the stories victims and their families shared is the frustration of going up to talk to a bishop and not being believed—or being believed but the priest was just taken out and put at another parish. That, I think, reflected how the Church dealt with addictions. If guys were alcoholics, they would get a fresh start and go someplace else. In some ways sexual abuse was perceived the same way, as, "You did something inappropriate. You shouldn't do that." It wasn't perceived as criminal. The Vatican has been really slow to understand this is really criminal behavior. I don't think John Paul had a sense of that. Benedict seems to have a better sense.

When the third friend mentioned above was removed from ministry, Father Frank became sacramental minister of his former parish. He and lay leaders of the parish tried a unique approach to reaching out to victims:

I was asked to follow him at that socially active parish. About a year later we organized a retreat for victims of abuse at a retreat center. I was part of that retreat. It was advertised in parish notices and the diocesan paper. We also extended personal invitations to sexual abuse victims we knew. But most of those who signed up to come were victims of domestic abuse. In other words, as it turned out, it wasn't so much clerical abuse as spousal abuse victims who responded, mostly women. But at least we made the effort to open that up to victims of any kind of abuse.

Below, Father Frank describes the emotions he experienced in 2002 when the scandal broke in his diocese and information became public. It was a difficult time for him because he was close with two priests, and acquainted with others, whose abuse he didn't previously know about. Father Frank also talks about the support that helped him cope during that time. He is quick to add, however, that what he has gone through is not comparable to the suffering experienced by sexual abuse victims:

> The scandal hit our diocese really strong. It was all the stages of grief. It was just like being in denial: "This can't be." I was in some ways disbe-lieving for a while because these were all guys I knew, or so I thought. I had worked with and been close to some of them. I was so angry. It made me sick, angry, sad, and guilty. It was a whole mix of emotions. There was just a lot of stuff stirring that I really had a tough time processing.
>
> Looking back on it, self-care is really important. Spiritual direction is really important. That helped me through a lot. I was still in a support group. We supported one another. And I did feel support from parishioners. They were there. That helped a lot. One of the gifts I was given is that I'm part of a married couples group. It's kind of a support group. They share what's going on in their marriages. They're trying to grow together. We meet for dinner and prayer maybe once a month or every six weeks. Their support was tremendously helpful. And family, they were very concerned about me. I felt a lot of family support, maybe with the exception of a brother-in-law that liked to push my buttons and make me mad as hell, just tease me about it. "Well who have you offended today, Frank?" Oh! I wanted to strangle him. [Laughs.] Some of the emotions are still raw today. Of course, I'm not a victim.

Asked what advice he would give to priests who, like himself, have ex-perienced emotional strain due to the scandal, Father Frank urges:

> Get the support of other priests. Join a support group. Reach out to other guys who are hurting. That stuff is important. You don't have to be doing it by yourself. Don't be afraid to reach out. And if you need counseling dealing with the anger and hurt, don't be afraid to ask for help. You're not the Lone Ranger.

Father George: Staying a Source of Support to a Friend

Father George is a diocesan priest. When he was a transitional deacon, he developed a close relationship with a mentoring priest who was about twenty years older. They became lifelong friends. Years later the friend,

Tom, was removed from ministry in the diocese because of a sexual abuse allegation. When more incidents came to light, Father George learned that he knew one of the victims and his family. This is Father George's story of being "at the center of many circles," as he puts it. He spoke with us about maintaining his friendship with Tom, reaching out to the victim, and how the experience has affected him personally:

> When I was ordained a deacon in the 1970s I was assigned to St. James parish for a six-month deaconate. Tom was the pastor there. Now this was a great assignment because I was born in another state. My family moved to this state when I was a teenager, but I never really got involved with the diocese. I didn't know any priests, any parishes. I was in the seminary for eleven years: high school, college, and theology. But in those days we didn't have summer assignments. When I went to the parish with Tom, we formed a very nice friendship, and he was the one who introduced me to the diocese. I got to know a lot of priests and parishes. We remained friends after my deaconate. I was from out of state and I didn't have any family here. He was from out of state too. He had no family in the diocese. So we would go out to dinner and enjoy each other's company. He was my mentor, my guide. And he was well respected by all the priests in the diocese. He had many friends. He had a great reputation as a pastor.
>
> During the 1990s I was on the personnel committee and an allegation of abuse against Tom came before one of our meetings. This first allegation was something that had happened many years before, and of course it wasn't made specific during the meeting; we weren't given all the details. I was very surprised about the whole thing. Those were the early days of all this. The problem of sexual abuse really wasn't in the forefront of our thinking in those days. So when I found out about this accusation I was skeptical. I was saying, "There's got to be something more to this. This is not Tom. I don't think it's true." I was erring on the side of Tom rather than the victim. I said, "What's going on here? What's the motivation?" All those questions you normally ask. I didn't have the background to understand, fully, the situation.
>
> Eventually, the bishop decided that Tom would have to retire and leave the diocese. The vicar for clergy knew that we were friends and he told me that he was going to go see Tom on a certain day to give Tom the news. He asked me if I would be willing to perhaps call Tom or visit him shortly thereafter because he would certainly be very devastated and shocked. And I agreed to do that. So at the time I picked up my phone and called him. I forget the exact words I used but something like, "I understand the vicar just left you and you got some very bad news." He started to get a little emotional, as did I. I said, "Tom, let's not talk about it on the phone.

Let me come over to see you." So I went over to his rectory and we decided to go out to dinner. I would say we spent maybe an hour and a half together. He wanted to tell me his version of the situation. I told him that would not be necessary. I really didn't need to know all those details. They weren't important to me. My goal was to try to be a support to him as a priest friend and do what I could to help him. We got into more practical details because he was asked to leave the diocese. He decided to go to his family home. He was not a big driver. He didn't like to drive even five miles, let alone hundreds of miles. So I offered to drive him to his home town.

I have stayed friends with him ever since then. My philosophy always was that—despite the fact that Tom did terrible, inexcusable, horrendous things and betrayed the trust of those put in him as a priest—he still needed support and I did not want to turn my back on him. Because, as I say, I was very close friends with him for all the years we were in the diocese together. The way I maintained our friendship once he went to his home town was by telephone, of course, and we went on vacations together now and again. Once in a while I'd go to visit him. That became harder and harder as life went on and I got more involved in my parish. Tom would come and visit me and stay there, which probably wasn't the greatest idea, looking back on it. In fact, one time he had a prolonged visit there. The bishop finally called me and said Tom couldn't stay there any more because his victim had made an agreement with the diocese that Tom would not come back. No one had told me that, so I didn't know. After that Tom never came back to the diocese again.

Tom has been laicized and presently is not in good health. Many of Tom's priest friends always ask me about him and want me to pass on their good wishes to him. A lot of his lay friends do the same. So this is not something between just me and Tom. People know I support him.

Going back to when I was a deacon, Tom was very good friends with a family named the Smiths. And therefore I became good friends with them because, again, I had nobody here and they would invite me to their home for Christmas, Easter, etcetera. They were a very hospitable, warm, friendly family. As I'm sure you're aware, where there's one allegation, there's often others. And as the years unfolded more allegations of abuse against Tom came out. In fact, one was very public. . . . The victim was one of the Smiths. So I had known him since he was a high school senior and had spent a lot of time with him and Tom. I knew that Tom had a friendship with him but absolutely no idea that anything else was happening. And neither did anybody else, as I'm finding out now. . . . Nobody had any idea what was going on, until this whole thing came out publicly.

The Smith family had long been members of the parish, though by this time the victim himself was a grown man who had moved out of state. Father George describes seeing him again after a long time:

> After the revelation, the victim's brother died. I had gone to visit him several times in the hospital because I knew his whole family very well. I was asked to have the funeral Mass, which I did. Of course the victim came to the funeral Mass. I was a little nervous about meeting him because I wasn't quite sure what kind of reception I would get—how he would feel about me, priests, the Church. As it turned out, we had a nice reunion. It was very cordial and friendly. It was a brief conversation at the funeral home and a brief one right after the funeral Mass. He said he would like to come and talk to me for a longer conversation, and I said, "You are absolutely welcome any time." Because he lives out of state, if that's going to happen or not, I don't know. But at least the possibility was mentioned.

In addition to personal and pastoral ramifications, Father George was also touched by the legal side of the situation when he was required to give a deposition:

> I had many connections with this situation, being friends with Tom, being friends with the victim and his family, and being the pastor of the parish where the abuse allegedly took place. I had to go have a deposition. I didn't know how it was going to go. My salvation was that the diocese provided me with a very fine lawyer. He spent a good three or four hours over several sessions preparing me and he went with me to the deposition. I was still quite apprehensive when we got there. There was a camera. There were a lot of people. There was a stenographer. There was my lawyer. There were other lawyers for various people. The questioner, Mr. Racine, was coldly polite. He never called me, "Father." He never called me anything actually. I always addressed him as, "Yes, Mr. Racine" or, "No, Mr. Racine." My lawyer told me that if you can be succinct with a "yes" or a "no," that is your best approach. He wasn't quite as courteous to me.
>
> It kind of got started before I knew it. We were probably a minute into it and I said, "Can I interrupt you for one minute? I meant to do this at the beginning but I didn't realize we started. Would it be okay with you if I say a prayer?" I had a little holy card of Saint Paul. "As you know, St. Paul also went to a deposition and he had to testify. So I want to ask the Holy Spirit to guide me and guide you and guide everybody else in this room. I brought a little holy card for all of you if you want to have one." So I think I took him off his game a bit. He said, "Of course. Do

remember Saint Paul told the truth. I would hope you would fiercely do the same thing." I said, "Of course." We said the Our Father and then we moved on.

Once I was into it for maybe five or ten minutes I felt a whole lot more relaxed and I felt the grace of the Holy Spirit with me. I was still cautious and weary, not knowing what the next question would be about, but in the very end it was not as bad as I thought it was going to be. I was there about two and a half hours. At the end of the agreed time, Mr. Racine wanted to ask more questions. My lawyer spoke right up. He said, "Well we can't do that. We agreed to this time limit." So he let me go.

Father George discusses how these experiences have affected his own faith:

> This whole experience has not affected my faith. I see this as basically a human weakness, a disease, a tragic flaw in a person who otherwise has very good qualities and was a good priest in many ways, did good things. It didn't shake my faith because I'm a pretty down-to-earth, practical person who knows the Church is made up of human beings. It did not affect my commitment to the priesthood either, maybe even strengthened it. We have to be more vigilant. We have to be more careful. We have to make sure all the Protecting God's Children safeguards have real meaning to them. We need to get behind them and make them happen.

Father Henry: Met with Scorn for Caring for People Who Had Been Abusers

Father Henry has been involved in the diocesan administrative side of the abuse problem. In the 1990s Father Henry's bishop appointed him to a position in which part of his responsibilities included working with other diocesan leaders to evaluate the status of priests accused of sexual abuse. Sometimes the response was to remove priests from ministry entirely. In other cases, it involved placing priests in treatment programs and then later returning them to limited ministry. Father Henry summarizes the diocese's policies regarding priests who had committed sexual abuse, policies that were already in place when Father Henry took the position:

> Several priests who had previously committed abuse had been in treatment and were back in specialized and supervised ministry. I and other priests in the chancery monitored them, and each had a support group. None had committed pedophilia; they had committed ephebophilia. Anyone diagnosed with pedophilia had been removed from ministry. There was never

any question or hesitation: if somebody had harmed a child, they were gone immediately. They were permanently removed from all ministry. However there had been very few true pedophilia cases in my diocese. Most cases involved arrested sexual development and involvement with adolescents. Usually the priests self-anesthetized with alcohol to give themselves the freedom to do this. In some instances it was a one-time event. When we learned of these incidents, the priests were given treatment, and if it was deemed successful by physicians, social workers, and psychologists, they were given limited ministry with the input of a lawyer. In hindsight we wouldn't do that; no quarter would be given to anybody who had abused in any way. But that's hindsight. We were adhering to the standards of the time.

There was a lot of work that went in to monitoring these priests. They had ongoing supervision in restricted ministry, usually hospital work. Only a few were ever in parishes, and that was only to say Sunday Mass, not to have any interaction with parishioners beyond that. This is the most important thing to know: *none* of these priests who were returned to ministry in the diocese ever re-offended. None. Of course, after the Charter was put in place, all of them had to be removed from ministry. We felt all that pastoral energy of working with these priests was to naught.

When the scandal hit in 2002, local news media and local law enforcement officials scrutinized the abuse cases in Father Henry's diocese and the procedures that had been in place. Much of the news coverage was extremely critical. Some news reports did not make it clear that known abusers in his diocese had been placed in supervised and restricted ministry. This allowed the public to infer that, as in some high-profile cases in other dioceses, priests had been returned to full-time parish positions, allowing them to claim further victims. Father Henry was singled out for individual criticism, but he was never contacted by the press and granted the opportunity to give his side of the story. Father Henry asked that we not share all the details of what happened during this period, in part because these events were extremely difficult and he wishes not to relive them. However, he describes some aspects of the scrutiny he endured as "the worst experience of my life." Below he talks about the local news coverage and the reaction of some of his parishioners:

We were trying to get priests help rather than just ditching them. There was pastoral outreach both to families and the accused. We operated from the Gospel perspective that you give people a second chance, and now we were met with scorn for caring for people who had been abusers. If it's wrong to help people like this, why would the Church have prison ministry? Why wouldn't we just let prisoners rot? The media brought shame not only on the priests who did this but on those of us who tried to be a priest to them. I was not asked to be interviewed by the media. They had no interest in giving our perspective. Anybody who was involved in this was described as reprehensible. Outreach to priests was viewed with scorn. Despite this I received a lot of support from parishioners. I had been in my parish for a number of years and at this point, people knew me. Those who had seen the stories but knew me realized they were slanted and written to be skewed and inflammatory.

Father Irwin: Therapist to Victims and Abusers

Father Irwin is a psychologist. He counsels a variety of individuals, some of whom have experienced trauma, including victims of sexual abuse perpetrated by clergy. Others are people with psychological disorders, many of whom are clergy. Father Irwin explains how he came to be an expert in these areas of psychology:

> It had a lot to do with, some would say, circumstance; I would say grace. In 1992 I happened to be in doctoral studies in psychology at [a state university]. That was when the first wave of the sexual abuse crisis hit us. It was the first time that we had any sort of national effort at a policy to deal with abusers in a systematic way. It was also around the time that Cardinal Bernardin was falsely accused. It was a big media attention-grabber. I happened to be studying with a professor who is a premier researcher in psychological trauma and an expert in the areas of neglect and physical and sexual abuse. She knew I was a priest. In a conversation in a hallway she said, "This would be an easy topic for you to research, if you'd be interested in collaborating with me on it." For legal and psychological reasons, the topic was a lot more complicated than I ever envisioned. I had to rewrite my dissertation proposal three to four times. I had access to potential subjects to study, but lawyers wouldn't allow me to actually interview hundreds of priests who were accused of sexual abuse. So I was forced to use archival data. It was a great blessing for me because if I had actually interviewed priests I would have been subpoenaed in the midst of the 2002 crisis.
>
> I finished my dissertation about a year before the story broke on January 6, 2002 in the *Boston Globe*. By that time I was at [a secular institution] doing my post-doctoral fellowship. I was watching and learning from national experts on how to deal with the crisis in a hands-on sort of way.

Father Irwin discusses his ministry with priests who have committed sexual abuse, their need for treatment, and his views about the approach the Church should take with them:

> It's an amazing ministry for me to be able to walk with and serve these individuals. Unlike what society paints these individuals to be, sex offenders, like any individuals with any mental disorder, need help. It's incumbent on us to see them as human beings who are struggling with a psychiatric disorder, as much as we'd like to vilify them and put them in tents under causeways.
>
> The majority of these men are feeling horrible about what they've done. Most offenders I've ever treated view it, in the psychological terminology, in an ego-dystonic way. In other words they despise this aspect of who they are and the fact that they've done this. That does not mean that without treatment and proper management of this disorder that they would not do it again. As a matter of fact they would be the first to say they need their program of recovery because they're plagued by this disorder or disease. It's rare, but it happens, that you meet an individual—and I've met priests like this—who are so troubled that they don't see any issue with offending a child. They see it as an ordinary part of who they are, as no different than waking up in the morning and going to sleep at night. Those are the most disturbing individuals I've ever treated. Those are the individuals we would call clear psychopaths and should never, as far as I'm concerned, be allowed to see the light of day or be in circumstances where they would ever have access to a child.
>
> I think, however, the majority of priests I've treated are willing and able to recognize this aspect of who they are as a problem and are willing to get help. They are willing to accept the monitoring and supervision that the religious order or diocese has structured for them so that they stay out of trouble and have no access to individuals to whom they might be attracted. To the religious orders' credit, they've incorporated these priests into the system. If you think about it logically, what's the best way to reduce risk in a sex offender? Is it to take away employment? Is it to create a system that makes him feel less than human? Is it that you make sure he doesn't have work or doesn't have shelter? What's the best way to reduce stress in any individual? You incorporate him into the normal aspects of what every human being does but monitor and supervise him accordingly.

Father Irwin describes the experience of counseling victims of abuse by clergy and the seriousness of the trauma they have faced. He also explains why some individuals who have suffered abuse at the hands of a priest nevertheless have chosen to seek counseling with him, another priest:

> I've worked clinically with several victims of clergy abuse, including Protestant, Jewish, and Catholic clergy. In each case, the similarities of their struggle are pretty striking. Their experience is not identical to ordinary trauma, if there is such a thing. What we see in these individuals, tragically, is what many people have called the "rape of the soul." It's hard enough when we see an individual who's been raped by a family member, such as a father, and they have to restore a sense of trust and regain a sense of safety in the world. Step back for a second and imagine that this child has viewed a priest, minister, or rabbi as a representative of God and then has to figure out how this representative of God has done this to them. That child feels as though God Himself or Herself has been the perpetrator. Is it possible to give that individual back a sense of stability, a sense of the sacred, a sense of meaning? It's a huge issue. It's an important area of research to figure out how to do this.
>
> Whether I'm treating depression or anxiety, or a person with a history of being abused by a priest, a priest psychologist is who I am. . . . Obviously, there are certain individuals who've been victimized by a priest who wouldn't come to me because I am a priest. However, certain individuals have sought me out *because* of it. They were looking to make sense of what happened to them, and in those cases it's been incredibly useful that I was a representative of the Church. I was able to hear their stories and help them begin to make sense of what had been an unfathomable reality. I think what these individuals have found in that particular relationship is the sense that there's somebody in the institution who hears them, who understands, who is willing to walk with them . . . in their suffering from what the Church has done—in their minds. It's very hard for a young child to distinguish the Church from this priest who also was an abuser.
>
> Returning to the Church is not the norm for most survivors of clerical abuse. Let's be very clear about that. For most people, their anger and their trauma may be irreconcilable with their faith. To allow themselves to walk into a church may be incredibly difficult. For many, to believe in God again is, I think, feasible but oftentimes they will not have any connection with organized religion. That's the price of what a few of our priests have done, destroying victims' sense of being safe in the world.
>
> No one ever sees the inner pain and the inner anguish these individuals experience when they ask the order or diocese to really come to grips with how this priest has offended them. However, if the institution takes responsibility for what this individual who has represented them has done,

it can become a very powerful instrument of healing and help them make sense of what has happened.

Father Irwin describes the positive outcomes he has seen in therapy with victims of sexual abuse:

> The wounds are always there, however healing can take place at a very deep and intimate level within the individual. Many victims of sexual abuse end up responding very well to treatment and attain some sense of "normalcy." On several different occasions after working in therapy for years with abuse victims, I've witnessed them meet with the perpetrator, who has also had treatment, and come to a point of reconciliation. It has given me an amazing sense of what the transformative nature of this work and what the transformative nature of grace is all about.

Finally, Father Irwin reflects on how being involved in this ministry has affected him personally and how it has been both challenging and fulfilling:

> It's been critical for me to have professionals in the field that I talk to about what I'm experiencing and feeling in regard to dealing with some very difficult men and some very difficult situations of horror from the victims of sexual abuse. I *have* to talk about what I experience every week with another professional. I *have* to get rid of the sort of toxic effects of that in me.
>
> I've been forced to realize that my life is in God's hands. How amazing for me to be in a situation in which, for ten years, I went through the desolations and consolations, the ups and downs, of doing a dissertation, graduating in 2001 thinking that my dissertation will end up on the library shelves gathering dust, then realizing that my life was not in my hands. I think the ability to abandon myself and this work into God's hands has been the single most amazing grace of this experience.

Conclusion

No single, unifying theme runs through the stories of these nine priests. This fact reflects that we intentionally sought men with varied backgrounds. It also reflects the fundamental reality that human experience is complex and sometimes can't be summarized in a bullet point. Nevertheless we see, in retrospect, a few commonalities among several of the priests profiled here. Among these are reactions to the scandal already alluded to in chapter 6, including the very human tendency for disbelief or shock when first learning of allegations against fellow priests as well as the spiritual conviction that men who have committed an act as terrible as sexual abuse nevertheless merit support and help.

We are struck by the fact that many of the nine priests profiled in this chapter have spoken with or otherwise reached out to abuse victims or their parents. For only one or two of the nine priests was this a notable reason that we initially sought to interview them. Yet many of the priests feel (and we agree) that their interactions with victims or parents are among the most important aspects of their scandal-related experiences. For Fathers Eric and Irwin, care for victims is more or less a natural outgrowth of their professional training or background. In some other cases, priests found themselves facing the unexpected decision of whether to reach out to victims or parents they had learned about. These priests typically felt trepidation—wondering how they might be received, not sure of the right thing to say—yet often the encounters seem to have turned out well. Certainly none of the priests express any regret. Perhaps this can stand as a source of encouragement for Catholics, priests and laity alike, who may be in a position to reach out to a victim they know. We conclude with the words of Father Eric, who, when asked to reflect on the scandal, urges that the response of the Church be focused not on itself but on care for victims:

> I think there's a great opportunity for the Church to come to a much more intentional, creative, healing path in its ministry. I'm afraid that the structure [of the Church] either doesn't know how to do that or is embarrassed by what's happened and wants to put this to rest as much as possible. It's just not going to go away, and I don't necessarily want it to go away. I want it to be an opportunity for something more to happen in the Church. I don't see that happening in the structure right now.

Chapter 8

Looking to the Future:
Who Is Encouraging the
Next Generation of Priests?

Be not afraid. The life of a priest is very fulfilling.

> —*A 32-year-old diocesan full-time associate pastor*

As both the laity and the episcopacy hold priests in utter contempt, I could not, in good conscience, encourage anyone to consider a vocation to the priesthood.

> —*A 53-year-old diocesan priest serving as an educator*

Let nothing deter you. Pray and consider all options: both diocesan and religious. Seek counsel of a faithful spiritual director.

> —*An 83-year-old religious order priest in active ministry*

As stated in the introduction, this research project is the most recently forged link in a chain of surveys that began in 1970. During the ensuing four decades, as described in detail in the previous chapters, the Catholic priesthood in the United States has changed both in terms of age and ethnic composition, as well as in terms of ideological perspective and overall attitude. Having pondered the satisfactions and the problems that priests report today and the challenges they deal with in their collaborative and multicultural ministries, plus the specific impact caused by the sexual abuse scandal that erupted in 2002, we conclude this book with an eye to the future as we carefully analyze priests' enthusiasm for promoting vocations.

Given the Catholic Church's reliance on ordained ministers to support its sacramental structure, the continual decline in the number of priests in the United States is obviously a cause for grave concern. The final question for the participants in this study addressed this important issue by asking, "What recommendation would you have for a young man who is discerning a vocation to priesthood today?" We intersperse many of the responses to that question throughout this final chapter as we search for signs that a possible reversal in the forty-year downward trend may be on the horizon.

We also analyze participants' answers to three other survey questions: (1) If you had your choice again, would you enter the priesthood? (2) When was the last time you encouraged someone to consider becoming a priest? (3) Have media stories of clergy sexual abuse of minors affected how much you encourage men to consider the priesthood? Responses to these three questions help us understand who among today's priests are actively encouraging the next generation of young men to respond generously to Christ's invitation to priestly service.

Previous Research on Vocational Encouragement

The baseline of this longitudinal study, as explained earlier, is the research that Greeley (1972) and his colleagues began conducting in early 1969 and completed in late 1971. In those immediate years following the conclusion of the Second Vatican Council, Greeley had correctly surmised that priests were not as enthusiastic about their vocations as they had been in prior years and that, as a consequence, they were not actively engaged in the recruitment of future generations of priests. The opening paragraph of chapter 14, titled "Recruiting for the Priesthood," merits highlighting here:

> Resignations from the priesthood are not the only or even necessarily the most critical problem that the Catholic priesthood in the United States faces today. It is generally accepted that there has been a dramatic slump in the number of young men entering the seminaries to study for the priesthood, and perhaps an even greater slump in the numbers of those finally ordained. . . . Many reasons can be advanced to explain this decline, but only one falls within the competence of this study: It may be likely that priests, who—as data in previous chapters have demonstrated—are extremely important in the encouragement of a priestly vocation, are no longer deeply committed to recruiting colleagues and successors. (Greeley, 1972:267)

Greeley discovered that priests' attitudes concerning vocational recruiting had changed drastically during the previous four to five years.

He asked the priests in his study to indicate which of the following four statements best described their attitude in 1965/1966 and then again in 1970: (1) I actively encourage boys to enter the seminary or novitiate, since I see the priesthood as a very rewarding vocation; (2) I encourage boys but advise them about the uncertainties surrounding the role of the priest today; (3) I neither discourage nor encourage boys, but allow them to make up their own minds; (4) Abstracting from their personal qualities, I tend to discourage boys from entering now and advise them to wait until the future is more certain.

What Greeley found was so alarming that it prompted him to state that the information he discovered "represents an *extremely serious* problem for the Catholic priesthood in the United States" (Greeley, 1972:269). Almost two-thirds (64 percent) of diocesan priests said that in 1965/1966 they would have fit in the first category of actively encouraging vocations but by 1970 only one-third (33 percent) felt the same way. The decline of active encouragement by religious order priests over that same period plummeted from 56 percent to 27 percent. While only 2 percent of diocesan priests and 3 percent of religious priests in 1970 (up from 0 percent and 1 percent, respectively, in 1965/1966) said that they would actually discourage young men from entering the seminary, the major shift of attitude was toward the middle two categories. Greeley described the third category, which by 1970 was the one with which the largest group of diocesan and religious priests (36 percent each) most identified, as the "hands-off" approach. Analyzing the responses by age categories produced even further concern for Greeley as the youngest cohort of priests (ages 26 to 35), who are typically the most enthusiastic, declined from 52 percent who actively encouraged vocations in 1965/1966 to only 21 percent by 1970. Those priests are the ones that we have classified in our current study as the last members of the pre–Vatican II ordination cohort and the first ones of the Vatican II ordination cohort. As we shall see, they continue to be the priests who are least likely to promote vocations today.

Satisfaction with Vocational Choice

Since, as Greeley (1972) observed, the more satisfied a priest is with his own choice of priesthood, the more likely he will be to encourage others, the first focus of analysis for this chapter centers on each priest's overall contentment measured by his response to the question about his willingness to enter the priesthood again if he was given the choice to do so.

Table 8.1
If You Had Your Choice Again, Would You Enter the Priesthood?
(Percentage in each category)

	Definitely Yes	Probably Yes	Probably or Definitely Not
All priests	75%	20%	5%
Ecclesial status			
Diocesan	74%	21%	5%
Religious	80	17	4
Birthplace			
Born in the United States	76%	20%	5%
Born in Europe or Canada	67	21	12
Other international	84	12	4
Generation			
Pre–Vatican II (born prior to 1943)	79%	17%	4%
Vatican II (born 1943–60)	70	23	7
Post–Vatican II (born after 1960)	80	17	3
Ordination cohort			
Pre–Vatican II (ordained before 1964)	81%	14%	6%
Vatican II (ordained 1964–77)	73	24	3
Post–Vatican II (ordained 1978–91)	70	23	7
Millennial (ordained 1992 to present)	81	14	5
Cultic model index			
Lowest quartile (ideologically "progressive")	55%	34%	11%
Second quartile	75	21	4
Third quartile	84	13	3
Highest quartile (ideologically "traditionalist")	90	9	1

As we showed in table 2.3 and repeat here at the top of table 8.1, the percentage of priests who would "definitely" or "probably" choose the priesthood again increased from 79 percent in 1970 to 88 percent in 2001, and then to 95 percent in 2009. Table 8.1 further presents closer scrutiny of priest satisfaction from various angles, each of which reveals a slightly different nuance.

Differences by Ecclesial Status

By focusing attention only on the first column of those who said they would "definitely" enter the priesthood again, some noteworthy differences immediately surface. For example, religious priests seem to be slightly more content with their life choice (80 percent) than their diocesan confreres (74 percent). In response to the open-ended question asking what they would say to a young man considering the priesthood today, a 72-year-old retired diocesan priest said that he would encourage a prospective candidate to "seriously consider joining a religious community, not the diocesan priesthood." Along those same lines, a 68-year-old active diocesan priest said he would encourage a young man to consider a religious vocation because there are "better opportunities for a variety of ministries in religious communities," and a 58-year-old active diocesan priest said he would mention that perhaps "a religious vocation may be more appropriate." While those were the only three diocesan priests who made such recommendations, the fact that not even one religious priest promoted diocesan service over religious life is noteworthy. A 58-year-old religious priest who serves as a spiritual director went so far as to say, "Do not join a diocese." While no other religious priest was as negative toward diocesan ministry as he was, many spoke positively of their own orders. For example, a 75-year-old retired religious priest emphatically wrote:

> Come and find out how rewarding the life and ministry in a religious congregation can really be!

Another retired religious priest, now 87 years old, made a glowing recommendation:

> The greatest gift of my life (besides my birth and the Catholic faith) has been my vocation as a religious priest in the Jesuits. I would enthusiastically support any man who felt a call to priesthood or religious life. Priesthood is an inspiring call to be a man "for others" in a significant lifelong role of helping to be in deep intimacy with Jesus.

A 61-year-old active religious priest warned, however:

> If coming to religious life, choose an established community with a distinct tradition such as the Sulpicians, Franciscans, Benedictines, Carmelites, etc.—not one of these dumps that are springing up today.

Another religious priest, who is 75, was less restrictive in his recommendation:

> If he is thinking of a religious order: check them all out.

Differences by Place of Birth

Priests born in Africa, Asia, or Latin America (those whom we identified earlier as "other international" priests) seem to be more content with their decision to enter the priesthood than those born in the United States, Canada, or Europe.

A typical piece of advice from enthusiastic other international priests in response to the open-ended question, "What would you say to a young man considering the priesthood today?" was "Go for it!" or "Be not afraid!" Such responses make it clear that they are very pleased with the decision they made to become priests. Perhaps due to a certain language barrier, the responses from the other international priests tended to be brief, such as when a 33-year-old priest from South America recommended, "Study. Pray. Work." Even when they did write more, they expressed themselves in pithy phrases as did this 46-year-old priest who was also born in South America:

> Pray much. Become very active in parish ministry. Go to confessional regularly. See a spiritual advisor on a regular basis. Read the Scriptures. Eat healthy. Exercise regularly. Read the lives of the saints.

Such upbeat advice was also expressed by many of those born in the United States. For example, an 81-year-old retired diocesan priest recommended:

> Have a strong literary (humanities) background. Achieve a personal maturity that makes one aware of strengths and weaknesses. Be an extrovert. Be positive about one's desire to serve. Learn another language. Don't take yourself too seriously—and learn to laugh at yourself. Trust in God.

Whether they expressed themselves eloquently or not, in English as their first language or not, the overwhelming majority of priests had many positive and encouraging things to say about the priesthood. Just 1.5 percent (11 out of 735 participants who responded to the final question) made only discouraging remarks that probably would turn a potential candidate away.

Parallel between Generation and Ordination Cohort Responses

Both the generation and ordination cohort subsections of table 8.1 reveal a kind of inverted bell curve effect. Seventy-nine percent of the oldest priests (those of the pre–Vatican II generation) as well as 80 percent of the youngest (those of the post–Vatican II generation) report that they would choose the priesthood again, compared to only 70 percent of priests from the Vatican II generation. Not surprisingly, a similar result is evident for ordination cohort.[1] These differences based on generation and ordination cohort surfaced repeatedly during the listening sessions. For example, a post–Vatican II generation priest passionately stated,

> If I knew that it was just going to be heartache from here on in, I'd still stay in just because of all of the joy that I've gotten out of it so far.

A few moments later, during the same listening session, a Vatican II generation priest spoke in the opposite tone (he was evidently hurt) and with a very different message:

> My experience of priesthood has been marred by some very significant, painful experiences. My greatest fear for anyone joining the priesthood in my diocese is that your talents would be ignored and not be well-used. You will be ultimately of no use. That would be a significant drawback because of the diocesan leadership.

Differences by Cultic Model Index Quartiles

Of all the subsections of table 8.1, the largest differences among respondents were according to the cultic model scale developed by Hoge and Wenger (2003). While only 55 percent of those priests who belong to the first quartile (the most ideologically "progressive") would "definitely" enter the priesthood again, a full 90 percent of the most "traditionalist" (members of the fourth quartile) would make the same decision.

---

[1] Logically, ordination cohort characteristics usually mirror generational trends. While it is possible that a priest of the pre–Vatican II generation could be a member of the millennial ordination cohort if he were a "late" vocation, it is impossible, for example, that a member of the post–Vatican II generation be ordained with the Vatican II cohort. For the sake of clarity, and due to their great similarities, we include the ordination cohort response rates in the tables of this chapter, but focus mainly on generational differences.

Table 8.2
When Was the Last Time You Encouraged
Someone to Consider Becoming a Priest?
(Percentage in each category)

	Within Last 6 Months	Within Last 6–12 Months	More than a Year Ago	I Have Never Done This
All priests	58%	16%	21%	5%
Ecclesial status				
Diocesan	59%	16%	20%	5%
Religious	56	16	23	5
Birthplace				
Born in the United States	58%	17%	20%	5%
Born in Europe or Canada	48	19	25	8
Other international	59	11	27	4
Generation				
Pre–Vatican II (born prior to 1943)	48%	17%	29%	6%
Vatican II (born 1943–60)	60	17	19	5
Post–Vatican II (born after 1960)	81	11	7	2
Ordination cohort				
Pre–Vatican II (ordained before 1964)	44%	17%	31%	8%
Vatican II (ordained 1964–77)	56	20	20	4
Post–Vatican II (ordained 1978–91)	62	13	21	4
Millennial (ordained 1992 to present)	76	12	9	3
Cultic model index				
Lowest quartile (ideologically "progressive")	45%	18%	27%	10%
Second quartile	56	16	23	5
Third quartile	59	20	19	1
Highest quartile (ideologically "traditionalist")	73	11	13	2

Encouraging New Priestly Vocations

It follows logically that the results in table 8.2 are for the most part similar to those found in table 8.1 because, as stated earlier, one would expect that those who are more content with their choice of priesthood would also encourage others more enthusiastically. However, there are a few differences. First, we would have predicted that religious priests would have encouraged vocations at a slightly higher rate than diocesan priests. In fact, diocesan priests were just slightly more active in this regard, perhaps due to the fact that they are more likely to be assigned to parish ministry, where they may have more frequent contact with young men who are considering a vocation. While many religious priests work at schools, many others are engaged in specialized ministries that focus on adults. Second, it appears that the other international priests encourage vocations at the same rate as those born in the United States, but Europeans and Canadians are the ones least likely to do so. Based on the data from table 8.1, one would have expected the other international priests to be the most active vocation promoters. Perhaps this is a language barrier issue. Finally, the previously mentioned inverted bell curve based on generation and ordination cohort disappears in table 8.2. The oldest generation and the oldest cohort are the ones *least* likely to have encouraged someone to consider becoming a priest during the last six months. While it seems contradictory that they would choose the priesthood again for themselves but would not vigorously promote vocations, perhaps this unexpected outcome is simply a product of their retirement status, which would limit their contact with potential candidates.

Once again, the cultic model scale shows that the most ideologically "traditionalist" priests are more active vocation recruiters than those who are ideologically "progressive." Almost three-quarters of conservative-minded priests have encouraged someone to consider the priesthood during the last six months, in contrast to less than half of the more liberal-leaning priests.

Next, we examine some of the most common themes among responses to the question about what advice priests would offer to a young man considering the priesthood.

The Most Common Advice: Pray!

The most repeated advice given by the priests in this study—be they "progressive" or "traditionalist," young or old, foreign-born or not—was simply to pray. For some, that was the only suggestion they offered. For others, it was the starting point of their strong endorsement for the call to priestly service. Here is a sampling of some of their advice regarding prayer:[2]

> Develop a life of prayer and service.

> Cultivate a strong spiritual life centered on Mass, daily prayer, etc.

> Pray the Scriptures and converse with priests who are varied in age.

> Regularly get away from the hustle and bustle of a media-driven society in order to listen to God and simply be.

> Open your heart to the voice of the Lord. Let Him encounter you in His love and respond as Samuel: "Here I am Lord, I've come to do your will!"

> Pray over it, but don't delay. The best discernment is done from inside the seminary or religious institute. Try it. You'll know (or they'll tell you) if it's not right.

> Take your time! Get involved in ministry. Take prayer seriously. Seek spiritual direction.

> Pray about it. Ask the Holy Spirit for light. Strive to live the Christian virtues. Make a daily plan for prayer. Attend Mass each day if possible. Confession every two weeks. Have a spiritual director. Begin to dialogue with a vocation director.

> Pray hard and be generous with God. . . . Have faith and trust that, no matter his sins and limitations, God can in fact call him to a life of purpose and joy as a priest!

> Prayer, prayer, prayer—liturgical and personal. Your connection to the Lord Jesus Christ is the friendship most sustaining to priests in good and bad times. Immerse yourself in Scripture. Do not expect an easy road. Seek to do the good that the Lord invites you to do to bring about the Kingdom.

> Don't ask, "What do I want?" rather, "What does God want of me?"

---

[2] In the vast majority of these quotations, we reprint each participant's entire statement verbatim. Only on a few occasions have we edited their text, either for the sake of clarity or brevity. While it would be enlightening to read the hundreds of individual statements, it would be impractical and cumbersome to publish them here. What is presented is simply a representative sample of the major points they mentioned.

The Second Most Common Suggestion: Get a Spiritual Director

After prayer, the second most frequent piece of advice was to find a good spiritual director. For many priests, this recommendation was coupled with an encouragement to pray and/or to get involved in some form of parish ministry. Here are a few representative samples:

> Get a good spiritual director. Pray. Keep close to the poor.

> Honesty, transparency with spiritual directors and superiors for a proper discernment.

> Have a good spiritual director. Have an active social life. Experience as much ministry as possible.

> With the help of a good spiritual director, he needs to face and work through his own prejudices and biases so that he can save all God's people, not just the ones he agrees with or likes. He needs to realize he must be a bridge, not a barrier, between God and God's people.

> Be involved in the life of the Church through the parish, have priest spiritual direction, engage in discernment activities of diocese or religious communities, and if possible do an annual retreat at a Jesuit Retreat Center. (That last one is what kept my vocation alive until I was ready to pursue it!)

> It may seem like stating the very obvious, but I believe *the most important consideration* is to truly discern whether or not the *Lord calls*. This is an activity best undertaken with the help of a trained and experienced spiritual director over a period of time.

Presuming that, through spiritual direction and other discernment, a young man determined that the Lord was in fact calling him, many priests encouraged,

> Follow your heart and listen to God's call.

> If God is calling, you'd better go. If God is not calling, you'd better not go.

> Trust in God. Find a priest who will guide you. Develop your spiritual life. Love the Church. Involve yourself with good lay people who will support you.

A Third Very Common Suggestion: Get to Know Many Priests

Besides encouraging a potential candidate for the priesthood to pray and to engage in serious spiritual direction, many priests highlighted the value of getting to know as many priests as possible. Aware that not all priests are inspirational, some of them issued warnings to stay clear of negative or unhappy priests.

> Get to know several priests and seminarians. Read Church history. Do volunteer work.

> Come to know good, solid, happy priests. Talk to a vocation director, pastor, and seminarians. Go to seminary as soon as possible—the more priestly formation, the better. Develop prayer life, attend Mass often if not daily.

> I would invite him to spiritual and social functions with positive priests— I would not subject him to griping, complaining priests. They turn me off, too.

> Talk to many committed, joyful, priests. Avoid negative or unhappy priests. Develop a strong personal prayer life. Make a clear decision about celibacy.

A Fourth Recommendation: Understand and Accept Celibacy

Another topic that was mentioned frequently in response to the open-ended question focused on celibacy. The majority of those who mentioned it did not question the validity or usefulness of this discipline. Rather, accepting it as a requirement for priesthood in the Catholic Church today, they talked about the importance of understanding the challenge involved in living a celibate life:

> Be especially convinced that you are emotionally ready to embrace celibacy for the rest of your life—freely and joyfully.

> Listen to the Holy Spirit. Consider the demands of celibacy. Foster healthy friendships with men and women. Take care of your physical and emotional needs. Foster healthy habits. Have refreshing hobbies and interests.

> 1) Think carefully about potential loneliness. 2) Be open and well-grounded in your sexuality. 3) Don't expect your identity to rest in your status or religious garb and experience of priestly life. 4) Embrace ambiguity and doubt. 5) Consult and respect the laity. 6) Smile and have a good sense of humor! 7) *Pray.*

> Pray, pray, pray, pray. Be comfortable with who you are—be aware of your sexuality and your sexual needs so that you are in control of them and they do not control you. Know what the virtue of prudence is! Know what the virtue of temperance is! Enjoy your ministry. Develop a priest support group. Develop a lay support group.

The following comment about celibacy is taken from one of the listening sessions:

> [I would ask if he has] a healthy view of his own sexuality. If you are to be a Catholic priest the expectation is to live a celibate life. Can you do that? Are you willing to do that? . . . Do you see a purpose for that? One of the difficulties most men experience is that they didn't do that piece when they started formation. . . . You didn't do your work early on where you began to integrate your sexuality into who you are as a person. God made you a sexual being. The Church is asking you to give this up as a gift in terms of ministering to God's people. You can do that or you can't. You have to make that decision for yourself and try to live to the best of your ability.

Suggestions Made by "Progressive" and "Traditionalist" Priests

While priests with varying ideologies seemed to agree on the four already-mentioned topics of prayer, spiritual direction, getting to know as many good priests as possible, and full acceptance of the celibate requirement, there were differences between the advice given by the most "progressive" priests and by the most "traditionalist" priests.

Many "progressive" priests emphasized the need to understand and fully embrace "servant leadership" so as to avoid falling into clericalism. Here are a few examples:

> Be realistic—about yourself, expectations, role and identity of priesthood, reasons you are seriously considering priesthood—Status? Ministry? Do you want to be a servant leader? Are you willing to sacrifice for the good of the community? Are you comfortable with your humanity?

> Priesthood is not about your status, but about serving people by proclaiming the good news and attending to their religious needs, and the commitment to and solidarity with the poor or oppressed.

> 1) To be determined to grow in respect and love for the people to whom you will be ministering. 2) To emphasize the servant aspect of the priesthood. (Jesus washed feet and in doing so, gave us an example.) 3) To view the Church as the Body of Christ or the People of God. All have something to give which is needed by the rest.

> They need to understand the call to servant leadership. We are too top-heavy with people dedicated to the institutional Church. We need to re-visit the documents of Vatican II so we understand the role of the laity and how we are to encourage them in their baptismal calling.

> Be a servant. Love the people. Be willing to learn throughout life. Follow the Spirit's movements. Test the call in prayer. Must be flexible. Do not get caught in the clerical culture.

> The most important things: 1) Deepen your spirituality. Have a loving relationship with Christ. 2) A love of Scripture. 3) Remember: Priesthood is not about personal privileges and control (or being served)—but service of others, especially of the poor.

"Traditionalist" priests emphasized a different set of topics, such as adoration of the Blessed Sacrament and devotion to the Blessed Virgin Mary. No "progressive" priest made reference to either of those two themes when giving advice to a potential future priest. The following comments were all made by "traditionalist" priests:

> Pray before the Blessed Sacrament each day if possible. Develop a devotion to the Blessed Mother. Learn to be generous and self-sacrificing.

> Speak to a priest who comes off as happy and fulfilled in his ministry. Give the seminary a wholehearted try in order to resolve vocational questions. Seek supportive family members and friends. Most of *all*, take time for quiet prayer, preferably in the presence of the Blessed Sacrament.

> Build a personal love with Jesus Christ through the sacrament of the Eucharist and of Reconciliation. Keep purity at all cost, as a priority of life. Find a trustworthy and holy spiritual director and visit congregations or diocesan seminaries to discern.

> Deepen your love for the Eucharist, the Mass, the Blessed Mother, the Church, and the Pope. Have courage; do not be afraid. The life of a priest is a life of joy and happiness. Do not look for supernatural signs of a vocation—the only sign you need is that God's people need you.

Differences in Timing between "Progressive" and "Traditionalist" Priests

The "progressive" priests recommend taking a slower approach to seminary entrance while the "traditionalist" priests typically advocate a "jump in now" mentality. Here are some statements from the more "progressive" priests:

> Finish college. Work a couple of years. Spend time learning Spanish. Spend six months in a poor nation like Honduras to understand people and their human condition.

Take a deep breath. Take your time. Study deeply the nature and mission of your choice. Make it your choice freely. Live with it till you die.

Experience life before you commit to a decision about priesthood, e.g., explore relationships, complete one's education, exercise financial responsibility, and know what it means to live independently.

Go to junior college first—get a job in the real world for a while. Pray for discernment.

The more "traditionalist" priests, however, were more inclined to encourage a young man to enter the seminary right away:

You won't know if God is calling you unless you take the leap. Jump in and put your trust in the Lord to reveal it to you.

It is the best profession for one's whole life. Go for it.

Go for it—you will be helped and there are great avenues for you to follow to become what God is calling you to become.

Mutual Warnings Concerning Opposing Theologies

The "progressives" and the "traditionalists" issued warnings, both directly and indirectly, about priests from the opposite end of the ecclesiastical spectrum in phrases such as these:

Beware of rigid priests/ministers. Respect your doubts. Enjoy your faith. Be open. Be honest. Be yourself.

Make sure they accept the Vatican II idea of Church and priesthood and not to try to go back to Trent!

The Church is like a big tree with old, dry, and dead branches and beautiful, vigorous, and green ones. Avoid the dead branches and look for the green ones. Seek a congregation or diocese and seminary where you can be holy; one which will be faithful to the Pope and to a demanding spiritual discipline.

Pray, stay closely involved with the Catholic community, study the Gospels, and find a diocese or religious community that is orthodox.

A Last Recommendation: Be Ready for Bumps and Surprises

Where the two extremes ("progressive" and "traditionalist") met again was in their agreement that while the priesthood can be challenging, it can also be very fulfilling and rewarding. They mentioned how wonderful it can be if properly lived but they also made these points:

Get ready for a bumpy ride; the Church has so many issues that need to be faced. Be ready to deal with many sides. Be flexible. Be prayerful. Be open.

Be aware of the realities of today's priesthood; a parish priest can no longer be free to do as much as he would like due to the priest shortage. Be prepared to be a pastor within five years of ordination, if not earlier! The people of God are wonderful! Love them and serve them, and they will love you and support you! It's a great life!

The Effect of the Sexual Abuse Scandal on Vocational Encouragement

The survey asked priests whether the scandal has affected how much they encourage vocations. As table 8.3 shows, more than half (52 percent) of all priests say it has had no effect on them. The following two comments are typical of the plurality of priests who say the scandal has had no effect on their encouragement of vocations:

> I'm still very supportive and encouraging of vocations. I still think we need good priests. The prior bishop asked us to ask each Confirmation student about a vocation in the Confirmation interview. I readily do that.

> The scandal hasn't diminished my love for priesthood or my encouragement of others to join it.

The generation and ordination cohort patterns that appeared in table 8.1 reappear in table 8.3, with the oldest and youngest generations slightly more likely than the Vatican II generation to have increased their encouragement in light of the sexual abuse scandal.

Once again, the largest difference appears when comparing priests according to ideology. This divide was also evident among the priests we interviewed. A religious order priest spoke about how he changed ministries soon after the scandal broke:

> Right around that time [2002] the provincial said, "I want you to teach the seminarians. Right now the American priesthood needs help." I said, "All right. Plan for me to help prepare new brothers and look after the brothers that I have." So after the sorrow and the anger [over the scandal] came a resolve. . . . I think it was Father Neuhaus that said, "The only response to infidelity is more fidelity." I said, "I think that's a good rallying cry, because the need for good priests hasn't gone away. I think there are men with the generosity to answer the call, even in difficult times."

Table 8.3
Have Media Stories of Clergy Sexual Abuse of Minors Affected How Much You Encourage Men to Consider the Priesthood?
(Percentage in each category)

	Yes, Much Less	Yes, Slightly Less	They Have Had No Effect	No, More Now
All priests	11%	22%	52%	15%
Ecclesial status				
Diocesan	13%	22%	51%	13%
Religious	8	22	52	18
Birthplace				
Born in the United States	11%	21%	53%	15%
Born in Europe or Canada	13	31	46	10
Other international	11	30	38	21
Generation				
Pre–Vatican II (born prior to 1943)	12%	23%	50%	16%
Vatican II (born 1943–60)	13	23	52	12
Post–Vatican II (born after 1960)	9	16	54	20
Ordination cohort				
Pre–Vatican II (ordained before 1964)	13%	18%	49%	20%
Vatican II (ordained 1964–77)	11	26	51	12
Post–Vatican II (ordained 1978–91)	10	24	54	13
Millennial (ordained 1992 to present)	13	15	54	18
Cultic model index				
Lowest quartile (ideologically "progressive")	20%	23%	53%	4%
Second quartile	11	25	51	13
Third quartile	8	25	54	14
Highest quartile (ideologically "traditionalist")	7	16	47	30

In contrast, two diocesan priests discussed their reluctance to encourage vocations in the wake of the scandal:

> What makes me tentative about encouraging vocations is: with what level of honesty can I encourage a young person to consider ministry in this radically dysfunctional organization which I have serious trouble trusting? Some of that attitude would be there without the sexual abuse scandal, but it's exacerbated by the scandal. I've been inside this for almost forty years and it's not a pretty picture. On the other hand, I love what I do. I want to do it as long as I can. When somebody comes *to* me, I certainly do not discourage them. Two weeks ago, a senior in high school in the parish came to me and said he was thinking about doing this with his life. I was supportive. But we're all the time being asked to give the diocese names of young men in the parish that we identify as potential candidates for priesthood. I've not been able to do that for a long, long time.

> It has definitely affected my desire to encourage vocations—and in a very negative way, quite honestly. I could not in conscience, at this stage with the way things are, encourage anybody I cared about to go into priesthood. I would be really strongly encouraging much discernment and caution because I think the biggest aftershock of the scandal is a sort of a conservative movement in the Church. There are a bunch of factors that have moved the Church in this direction but the scandal is a strong motivating factor.

What about priests of the millennial ordination cohort who were discerning their own vocation to the priesthood in 2002? How did the scandal affect their own resolve to become priests? Only three of the men we interviewed were in formation at the time the scandal broke. None of the three told us that the scandal caused him doubts. Of course, given that we have only interviewed priests, we would not have spoken with anybody who permanently left the seminary because of the scandal. A priest who, in 2002, was preparing for ordination in an order whose charism centers on ministry to young people remembers:

> It didn't cause me to second-guess my vocation. That did happen with a few guys behind me in formation. One left and later came back. A couple others left and didn't come back.

Another of the priests who was in the seminary in 2002 says:

> It didn't shake me to the core. It did make me question, in one sense, the discipline of celibacy.

The priest quoted earlier who became a seminary professor in 2002 told us he didn't perceive that the scandal dissuaded any of the seminarians he taught or any other men who have approached him about the priesthood:

> I haven't met any young man who has inquired about religious life or priesthood who was reluctant because of the scandal. I haven't met anyone who says, "I'd be a priest except for the scandal." That hasn't kept them away.

A religious priest who was a vocations director in the early 2000s recalls questions he received from men considering the priesthood. While they had concerns about the scandal in his order, some of their reactions surprised him:

> Unquestionably it came up with a fair amount of candidates. They would ask if this community had been impacted by it, if men had been removed from ministry. I'd tell them the truth that we did have some men who were removed from ministry for this. They would want to know how we responded. I would tell them that it's been a very dignified response—I mean, it's been appropriate . . . obviously they're on safety plans; they have very restricted lives now. Yet at the same time they're treated with dignity and respect because they're our family members. They continue to be counted as one of us. I think that has been almost a point of healing for some men who've been interested in our religious community as their vocational choice. They're thinking that, "Gosh, if this is the way they treat the worst among them, then maybe they're a healthy group and they stand by what they purport in terms of the Gospel message." So it was kind of helpful for inquirers to learn that we just didn't evict men, we didn't put them out on the street. That was something that surprised me. I thought they would think, "If anybody in your group has been removed from ministry, I don't want to join the group." It was, in some measure, something quite opposite of that.

Conclusion

In many ways this chapter has been about the passing down of wisdom. Men with the benefit of experience have offered their ideas to those of a younger generation considering becoming a part of their unique life and brotherhood. During an interview discussion about priestly fraternity, a diocesan priest in his 40s emphasized the importance of intergenerational ties among priests and learning from those who have gone before:

Last Friday our presbyteral council had a day of recollection. The speaker was talking about fraternity, brotherhood, and the need for support. We were at this retreat house. It's a Jesuit place and they have a cemetery there. One of the older fellows, he's 84 years old, was walking around and he called me over. He was looking for a grave of a priest. I happened to have just walked by the guy's grave so I showed him where it was. He said, "This was my great uncle." I looked down. The guy was ordained in 1864. This older priest told me his great uncle had taught at one of the Jesuit high schools in town and had taught a lot of the professors he had in the 1940s in the seminary. Then he started telling stories about those old-timers and the professors and seminary life. It was interesting how our lives are intertwined. My reflection to the group that afternoon was that there are fewer and fewer of us. When I was first ordained twenty years ago, I was footloose and fancy free. I really wasn't that interested in the fraternity. I was out to conquer the world. I didn't care what anybody else did. I had my plan. I didn't go to a lot of priest things. I didn't do priest support. I was kind of an independent fellow. And I said how much that's changed for me. Now I participate in priest fraternity groups and support groups. I try to get to any kind of social thing where I can be with other priests to just talk and encourage each other, to have that fraternity. My fear is that, as we get fewer and fewer of us and we have more and more hats we wear, we just don't have time. . . . My biggest concern is we forget stories. We forget the giants that have gone before us and the characters that have really tried to be faithful to their ministry and service to the Church and the Lord.

As we end our reflections, it is helpful to call to mind the conclusion that Father Greeley arrived at forty years ago: "If priests are among the most effective recruiters of other priests and if their enthusiasm for recruitment has undergone a considerable decline, then it is not likely that the present vocation crisis will cease unless there is once again a return to some higher level of enthusiasm for vocational recruiting among the clergy" (Greeley, 1972:269). As we have seen in this chapter, there are signs of a renewal in vocational recruiting by priests, especially among the post–Vatican II generation who are actively and happily promoting the priesthood. Perhaps their happiness will attract more men to consider priesthood, which, in time, will help prevent today's priests from feeling so overworked. This is a change we can all embrace and support.

Reflections from an Archbishop

Archbishop Gregory Aymond*

Although this deeply interesting milestone study of priests—with a comprehensive 360-degree perspective of and by Catholic priests themselves—will be greatly appreciated by scholars of the Church and sociologists, the ultimate beneficiaries of the work will be *all* Catholics. For in the stories of our priests, we hear the stories of our Church. In their disappointments and shortcomings, we see our own. In their victories and contributions are the fruits of the new evangelization of the twenty-first century.

As a bishop who shepherds the priests of an archdiocese with a full and happy heart, I can say, with certainty, that this study is well worth reading. I also suggest that this study will have a significant impact on how we see vocations and how we can appreciate more fully the priests who serve our Church with great love, enthusiasm, and integrity.

Yes, as in every walk of life, there are some coworkers who are not happy every moment of every day, some who are deeply dissatisfied and question what they do and who they are. But I am one bishop who can testify—indeed, loudly proclaim—that in my own experience, in my work with brother priests in more than one diocese for more than three dozen years, I have known them, as a whole and as individuals, to be an exceptionally devoted and motivated cadre of men, in ways that are described in great detail in this study.

Any of them—any of *us*—will so testify and have done so quite eloquently and honestly in these pages.

---

*Archbishop Gregory M. Aymond is the fourteenth archbishop of New Orleans and serves as chairman of the USCCB Committee on Divine Worship.

But the aim of this study is certainly not to glorify any priest, nor priests as a class. Though priests are to a distinct degree set apart from others by the nature of their vocation, they are called by Christ to serve among and with and for the people of God. Any priest who seeks to be seen "above" those in the pews and any layperson who seeks to put him on a pedestal in that manner are not serving the people or the priesthood in so doing.

The aim of the research herein is to quantify from a sociological perspective what priests actually experience and what their attitudes are today, in a particularly challenging environment. Like all people, priests are confronted with rapid, sometimes dizzying and disorienting, change— within the Church and outside those sacred walls.

So, how are they doing? How are they coping with myriad responsibilities and demands? How are their parishes doing during these times? Where do we as a Church stand in relation to our ministers, and where are we going over the next decades?

In this study, authors Mary Gautier, Paul Perl, and Stephen Fichter answer these important questions. They discuss demographic trends that are about to affect many dioceses and parishes in the United States. The point that a large number of priests will be retiring is factual and this will affect the way in which parish life is lived out. Even though in many dioceses the number of seminarians is increasing, there will be a period of time that will be very challenging before us in the United States and we must be prepared to face this reality with faith.

Even though priests would in general state that they are overworked, at the same time they are overwhelmingly satisfied with their way of life and the ministry that they do. It is also interesting to note that when priests pastor multiple parishes, this becomes very challenging and wearing on them and they find it difficult to establish meaningful relationships.

The demographic trends suggest that we are just about at the crest of a sea change in parish life. Many dioceses have invited priests from other countries to join their presbyterate to help satisfy the shortage of priests. The study discusses this issue and how priests who are not US-born do face some challenges in terms of culture.

Half of the priests now serving will be retiring out of the picture in the next ten years. Parish life as we know it will be radically different. We are already living that change in many parts of the country but the national data help to put it into perspective, so that what is perceived as decline and diminishment in one part of the Church is balanced by creativity, innovation, and new life in another part of the Church. Regardless of how you define what is going on in the Church today, there is no possibility of a return (at least not in the next few generations) to the luxury of an abundance of priests and religious in service to the Church.

Nevertheless, priests today are overwhelmingly satisfied with their chosen life and with the work they do. The authors demonstrate that this satisfaction is not due to increasing age, nor attrition of discontented priests, nor more traditionalism among some priests. Rather, the data show that priests are happy because they find fulfillment in their ministry; they are satisfied because they believe that what they do makes a difference in the lives of others.

Among the challenges in priestly life today, we would expect overwork to rank at the top, particularly in light of diminishing numbers and a rapidly aging clergy. However, while overwork is at least "somewhat" of a problem for half, the authors find that loneliness and lack of opportunity for personal fulfillment are better predictors of priestly dissatisfaction. The tipping point, meaning the point at which overwork impinges on personal satisfaction, comes when priests pastor multiple parishes. When a priest's time is spread so thin that he no longer feels that he can establish meaningful relationships with parishioners, then he feels the pressure of overwork.

Most priests recognize the diminishment of the clerical workforce and are supportive of the variety of measures that have been put in place to share the workload, such as international priests, permanent deacons, and lay ecclesial ministers. Few say they have a problem working with international priests and most favor an increase in collaboration with permanent deacons and lay ecclesial ministers. While some express concern that many international priests and the most recently ordained priests share less enthusiasm than older priests for collaboration in ministry, the data show that these groups are still solidly in favor of increased collaboration in ministry. It is encouraging that priests are very open to collaboration and sharing their ministry with permanent deacons, lay ecclesial ministers, and international priests.

International priests are somewhat younger, on average, than US-born priests, harkening back to earlier times when young men in their very early 20s were commonly ordained to the priesthood. They tend to be somewhat more traditional in ecclesiology and deferential toward hierarchy. At the same time, they are much more open than US-born priests to learning more about ministry within the multicultural setting that is the US Catholic Church today.

In the Archdiocese of New Orleans, Louisiana and environs, for example, we currently have an office of black Catholics and Hispanic ministry, and special apostolates for Vietnamese, Filipino, and Korean Catholics. We have a tradition of racial and ethnic diversity that dates to the colonial era and has continued through various waves of immigration over the past century—and especially in the past few decades. Our mission statement on racial harmony serves as a call to action in this regard:

> The Office of Racial Harmony and the Archdiocesan Implementation Committee are fully committed to assisting all parishes, schools, administrative offices and individual Catholics of the Archdiocese of New Orleans to faithfully explore ways to promote racial harmony so as to build a more loving, accepting, and respectful community. We are dedicated to addressing the sin of racism and to working to change hearts and minds so that the rich blessings of multiculturalism, diversity, and ethnic inclusion will be appreciated.

The priesthood in the Archdiocese of New Orleans and across this nation is called to minister to widely diverse populations, sometimes within individual parishes, which are rarely, if ever, organized along national lines as they were during the nineteenth- and twentieth-century waves of European immigration. Times change. People change. Yet the mission of the Church and her priests remains ever the same: to bring the good news of Jesus Christ to every person of every background and culture on the face of the earth.

The authors address the sexual abuse crisis in the words of faithful priests who have lived through it. They discuss some of the emotional reactions they experienced as well as the scandal that unfolded around them. Many describe personal trauma and faith-shattering revelations about priests they had known for years. Others describe the support they found in brother priests, supportive bishops, and faithful laity that sustained them through one of the most exceptionally difficult periods in the history of the Catholic Church in America. The study presents the impact of the scandal from a unique perspective and discusses how it has affected priests' lives and ministry.

We can also learn how to support our priests in a new era of accountability and vigilance in the protection of God's most precious gift to our world: the children whom Jesus calls so poignantly to come to him.

The final chapter, on vocations to priesthood, demonstrates that despite the trauma of the sexual abuse crisis, the diminishment of the clergy, and the increasing complexity of parish life today, priests continue to recommend the priesthood as a vocation. Most say that the sexual abuse crisis has not affected how much they encourage men to consider the priesthood. More recently ordained priests are even more likely than those who have been serving for many years to say they have recently encouraged someone to consider priesthood.

Each age of the Church, throughout its long history, has faced particular challenges, both within and without the Body of Christ. In early centuries, persecutions resulted in many martyrs among the presbyterate, as well as among the Christian population at large. In the Middle Ages and through the time of the Protestant Reformation, it became clear that the Church was called to reform herself, resulting in the formation of many new religious movements and the Council of Trent. In more recent times, just fifty years ago, Pope John XXIII was inspired by the Holy Spirit to convoke the Second Vatican Council, which aspired to bring the Church into the modern age while clarifying the spiritual and institutional roles of bishops, priests, religious, and laity in new ways. The influence of Vatican II is evident in this study of the priesthood by CARA—indeed, by the very existence of the study and its predecessors over the past forty years.

Through means of Scripture, tradition, and the magisterium of our Church, in the Holy Father and in the college of bishops (whether they are gathered in council or in the daily ministry of their office), each Christian is called to his or her vocation. We believe priests are called in a special way to a special task among the faithful. We also know that priests, as ministers and fellow believers, take on immense responsibilities for the Church and her people.

They are not alone in their work. We cannot leave them alone but must invite them into our hearts. For they need and want to be as one with the people. Saint Paul reminds us too that God is always with us when we stand together in faith, priests and laity:

> He will keep you firm to the end, irreproachable on the day of our Lord Jesus. God is faithful, and by him you were called to fellowship with his Son, Jesus Christ our Lord. (1 Cor 1:8-9, NABRE)

As God is faithful, let us be faithful and ever willing to listen to our priests, to help and support them, to love them as they love us. This remarkable book will help us hear what they have to say to us in our time—and for all time. For, like Christ, we know that they will be with us until the end of time.

Reflections from a Former Seminary Rector

Msgr. Jeremiah McCarthy*

It is a pleasure to contribute to this fine volume. While acknowledging significant challenges facing priests today, the book also provides abundant good news about the US priesthood. The high rates of satisfaction reported by priests in their ministry continues to be a surprisingly counter-intuitive finding in light of the daunting challenges posed by declining numbers of priests, a growing Catholic population, and increasing workloads.

After stratifying the clergy into four age cohorts (pre–Vatican II, Vatican II, post–Vatican II, millennials), the CARA study analyzes the cohorts through the interpretive lens developed by the late Dean Hoge, namely, the contrast between two different visions of priesthood, the "servant-leader" and the "cultic" models. This interpretive matrix provides some interesting insights about different attitudes among these cohorts with respect to collaboration, sources of satisfaction in ministry, the expanding role of international priests, the need for intercultural competency, and the effects of the sexual abuse scandal. Hoge's central observation about the contrast in attitudes between older "servant-leader" priests and newer "cultic" priests focuses on the varying ways in which these two cohorts view priestly identity and ministry. The servant-leaders, having been raised in a period of strong Catholic identity and community, assume the basic contours of the priestly role but are generally apt to pursue more collegial, collaborative, and open styles of leadership. The cultic-oriented priests, raised in the climate of change and ferment of the post–Vatican II era, prefer more traditional understandings of priestly

* Msgr. Jeremiah McCarthy, PhD, is executive director of the National Catholic Educational Association Seminary Department.

identity and authority coupled with concern for strong, clear delineations of roles and responsibilities between priests and the baptized faithful.

The book provides some interesting contrasts in perspective and emphasis based upon the cohort framework. The data indicate that there is still some significant variation with respect to issues of collaboration and working with women and the lay faithful. For the good of the Church, this gap must shrink (see table 4.5, "Attitudes about the Priesthood and the Church Today, by Ordination Cohort"). While the data suggest, positively, that there is a growing convergence among the cohorts of priests with respect to important issues of priestly identity and ministry, nonetheless, more efforts to strengthen this common sense of purpose are crucial.

The survey takes note of the significant stress priests are experiencing in light of the shortage of priests, especially with expanded workloads (see table 4.2, "Importance of Selected Problems on a Day-to-Day Basis, by Ordination Cohort"). One conclusion deserves comment: "Although it is perhaps less of a problem for them on a daily basis, conflicts with parishioners or laity about issues may become even more frequent as there are fewer priests ministering to more Catholics." From a personnel management perspective, given this present and emerging reality (e.g., stresses occasioned by parish closures in many dioceses as the Catholic population shifts from its Eastern and Northeastern roots to the Southern and Western United States), investment in conflict resolution skills and other human resource skills may help to address these difficulties.

On the other side of the equation, millennials were 13 percent more inclined to affirm the ontological difference of the ordained ministry and to uphold the distinction between priests and laity in the Church than older cohorts. Eighty-one percent of all priests serving in 2009 support collaboration with the laity, and 77 percent support the contention that the Church "needs to move faster in empowering lay persons in ministry." With respect to the empowerment of women, the survey identifies an important source of tension and conflict since more than 80 percent of lay ecclesial ministers are women. The report states, "In fact, there are some indications that the attitudes of the more recently ordained cohort may be less accepting of collaborating with women in Church ministry."

This finding, coupled with the observation that "members of the millennial cohort are more likely than the older priests to agree with the statement, 'It is essential to uphold the distinction between priests and laity in the Church,' " requires ongoing interaction between priests and bishops to find calm and constructive patterns of collegial partnerships rather than status/power disputes to govern the relationship between priests and the baptized faithful.

There are implications in these findings for seminary formation. It is essential that seminarians demonstrate a capacity to effectively and appropriately relate with women and all laypersons with whom they will be serving in the Lord's vineyard upon ordination. Clarity and strength in affirming one's priestly identity are important virtues, but they are not to be purchased at the expense of minimizing the dignity and rights of the baptized faithful. For vocation directors and psychologists involved in the screening and admission of candidates, there should be a clear expectation that the testing process assesses a candidate's capacity for affective maturity or "emotional intelligence" as a condition for admission to the seminary.

The emphasis on human formation in *Pastores Dabo Vobis* (Pope John Paul's 1992 encyclical on priestly formation) is an affirmation that candidates for the priesthood must have solid interpersonal skills and a capacity for affective maturity in order to benefit from the spiritual, academic, and professional training provided by the seminary. From my experience in seminary formation, to the extent that students lacked essential human formation skills, these deficits were usually displayed as a debilitating form of rigidity in ordinary interpersonal encounters and pastoral settings. In responding to these challenges, I think that it is important for seminary formation personnel to observe an essential distinction between a legitimate concern for orthodoxy and the behavioral issue of pastoral rigidity.

The Church's great theological tradition can be imagined as a big tent that welcomes diverse, complementary theological perspectives, from Augustine to Aquinas, from von Balthasar and de Lubac to Congar and Rahner. In order to sustain a theological engagement with this great tradition, not only must one bring to the table astute, critical thinking skills, but also a disposition to listen and to learn. The title of one of Jacques Maritain's books, *Distinguish to Unite, or, The Degrees of Knowledge*, captures the balance that is essential for dialogue and shared understanding. We make distinctions and stake out intellectual positions in service of a more comprehensive, unified grasp of truth. Intellectual integrity requires the courage of our convictions but also the capacity to recognize that our grasp of truth is always partial and finite. In Charles Davis's book *The Temptations of Religion*, one of these temptations is the "lust for certitude." A rigid insistence on one's own point of view all too often can result in polarization and harmful disunity in a parish. Consequently, a good question that seminary formation staffs frequently ask is the following: Can this seminarian, notwithstanding his theological preferences and sensibilities, exercise priestly ministry with compassion, skill, and sensitivity to pastoral complexity? Humility is an intellectual virtue as well as an essential human formation skill.

Father Ron Rolheiser, OMI, quotes the emeritus Archbishop Joseph MacNeil of Edmonton, Alberta, Canada, to the effect that priests are not "ecclesial robots" but wise and discerning pastors who know how to apply the constant teaching of the Church in the face of contemporary challenges. The "my way or the highway" syndrome, unfortunately, can come from either the left or the right to the detriment of effective pastoral ministry and service. What the Church cannot afford is a priest who operates as an ecclesial policeman rather than a shepherd of souls. Seminaries must ensure that seminarians acquire the interpersonal and spiritual skills essential for effective ministry.

My thirty-nine years of priestly ministry have given me the privilege of working with priests from different age cohorts and serving with them in parishes across the country. Happily, and gratefully, I cherish the experience of serving with hardworking, dedicated millennial priests who take care of their parishioners with zeal, make themselves available with incredible generosity, and display a commitment to personal holiness and daily prayer that is truly edifying. To the extent that there are contrasting (and sometimes conflicting) differences in style and substance among the cohorts of priests identified in the survey, the solution, I think, lies where it always does: namely, more dialogue, patience, understanding, and a commitment to work together. The wisdom of Rabbi Gamaliel is as necessary today as it was in the life of the early Church: "For if this endeavor or this activity is of human origin, it will destroy itself. But if it comes from God, you will not be able to destroy them; you may even find yourselves fighting against God" (Acts 5:38-39, NABRE).

Rabbi Gamaliel provides priests with an example of patience and forbearance as we continue to learn from one another, support one another, respectfully challenge one another, and, in so doing, more effectively serve God's holy people.

For bishops, in particular, the report provides some challenging observations about leadership as well as encouragement for initiatives to strengthen priestly morale and solidarity. The finding that 64 percent of all priests (table 3.1) are concerned about the "way authority is exercised" deserves careful attention. A careful analysis of this discovery indicates that for priests who experience "little or no support" from their superiors (i.e., either bishop or religious superior), 59 percent say the way authority is exercised in the Church is a great problem. For a significant number of priests who disagree strongly that "they are a member of the bishop's team," the number registering strong dissatisfaction rises to 71 percent.

Correlatively, for priests who have a positive and happy relationship with their bishop/superior, there is a desire for more democracy in the Church, not necessarily for themselves, but for more inclusive relationships with the lay faithful.

The findings suggest that it might be useful for the issue of authority and administrative style to be an ongoing discussion item for collegial conversation between a bishop and his priests at regular meetings of the presbyteral council. This kind of structured conversation could be a way to help those who feel alienated from the "bishop's team" to develop a greater sense of ownership and trust in the way things are handled. The desire for greater "democracy" in the Church suggests a yearning for a greater sense of consultation and inclusion in the governance of the Church. I find that this longing coheres with the substance of the findings in the book concerning the attitudes and concerns of priests with respect to collaboration.

What is striking to me as I read through the text is a sense of admiration and gratitude for the dedication and zeal of my brother priests. In the face of so many challenges, they are happy men. Yet, in the midst of this good news, I also experienced a rising sense of alarm. How long can we continue to manage the crisis in priestly numbers by restructuring our parishes into ever larger megaparishes, importing generous international priests, and assigning priests to be pastors of multiple parishes and cluster arrangements? To these questions, there are no easy answers. This research, like all good research, provides a clear picture of reality, a baseline of evidence from which constructive action can flow.

The book raises an important issue, first astutely identified by Father Andrew Greeley in his early sociological studies of the priesthood in the 1970s. The data gathered by Greeley and his colleagues, and attested to consistently in every study of priests since then, demonstrate that priests are happy in their ministry. However, paradoxically, priests are less inclined to recruit for their profession. This finding is a perplexing anomaly that suggests the need to develop an ongoing, dynamic culture of vocational discernment and recruitment. While there is evidence of greater promotion of vocations to the priesthood, among postconciliar and millenial cohorts, efforts to strengthen the ministry of vocation directors as well as the promotion of ongoing formation of priests are essential for a healthy and effective priesthood.

The statistics about priests are sobering. The average age of diocesan priests is 64, and as the report ironically observes, they are within a year of receiving their first Social Security checks. The pre–Vatican II priests (ordained 1940–60) are well into their senior years, and are being joined in retirement by the boomer generation that is the Vatican II cohort. By 2050, the number of active priests will be half of what it is today, based on long-term trends. In citing these figures, I by no means subscribe to despair. The enormous increase in the numbers of permanent deacons and an energetic and dynamic corps of lay ecclesial ministers along with an explosion of lay leadership are trends to celebrate.

However, the graying of the priestly corps is extremely worrisome and is not going to be easily reversed. The gift of ministry requires the healthy complementarity of the ordained priesthood and the priesthood of the baptized faithful. Indeed, paragraph 10 of *Lumen Gentium* reminds us that these priestly expressions, while essentially distinctive in nature, are, however, "ordered to one another." Each of these expressions is essential for the Church to achieve its mission. Let me be clear. We must affirm the growth of lay ecclesial ministry and continue to celebrate the gifts of the baptized faithful. However, no amount of increase in lay ecclesial ministry can substitute or make up for the absence of an ordained priesthood. Recruitment of candidates for the priesthood is imperative for the health and well-being of the priesthood and for the Church, which cannot function without it.

The two chapters devoted to the sexual abuse scandal are, in surprising ways, yet another confirmation of the strength and resilience of the priesthood. The powerful vignettes of the suffering of victims evoke sadness and deep sorrow at the incalculable harm that has been done to them. The suffering experienced by good priests is also part of this tragedy. Moreover, the nine priests who share their stories about ministering to a wounded Church are eloquent witnesses of grace, healing, and mercy. They are a tribute to the finest traditions of the priesthood. No wonder the Catholic faithful love and revere their priests even as they grieve the failures perpetrated by some of them and the scandalous evasion of leadership responsibility by bishops who failed to protect the innocent from the criminal predations of abusers.

An important take-away from these narratives is the need for ongoing evaluation of the justice and fairness of the Dallas Charter adopted by the bishops in the aftermath of the scandal. While no one questions the need for the protocols that have been established (safe environment training, maintenance of professional boundaries, prompt reporting to civil authorities, and active intervention on behalf of victims), even so, the "zero tolerance" environment leaves priests feeling vulnerable and without support in the event of a false accusation.

The recently released John Jay study (*The Causes and Context of Sexual Abuse of Minors by Catholic Priests in the United States, 1950–2010*) is an insightful complement to this book's compelling vignettes about the impact of the crisis on today's priests. They have truly "stood at the gates" and provided heroic witness for a battered and demoralized Church, and I don't think that we can repay them with enough gratitude. Comparing the CARA and Jay reports provides both hope and challenge.

In particular, the John Jay study highlights the enormously good work that has been accomplished in seminaries in the area of human formation for chaste celibacy and solid instruction in the moral and spiritual resources for healthy psychosexual development. While these findings are not directly connected to the central focus of the two chapters devoted to the abuse crisis, they provide an important perspective that complements the stories of the priests who are featured in the interviews.

What I found most insightful in these nine narratives that links them to the John Jay report was the importance of honesty and transparency in communicating with parishioners and reaching out to victims. The same virtues of honesty and transparency apply to formation in chaste celibacy. The old adage in therapeutic circles is that you are "only as sick as your secrets." One of the enduring lessons of this awful episode in the life of the American Catholic Church is that "the devil loves the dark." A culture of secrecy, of hiding from the truth, contributed to the perpetuation of this scandal, tragically, for far too long. We are still coming to terms with the depth and scope of the abuses that took place and we are still in need of accountability for those who did not exercise the leadership that was expected of them.

Going forward, we should be grateful that we have healthy seminaries that have been proactive in the area of human formation with solid training in celibate chastity following the clear emphasis on human formation in Pope John Paul II's landmark encyclical *Pastores Dabo Vobis* (1992). The John Jay study notes:

> Over the past twenty-five years, a remarkable intensification of human formation and deeper understanding of the importance of its role are evident in almost every seminary. Over the same period, the total number of accusations of sexual abuse of a minor by a Catholic priest has fallen from 975 for the period of 1985 through 1989 to 253 for the period of 1995 through 1999, and then 73 for the period of 2004 through 2008. An awareness of the problem of sexual abuse surely informed the development of the curriculum, but the benefits to seminarians may be seen in the continuing very low levels of sexual abuse of minors.

These findings confirm that good work is being done in seminaries, and this good work will continue to strengthen the priesthood. Pope John Paul's emphasis upon human formation has had a dramatic and powerful impact on seminary education throughout the world. The importance of this foundational pillar of priestly formation (along with the intellectual, spiritual, and pastoral dimensions articulated in *Program of Priestly Formation*, 5th ed.) cannot be underestimated.

By way of conclusion, this book affirms the strength and resilience of priests in a time of considerable stress and transition in the US Catholic Church as well as in American society and culture at large. The late Msgr. Phil Murnion, long-time director of the National Pastoral Life Center in New York, was a splendid example of the qualities of dedication and service that characterize good priests everywhere. While he was always clear about the identity and essential role of the priest, he was equally passionate about the essential need for priests to work collegially and to honor all the gifts of the lay faithful. As he often used to say, "Priesthood is not a license for private practice."

The data, complemented by the engaging and compelling interviews with priests, make the case for priests to work collaboratively with the lay faithful to fulfill the Church's mission. The common bond of priesthood joyfully links all the cohorts of priests who are the subject of the study. The study affirms that our truly overworked priests, who, nonetheless, spend their lives so faithfully on behalf of God's people, are genuinely, authentically, happy men. The CARA study invites us to do everything we can to ensure that the priesthood, this priceless resource and jewel of the Church, is sustained and strengthened for the good of us all.

Reflections on a Changing Ministry and Changing Ministers

Sister Katarina Schuth, OSF*

The availability of data on priests in the United States collected over a period of forty years provides an exceptional opportunity to notice similarities and differences and make recommendations based on patterns of change. The current research by CARA is presented in a way that allows for these comparisons and at the same time introduces fresh insights particular to the evolving situations in which priests find themselves at this time. Many themes are explored in the research, but this commentary will focus on a few previously identified but recurring themes of note and several contemporary ones of enormous significance for the future of the Church. Among the themes occurring repeatedly through the years are the positive attitudes toward priestly life and ministry, with some slight shifts among various age cohorts. The sources of support for priests are noteworthy; some have remained constant, but with recent problems others have shifted. The clergy sexual abuse scandal has tested the relationship of priests to their bishops and superiors. Among the contemporary themes comparatively new to the research are findings related to the changing structures of parishes. All of these themes are interrelated and thus have a powerful impact on priestly life and ministry.

The Attitudes of Priests toward Priestly Life and Ministry

It is an immeasurable source of reassurance and hope that at a very high rate priests cherish their choice of priesthood as a way of life and continue to enthusiastically embrace the ministry of their vocation. The

---

* Sister Katarina Schuth, OSF, PhD, holds the Endowed Chair for the Social Scientific Study of Religion at St. Paul Seminary School of Divinity, University of St. Thomas, St. Paul, Minnesota.

data demonstrate their general satisfaction in several ways, for example, 97 percent say they *will definitely or probably not leave the priesthood*, a rate that has increased from the 88 percent who said so in 1970. Since 1985, it has been at 93 percent or higher. Ninety-five percent say they would *definitely or probably choose priesthood again*, another encouraging measure, which is up from 88 percent in 2001 and much higher than the 79 percent in 1970.

In a comparable study of 911 priests who serve more than one parish, 90 percent said they would definitely or probably make the same choice again, even as they minister in what many priests would consider more complex and demanding situations (Schuth, 2006:213). Yet these highly positive numbers are tempered somewhat when the cultic model index, as defined in chapter 2 and as computed in table 8.1, is applied. Among the lowest quartile of the index, representing priests who are ideologically more progressive, 89 percent say they would definitely or probably choose to enter priesthood again, while among those in the more traditionalist camp, 99 percent say they would make the same choice.

From a slightly different perspective, a third measure of priests' attitudes concerns their overall happiness, which no doubt takes into account aspects of both their life and their ministry. Though differences in wording do not allow the possibility of making long-range comparisons, in the 2009 survey 97 percent of priests say they are very happy or pretty happy, of whom 61 percent say they are very happy. Previous surveys from 1970 to 2001 showed an average of only 38 percent who said they were very happy, a figure closer to the 42 percent in the survey of priests serving more than one parish (Schuth, 2006:212); however, in the latter study 92 percent of priests responded that they were very happy or fairly happy, comparable to the 2009 CARA study. The degree of happiness seems to have increased, though not the overall percent of those who fall into both categories of very happy or pretty happy.

Although no single question was asked about overall satisfaction with priestly ministry, more complex data provides insight into sources of satisfaction. Three measures are indispensable: first, the joy of administering the sacraments and presiding over the liturgy is considered to be of great satisfaction to 94 percent of respondents; satisfaction with preaching the Word is second with 83 percent saying so; and third is being part of a community of Christians who are working together to share the Good News of the Gospel with 73 percent saying it provides great satisfaction.

The first and third of these measures have increased by 10 percent or more since 1970; the second item has been measured only since 1993 and has increased only slightly. Two other sources provide other perspectives on the topic considering satisfaction in general. One is a 2001 Pulpit & Pew survey of pastoral leaders that shows 79 percent of Catholic priests are very satisfied with their current ministry, far more than the 47 percent of satisfaction of those in other professions. The other source is from the study of priests serving multiple parishes, which shows that 94 percent are very or somewhat satisfied, of whom 57 percent say they are very satisfied (Schuth, 2006:192).

What might be made of the data that indicate the increasingly positive responses to these questions about priestly life and ministry? The CARA study provides some potential answers based in part on age and ideological disposition. Some of the most revealing data can be found in table 2.4, which shows satisfaction by age and by year. Relative to age, every survey since 1985 indicates that as age increases, those who would definitely not leave the priesthood also increases. Across the years of the survey, as expected, the highest percentage of those who say they would definitely not leave are in their 70s and older. Only those in their 60s show a decline, moving from 91 percent in 1985 to 85 percent in 2009. More telling is the astounding increase within the two youngest cohorts of those who definitely would not leave; for example, those in their 30s moved from 37 to 88 percent and those in their 40s from 44 to 73 percent.

One possible explanation for the overall improvement derives from the percentage of priests who fall in various categories relative to the cultic model index. Table 2.5 shows that of those in their 30s, 32 percent are in the two quartiles representing the progressive side, and 46 percent of those in their 40s are in those two quartiles. By contrast, 60 percent of those in their 50s and 60s lean toward the progressive side. Those over 70, however, are somewhat more similar to the younger groups. As the tendency toward orthodoxy increases among the youngest groups, so too do all the measures of satisfaction. The youngest groups, it appears, experience support for their views of priesthood and the direction of the Church. They believe their traditionalist models of priesthood are more compatible with Church authorities than most of their older counterparts, who sometimes feel that their views are dismissed.

Other factors also may come into play. One of the ministries ranking among the lowest in terms of satisfaction (at 30 percent) is organizing and administering the work of the Church. Older priests are more likely to be pastors of very large parishes that require considerable administrative time and skill and so often are somewhat disappointed with that form of ministry. Further, a rather important source of satisfaction for priests is the sense of well-being that comes from working with like-minded priests. Again, rather frequently older priests have complained that their views of Church and ministry are not attuned to the younger priests who have been ordained in recent years. As they experience lack of appreciation of their understanding of Vatican II in parish ministry, their enthusiasm is somewhat diminished, especially when compared with the younger cohorts of priests. Important to remember is that these are differences of degree among various groups of priests. Overall, the four measures of satisfaction are on the rise, with increased probability of remaining in the priesthood, increased proportions that would choose priesthood again, higher levels of happiness, and many sources of great satisfaction with ministry.

Sources of Support for Priests

Over the past four decades, some significant sources of support that priests have counted on are still as important as ever and some new sources are emerging as changes in life and ministry evolve. Among the elements, the support of priests for each other is consistently mentioned as essential for their well-being. They especially appreciate fraternity with those whose views about Church and ministry are compatible with their own. A total of 77 percent of priests born in the United States say they experience strong or somewhat strong support from their brother priests. On average, about 15 percent fewer priests born outside the United States feel the same. Of all respondents, 71 percent report that of great importance is the sense of well-being that comes from living the common life with like-minded priests and 60 percent say it is from working with those whose views are compatible. Yet some conditions are impinging on the strength of that support as reported in several chapters. In many dioceses, fewer priests are sparsely distributed across the area, so it is often difficult to arrange regular meetings. Another constraint comes with increasing workloads for priests serving very large parishes or several parishes at once. Additionally, even when priests are in closer proximity, they may not be as inclined to gather for recreation and relaxation because of differences in cultural backgrounds and ideological perspectives, a separation that is sometimes related to age cohorts as well. Perhaps these conditions help explain why 40 percent of respondents identified the loneliness of priestly life as somewhat of a problem or a great problem.

Another source of support that priests have counted on through the years is their relationship with their bishops and major superiors. While many still experience support, a sizeable minority of 35 percent say the lack of support is somewhat of a problem or a great problem for them. The survey links this response with the attitude of priests about "the way authority is exercised in the Church." On this topic, 64 percent of priests believe the exercise of authority is somewhat of a problem or a great problem. The 30 percent who say it is a great problem have disapproving attitudes about superiors (table 3.2); for example, 59 percent say they receive little or no support from the bishop and 68 percent have very little confidence in the diocesan bishop. A high 71 percent disagree strongly with the statement, "I feel that I am a member of the bishop's team." These same 30 percent who see the way authority is exercised in the Church as a great problem have similarly negative attitudes about democracy in the Church, for example, agreeing that parishes should be able to choose their own priest (64 percent) and priests should choose their own bishop (59 percent). These assessments suggest that troubling tensions exist between these priests and their bishops or superiors.

The reasons for the problems may arise from sources related to the present circumstances in the Church. In many dioceses, the shortage of priests often results in parish closures and the assignment of one priest to several parishes. This situation no doubt exacerbates the misgivings about the relationship with bishops since priests are on the front lines managing the distress and anger of parishioners when their parishes are clustered or closed. Priests express their frustration when they believe their plight is not understood or their ministry is not appreciated. Since the 2002 Dallas document titled Charter for the Protection of Children and Young People, some priests feel further distanced from and less supported by their bishops. Others recognize the difficult position of the Church regarding the sexual abuse scandal but wish the situation would have been handled differently by the bishops. Especially controversial is the zero tolerance policy, which is resented by many priests. The responses in the CARA survey, especially the representative anecdotes, indicate how wide a net and how great a pall was cast by the difficulties and complications in the aftermath of the abuse situation. The quotes suggest that priests were touched by the scandal in numerous ways—by accusations against friends or immediate colleagues in ministry, by being assigned to parishes where priests had been removed because of accusations, by having to deal with families of children who were abused, and by a nagging fear that they might be falsely accused. Many of these priests express their disapproval of the way their leaders—bishops and other diocesan officials—handled both victims and those who were accused, but at the same time they acknowledge how difficult it is to be fair with limited information about individual cases.

Even as some of the traditional forms of connection and support may be lessened for some, other priests are finding new strength in their relationships with parish staff and parishioners. Among the most important sources of satisfaction the survey identifies, several involve working with a wide variety of people and being part of the community with them. In research on priests who serve more than one parish (Schuth, 2006:194–95), 96 percent of the priests said they were somewhat or very satisfied with their relationships with parishioners and in the same proportion they said this was true of professional staff. Their comments reinforce the perception that those closest to them provide the greatest support in their daily life and ministry. At the same time, families offer considerable encouragement and comfort to those who are fortunate enough to have them nearby. For international priests, the absence of their loved ones leaves a considerable lacuna that should not be overlooked.

The Effects of Changing Ministry: Personnel, Structures, and Membership

As noted, the survey reaffirms the notion that priests are highly satisfied with the nature of priestly ministry, even as many of them find the scope of responsibilities to be overwhelming and the adjustments they need to make to address the changing reality to be demanding. First of all, the personnel they encounter are constituted very differently from several decades ago when priests and religious were well-represented in parishes. These days a typical large parish will have more lay ecclesial ministers and smaller parishes have more lay volunteers than in the past. Adapting to collaboration with lay staff works well for many priests, but others are hampered by their inadequate preparation for working collaboratively, by ideological differences with staff members, or even by aversion to the concept of lay ecclesial ministry. Further, only the largest parishes have more than one priest and so generally the companionship they might have enjoyed while working with other priests in the past is diminished. At the same time, priests are becoming pastors at a younger age. Some welcome this responsibility and thrive in the position, but others would be more effective if they had the opportunity to be mentored for a few more years as an associate.

Moving Forward

In this essay I have reflected on three main topics: attitudes toward priestly life and ministry, sources of support for priests, and changing ministry. In many respects, the findings of the CARA survey are encouraging and positive directions are being fostered. At the same time, in some areas new concerns have arisen, opening opportunities for development and/or correction.

First, concerning attitudes of priests about their life and work, research studies through the years have yielded highly positive results and the CARA study reaffirms these findings. Priests are generally very happy with their choice of vocation and they experience enormous satisfaction with their ministry. These elements are the essence of priesthood and must be maintained. However, some cautions might be appropriate. As ministry changes, involving fewer priests and more lay ecclesial ministers, it will be necessary for Church leaders to assess the effects on the lives of priests and on the nature of their ministry. Further, as differences deepen among priests of various age groups and ideological preferences, it would seem wise to cultivate a spirit of appreciation and respect among priests and to soften hardened views about matters that are not doctrinal.

Second, concerning sources of support for priests, the record shows that some are stable and others are in flux. The strongest base of support comes from the fraternity that priests enjoy. Some of those ties are deeper than ever, but several threats impinge on this great strength. Because of fewer priests in many dioceses, especially where they are located at great distances from each other, opportunities for getting together are lessened. If age, cultural backgrounds, and perspectives about ministry also differ, even more difficult is the prospect of finding compatible relationships. Dioceses, groups of priests, and individuals are making efforts to alleviate some of the concerns by encouraging several pastors to live together, or by careful attention to placement of priests so that they are in proximity to at least some others who are part of their cohorts and friendship groups. Needing much more attention in the years ahead is the plight of international priests. Surveys show they find less support than they would like from American-born priests, they struggle with acceptance in parishes because of language and cultural barriers, and they lack sustenance from their own families. Since the predictions for the future are that eventually almost half the priests will come from other countries, they need to be more successfully incorporated into presbyterates and their sources of support bolstered.

Another source of support experiencing difficulty is the relationship some priests have with their bishops in the aftermath of the clergy sexual abuse scandal. Though many current bishops were not in office at the time of the Dallas Charter in 2002, a negative feeling still prevails about the provisions of the document. It seems advisable that some form of reconciliation between priests and bishops around these issues might be attempted. Bishops may wish to be proactive in resolving the rift that still exists.

Finally, as ministry changes, pressures and tensions tend to increase. Among the concerns are pastoring larger parishes and clustered parishes, having fewer companionable priests in close proximity, and working effectively with lay staff, both paid and volunteer. It seems desirable that seminary education and formation attend to these shifts in a more direct way. These ministerial situations are not likely to return to earlier patterns, so preparing seminarians for the future should include more appreciation for the ministry of administration, acceptance of a wide variety of priests, and gratitude for laypeople who give generously of themselves in full- and part-time ministry. The positive factors in place, combined with a firm foundation in prayer, should yield even more effective ways of spreading the Gospel in the years to come.

Reflections on the Happiness of Priests and the Impact on Parishes

Dianne M. Traflet*

One of the great treasures of our faith is true Christian joy—a certain happiness that by its very nature must be shared. It radiates from self-possession, is honed by self-sacrifice, and is expressed in self-donation. This study of Catholic priests presents such an image of happiness, providing more than snapshots of happy moments in daily service to the Church but multidimensional portraits of meaningful and fulfilling lives. At a time when studies show declining happiness in the general population, what can be learned from priests who are indeed happy? An astounding 97 percent of the responding priests report that they are either somewhat or very happy with their lives as priests, with 61 percent noting that they are "very happy." Considering that 90 percent of the diocesan priests in this study work in parishes, what might be the implications for the parish community?

A clue to the impact of a priest's happiness upon parish life may be gleaned throughout this study's statistics and stories. Certainly, as stated in the survey, three key themes of service, meaning, and community often emerge in analyses of happy lives. So too do these themes appear in the lives of these happy priests, along with five additional, complementary factors: humility, accompaniment, spirituality, mutual support, and collaboration. Might these factors also point to the building of a thriving parish? Let us look more closely at each.

* Dianne M. Traflet, JD, STD, is associate dean, assistant professor of Pastoral Theology, and founder and codirector of the Institute for Christian Spirituality, Seton Hall University, South Orange, New Jersey.

The key starting points, as St. Augustine would emphasize, are "the foundations of humility. The higher your structure is to be, the deeper must be its foundations." Before a priest can expect his work to be fruitful, he must understand and embrace humility; before a parish can be a bright presence in the Church today, it must lay a solid foundation of humility. How might priests and parishes express that humility? This study presents a manifold response: approach ministry in a spirit of collaboration; recognize and appreciate each other's gifts and talents; delight in each other's successes; and grow with one another in prayer, friendship, and mutual support.

While the survey does not ask the question, Are you humble? (how difficult it would be to answer that humbly!), it does provide veiled answers in such words as "gratitude," "invited," "service," and "instrument." All suggest that the happy priest is a humble priest, a servant-leader. His is a deep humility that shuns any hint of authoritarianism, and seeks dynamic collaboration. Thankful for his vocation and for God's continued work on his soul, the humble priest clings to Christ, recognizes his own weaknesses, and welcomes input from both fellow priests and the laity. He desires that his life and ministry reflect the presence of Christ. As explained by one priest, "People do have that expectation of meeting Christ in me. That's thrilling. It's very humbling too because I'm very acutely aware of my own flaws and weaknesses. Somehow God in His providence is able to use me."

This is the type of humility that stands in awe at the power of God's mercy on a repentant soul: "There's just nothing like that one-on-one personal, intimate moment of being an instrument of God's mercy." Far from being detached observers of this divine work, priests bear witness to conversions with emotion; as one respondent described, "It just breaks me to pieces and melts my heart because the prospect of coming home, coming back to God's embraces, is just amazing." Referring to a person who had not been to confession in three decades, a priest explained, "To be able to help heal somebody from their wounds is just absolutely powerful and very humbling."

As these few quotes attest, many of the surveyed priests speak about their vocations with lively enthusiasm, using dynamic words such as "thrilling," "amazing," and "absolutely powerful." These words suggest more than happiness; they paint a picture of exclamation marks and exuberant spiritual adventure. The enthusiasm of happy priests can be a service in itself, helping to jump-start and fuel our good efforts, and ultimately contributing to the building of a community of faith and abiding friendships. Happiness, then, never isolates or turns inward but rather invites and welcomes community.

The responding priests clearly feel privileged to participate in the various milestones of those they serve. As one respondent indicated, "the greatest joy is being invited into people's lives because I'm a priest, not because of who I am, whether it's in joyful times or sad times. It could be anointing someone in the hospital or in their home. Or working with a family after death. Or it can be a couple's first baby, a wedding, a fiftieth wedding anniversary, different things like that where I've truly felt a part of people's lives." Parishioners may expect that these parish priests will not be burdened by hospital visits and other ministerial duties; they will welcome opportunities to be present to those who are suffering. These times of accompaniment often are edifying to the priests themselves who find inspiration in the "faith of the people and their attempts and willingness to lead good lives."

This accompaniment is the second key building block of happiness and the thriving parish. It is likely that many of those who serve in administrative roles, rather than in parishes, miss that opportunity to accompany others, and the resulting relationships that emerge from such journeys. One priest noted, "I miss terribly the relationships and being part of people's lives—the incredible, awesome gift it is to be welcomed into people's lives like no one else is . . . to really be that presence of God in those traumatic and joyful and sad times of life."

These words suggest a purposeful accompaniment, that is, a focused effort to be present to others and to unveil God's presence, particularly in times of darkness and confusion. This type of accompaniment is not reserved for momentous times but the daily struggles and vicissitudes of life with their disguised potential for transformation, conversion, and discernment. Perhaps this priestly ministry is best described as participation in ongoing pilgrimages, sacred journeys that have the capacity to deliver lasting, poignant memories, not just of sights, but insights—those images and ideas that touch our hearts, and stir our consciences to lead better lives. Humbled and happy to play a role in an individual's interior pilgrimage, one priest explained, "You can say to someone, 'Your sins are forgiven. You have a new beginning. You can leave here a new man, a new woman.'" Seen in this light, priestly ministry is a constant opportunity to witness to and embrace the springtime of new life.

Such springtime defies age; as noted by one respondent, "I truly love being a priest. Not that I haven't had struggles like we all do, but what a joy this road has been for me. I'm only sad about not having too many more years left, but I will use each day to embrace the Lord more deeply in my own life and share that presence with any who seek Him in my work as a priest." His words speak not only to the desire to serve even after retirement age but also to the continual need "to embrace the Lord more deeply" at any age, and in all ministries. Surveyed priests recognize that their hectic work lives demand rich spiritual lives, for accompaniment is not just about journeying together, but journeying with God, with eyes focused on him, wills surrendered to his. This accompaniment is about *God*'s company; it requires learning to rely on God's directions, to follow his voice and receive his life. It is to be open to a new life in God, and to be ready and eager to share his life with others. This is a faith-filled accompaniment, *cum pane*, nourished by the Eucharist, the "focal point of the spiritual life."

Spirituality, the third building block of happiness and parish life, is at the heart of priestly ministry. Ninety-four percent of priests in this study report that administering the sacraments are sources of joy, and 83 percent report satisfaction in preaching the word of God. One priest captured this joy in the following statement: "I really would like to think that I work hard preparing my homilies and gathering people for prayer and celebrating the Eucharist in a way that gives people experience of God's grace in their lives. That, too, is a rich blessing." The surveyed priests clearly enjoy praying with their parish community. They are eager to pray for others, and are grateful to accept prayers on their behalf. They desire the primacy of prayer, not only to nourish themselves, but also those whom they serve. Overworked, though, they find it difficult to find time to get away from the day-to-day demands of their ministry. They realize that solitary and quiet prayer leads to more fruitful ministry, and to the experience of their work as a "rich blessing." Ultimately, significant time for prayer has the capacity for giving deeper meaning to their priestly ministry, and consequently, a deeper sense of fulfillment and satisfaction.

These priests recognize the need of supporting family, friends, parishioners, and fellow priests. This is the fourth building block of happiness and a thriving parish: mutual support and encouragement. Seventy-seven percent of those born in the United States say that they receive either strong or somewhat strong support from their brother priests (though those born in other countries report receiving less such support— 66 percent of the European or Canadian priests and 59 percent of other international priests). Priests welcome honest feedback and advice by brother priests; explained one respondent, "I definitely like sharing life on a daily basis with [my religious community] and doing so in a way that is grounded in prayer, ministry, and a common life. It's a place where I can be challenged and sometimes stretched, be repeatedly welcomed to the human race in terms of humility where my brothers invite me to grow."

Respondents lament that with the priest shortage, and with near-empty rectories, there are fewer opportunities for regular conversation among brother clergy. This presents a difficult challenge: "I'm surrounded by people *continuously*, but very few are my peers. . . . I can't unburden myself about my stresses. I can really only do that with another member of my order. When I had another priest living with me, we would get together every evening and just talk for an hour, just review the day and compare notes and complain and laugh and cry together. That was a really wonderful experience of community."

While priests express the need for priestly camaraderie, they also are very appreciative of the support and encouragement of laypeople. More than 80 percent of all priests say that they receive strong or somewhat strong support from nonpriest friends, with 94 percent of US-born priests reporting such support. This statistic is particularly poignant when looking at how priests relied on the encouragement of the laity during the scandals. One priest who was falsely accused was enormously grateful for the trust and kindness that the parish showered upon him: "What kept me going was the fact that the parishioners banded together. . . . If I didn't have their support I probably would have left priesthood. . . . they did not waver as to my innocence. . . . [Support] was overwhelming. They held a prayer vigil every Sunday night. . . . Signs [of support] went up on lawns." When the priest was exonerated, parishioners held a huge celebration, a homecoming of sorts, the kind that reveals the happiness not just of a community but a family.

This moral support seeks to build up the other, while building a community of faith and a spiritual family. The fifth and final building block of happiness is collaboration, the type that is generated and propelled by humility. Statistics point to the satisfaction priests experience in "working together," and to their desire to collaborate with the laity. Seventy-three percent of the surveyed priests note satisfaction in "being part of a community of Christians who are working together to share the Good News of the Gospel." This statistic is affirmed by one priest who stated, "It is a meaningful life, working with people to form hearts and minds in the spirit of the Gospel."

Such work does present challenges, including "unrealistic demands and expectations" of laypeople (53 percent of respondents find this to be somewhat or a great problem) and difficulty in reaching out to people (58 percent of respondents find this to be somewhat or a great problem). These statistics seem to point to overwork, and to the great desire of priests to evangelize and make a difference in others' lives. Perhaps this is why the statistics show an extremely large percentage of priests who express recognition, appreciation, and reliance on the gifts and work of the laity. Eighty-one percent of the responding priests "somewhat" or "strongly" agree that parish life would be aided by an increase in full-time professional lay ecclesial ministers. Seventy-seven percent note that the Catholic Church needs to move faster in empowering laypersons in ministry. "Clearly," explained one priest, "the church is more collaborative today. . . . More [parishioners] are getting more and more involved in more things and that's exciting to me." These priests are enthusiastic about the prospect of both lay participation and lay leadership, as noted by one priest: "I think we need to find leadership from within the people . . . rather than imposing our will on them or telling them what is going to happen." Another priest discussed how his parishioners assumed leadership responsibilities after he "invited or called them to a deeper level of involvement . . . people have really taken leadership roles in adult education, peace and justice . . . , and a men's spirituality group."

The respondents appreciate how the gifts and talents of the laity build the Church today, sometimes quite literally. One priest noted that he relies on the talents of parishioners to "help and direct building and renovation projects," and so much more; they are involved in such work in his parish as "pastoral council, finance council, consulting trustees," and leadership roles in the grammar school. He concludes, "I couldn't imagine doing what I do without the help of lay people." In the past decade, in particular, the collaboration among priests and laity also involves rebuilding, renewing, and reenergizing—efforts that seek to restore confidence and to contribute to the mission of healing the broken bonds of trust.

All five factors (humility, accompaniment, spirituality, mutual support, and collaboration) help us to understand how priests were able to answer the survey questions so positively despite experiencing devastating pain during the "heartbreaking" and "horrifying" scandals that began to explode in 2002. This pain showed a wide range of deep emotion: anger at the perpetrators, initial disbelief and shock, and deep sympathy for the victims. How did priests, a number of whom were falsely accused, continue to serve, even enthusiastically? One statement by a parishioner captures the essence of support and collaboration at the service of the Church. Several months after news of the scandals broke, a woman confronted her parish priest: "Father, when you walk down that aisle, you pick your head up and you look at us. You haven't done that for months. We love you. We care about you. You *look* at us when you walk out." Consider the image of that priest at the end of Mass; he had just exhorted the community to "go in peace to love and serve the Lord," and then he proceeded down the aisle as a prisoner of his anxiety and fear. Far from reflecting the love and peace he just proclaimed, he projected isolation and self-absorption. The parishioner, seeing this, became an instrument of healing; she accompanied the priest in a time of great anxiety and sadness and she supported him in the way that Christ once spoke to Peter: "Arise. Be not afraid." The parish priest had the humility to listen and to take his parishioner's words to heart. In a few sentences of kind reproach, the parishioner had helped to build the Church.

The story is a helpful reminder that isolation suffocates happiness; community resuscitates it. According to St. Bernard of Clairvaux, "We all need one another; the spiritual good which I do not possess, I receive from others. In this exile, the Church is still on pilgrimage and is, in a certain sense, plural; she is a single plurality and a plural unity. All our diversities . . . make manifest the richness of God's gifts."[1] While this study of Catholic priests is not designed to be an analysis of the laity, it gives an emerging and encouraging picture of the laity at work in service to the Church. Interspersed in the stories of priestly ministry were words of appreciation for the encouragement, inspiration, and faith of parishioners, along with words of respect and admiration for their leadership skills and talents.

The study reminds us that we are a Church on pilgrimage, glimpsing both light and shadows, and experiencing both inspiration and disillusionment. Sometimes, parched and tired, we continue on our way, fellow pilgrims, humbly open to transformation. Our happiness emerges often when we least expect it. It is discovered, as these surveyed priests attest, when the search for meaning supplants the search for happiness. When

---

[1] St. Bernard of Clairvaux, *Apologia to William of St. Thierry*, 4, 8, as cited by John Paul II, apostolic exhortation *Vita Consecrata* (Vatican City: Libreria Editrice Vaticana, 1996), 52, 118.

this happens, the parish is more likely to become what Pope Paul VI hoped, "a village fountain," where we all may encounter Christ with our fellow laborers and where we, priests and laity alike, may echo St. Peter's words to Christ: "Lord, it is good that we are here" (Luke 9:33, ESV).

References

Anderson, George M. 2008. "The Future of a Multicultural Church: Allan Figueroa Deck on Ethnic Ministry." *America*. September 22. Available at http://www.americamagazine.org/content/article.cfm?article_id=11064.

Associated Press. 2007. "Jesuit Order Settles Suit on Sex Abuse in Alaska." November 19.

Berry, Jason. 1992. *Lead Us Not into Temptation: Catholic Priests and the Sexual Abuse of Children.* Urbana: University of Illinois Press.

Berry, Jason, and Gerald Renner. 2004. *Vows of Silence: The Abuse of Power in the Papacy of John Paul II.* New York: Free Press.

Bleichner, Howard P. 2004. *View from the Altar: Reflections on the Rapidly Changing Catholic Priesthood.* New York: Crossroad Publishing Co.

Brooks, Arthur C. 2008. *Gross National Happiness: Why Happiness Matters for America—and How We Can Get More of it.* New York: Basic.

Burns, James. 2008. "Ministry Seeking Understanding: Assessing the Impact of Traumatic Experiences in Roman Catholic and Other Clergy." Paper presented at the Religious Research Association/Society for the Scientific Study of Religion joint annual conference. Louisville.

———. 2010. "Examining Well-being, Satisfaction and Burnout in a Variety of Catholic Clergy." Paper presented at the Religious Research Association/Society for the Scientific Study of Religion joint annual conference. Baltimore.

Butterfield, Fox. 1992. "New Sexual Misconduct Charge against Ex-Priest." *New York Times.* September 24: A25.

Carroll, Jackson W. 2006. *God's Potters: Pastoral Leadership and the Shaping of Congregations.* Grand Rapids, MI: Eerdmans.

DeLambo, David. 2005. *Lay Parish Ministers: A Study of Emerging Leadership.* New York: National Pastoral Life Center.

Doyle, Thomas P., A.W. Richard Sipe, and Patrick J. Wall. 2006. *Sex, Priests, and Secret Codes: The Catholic Church's 2,000 Year Paper Trail of Sexual Abuse.* Los Angeles: Volt.

Dulles, SJ, Avery. 1974. *Models of the Church.* New York: Doubleday.

Easterlin, Richard A. 2001. "Income and Happiness: Towards a Unified Theory." *Economic Journal* 111:465–84.

Euart, Sharon. 2010. "Canon Law and Clergy Sexual Abuse Crisis: An Overview of the U.S. Experience." Washington, DC: United States Conference of Catholic Bishops.

Fichter, Joseph H. 1968. *America's Forgotten Priests: What They are Saying.* New York: Harper and Row.

Fox, Thomas C. 2002. "What They Knew in 1985." *National Catholic Reporter.* May 17: 1.

Froehle, Bryan T., and Mary L. Gautier. 1999. *Pastoral Ministry in a Time of Fewer Priests.* Washington, DC: Center for Applied Research in the Apostolate.

Gautier, Mary L., ed. 2009. *CARA Catholic Ministry Formation Directory 2009.* Washington, DC: Center for Applied Research in the Apostolate.

Gautier, Mary L., and Paul M. Perl. October 2000. *Special Report: National Parish Inventory.* Washington, DC: CARA at Georgetown University.

Gautier, Mary L., and Mary E. Bendyna, RSM. 2009. *When we can no longer 'do': A Special Report on Issues in Retirement for Diocesan Priests.* Washington, DC: Center for Applied Research in the Apostolate.

Gautier, Mary L., Mary E. Bendyna, RSM, and Melissa A. Cidade. 2010. *The Class of 2010: Survey of Ordinands to the Priesthood.* Washington, DC: Center for Applied Research in the Apostolate.

Globe Spotlight Team. 2002. "Scores of Priests Involved in Sex Abuse Cases." *Boston Globe.* January 31: A1.

Goodstein, Laurie. 2003. "Decades of Damage: Trail of Pain in Church Crisis Leads to Nearly Every Diocese." *New York Times.* January 12: A1.

Gray, Mark M. 2010. "Steady Change: A Future with Fewer Catholic Priests." *Our Sunday Visitor.* June 27: 9–12.

Gray, Mark M., and Paul M. Perl. 2005. "Public Reactions to the News of Sexual Abuse Cases Involving Catholic Clergy: A Comparative Review of Research." Washington DC: Center for Applied Research in the Apostolate. Available at http://cara.georgetown.edu/pubs/CARA%20Working%20Paper%208.pdf

Gray, Mark M., and Paul M. Perl. 2008. *Sacraments Today: Belief and Practice among U.S. Catholics.* Washington, DC: Center for Applied Research in the Apostolate.

Greeley, Andrew M., and Peter H. Rossi. 1966. *The Education of Catholic Americans.* Chicago: Aldine Publishing Co.

Greeley, Andrew M. 1972. *The Catholic Priest in the United States: Sociological Investigations.* Washington, DC: United States Catholic Conference.

————. 2004. *Priests: A Calling in Crisis.* Chicago: University of Chicago Press.

Gregory, Wilton D. 2008. "Catholic Preaching in the Multicultural Context of the United States of America." The Roman Catholic Archdiocese of Atlanta web site. Available at http://www.archatl.com/archbishops/gregory/writings/2008/01-13-08-multicultural.htm.

Hoge, Dean R. 1994. *Project Future Directions.* Chicago: National Federation of Priests' Councils.

————. 2002. *The First Five Years of the Priesthood: A Study of Newly Ordained Catholic Priests.* Collegeville, MN: Liturgical Press.

————. 2006. *Experiences of Priests Ordained Five to Nine Years.* Washington, DC: National Catholic Educational Association.

Hoge, Dean R., Joseph J. Shields, and Douglas L. Griffin. 1995. "Changes in Satisfaction and Institutional Changes of Catholic Priests, 1970–1993." *Sociology of Religion* 56:195–213.

Hoge, Dean R., and Jacqueline E. Wenger. 2003. *Evolving Visions of the Priesthood: Changes from Vatican II to the Turn of the New Century.* Collegeville, MN: Liturgical Press.

Hoge, Dean R., and Aniedi Okure. 2006. *International Priests in America: Challenges and Opportunities.* Collegeville, MN: Liturgical Press.

John Jay College Research Team. 2011. *The Causes and Context of Sexual Abuse of Minors by Catholic Priests in the United States, 1950–2010.* Washington, DC: United States Conference of Catholic Bishops.

Los Angeles Times Poll. 2002. Richardson, Jill Darling. "Priests Satisfied With Their Lives." *Los Angeles Times.* October 20.

Morris, Charles R. 1997. *American Catholic: The Saints and Sinners Who Build America's Most Powerful Church.* New York: Random House/Time Books.

Murnion, Philip J. 1992. *New Parish Ministers: Laity and Religious on Parish Staffs.* New York: National Pastoral Life Center.

————. 1999. *Parishes and Parish Ministers: A Study of Parish Lay Ministry.* New York: National Pastoral Life Center.

Paulson, Michael. 2002. "Most Catholics in Poll Want a Resignation." *Boston Globe.* April 17: A1.

Perl, Paul, and Bryan T. Froehle. 2002. "Priests in the United States: Satisfaction, Work Load, and Support Structures." Washington, DC: Center for Applied Research in the Apostolate. Available at http://cara.georgetown.edu/pdfs/Priest_Paper5.pdf.

Pew Forum on Religion & Public Life. 2007. *The U.S. Religious Landscape Survey.* http://religions.pewforum.org.

Pope Benedict XVI. 2008. Homily at Mass in Washington Nationals Stadium. Vatican City: Libreria Editrice Vaticana.

Reuters. 2010. "Women Priests and Sex Abuse Not Equal Crimes: Vatican." July 16.

Schemo, Diana Jean. 2000. "Priests of the 60's Fear Loss of Their Legacy." *New York Times.* September 10: A1.

Schoenherr, Richard A., and Lawrence A. Young. 1993. *Full Pews & Empty Altars: Demographics of the Priest Shortage in United States Catholic Dioceses.* Madison, WI: University of Wisconsin Press.

Schuth, OSF, Katarina. 1988. "American Seminaries as Research Finds Them." *U.S. Catholic Seminaries and Their Future.* Washington, DC: United States Catholic Conference.

———. 2006. *Priestly Ministry in Multiple Parishes.* Collegeville, MN: Liturgical Press.

Secretariat of Child and Youth Protection. 2009. International Priests 2009. Washington, DC: United States Conference of Catholic Bishops.

Stammer, Larry B. 2002. "Most Priests Say Bishops Mishandled Abuse Issue." *Los Angeles Times.* October 20: A1.

Steinfels, Peter. 1992a. "Church Panel to Investigate Sexual Abuse Charges." *New York Times.* September 22: A21.

———. 1992b. "Inquiry in Chicago Breaks Silence on Sex Abuse by Catholic Priests." *New York Times.* February 24: A1.

United States Conference of Catholic Bishops. 2005. Child and Youth Protection Resources web page. Washington, DC: USCCB. Available at http://www .usccb.org/issues-and-action/child-and-youth-protection/resources/.

———. 2006. *Program of Priestly Formation.* Fifth Edition. Washington, DC: USCCB.

———. 2008. Embracing the Multicultural Face of God: Recognizing Cultural Diversity in the Church. Washington, DC: USCCB.

University of Chicago News Office. 2007. "Looking for Satisfaction and Happiness in a Career? Start by Choosing a Job that Helps Others." April 17. Press release. Available at http://www-news.uchicago.edu/releases/07/070417.jobs .shtml

Watanabe, Teresa. 2002. "Young Priests Hold Old Values." *Los Angeles Times.* October 21: A1.

Woodward, Kenneth L. 1994. "Was it Real or Memories?" *Newsweek.* March 13: 54.

Index

NOTE: Page numbers followed by "t" denote tables. Page numbers followed by "n" indicate footnotes.

active priests, 11–14, 15t, 45, 56, 69, 101t, 126, 214. *See also* retirement, priests in; semi-retirement, priests in
Ad Hoc Committee for the Study of the Life and Ministry of the Priest, 123
African American priests, 7–8, 10, 21, 22, 36, 98, 206
African priests, 7–8, 10, 98
age of priests, 1, 2–6, 12, 17, 32, 206; average at ordination, 5–6
alcoholism, 160
alter Christus, 33t, 40
American Catholic Priesthood Study, 3n
Anglo/white/Caucasian priests, 6–8, 10t, 97
ARDA, *see* Association of Religion Data Archives
Asian American/Asian/Pacific Islander priests, 7–8, 10
Asian priests, 7–8
associate pastors, 15–16, 18, 21, 28, 38, 40, 42, 45, 54, 57, 73, 75, 77, 79, 98, 102, 157, 167, 170, 184, 223. *See also* pastors
Association of Religion Data Archives (ARDA), 3n

authority, 55, 76, 105, 165, 166, 210; problems with the exercise of 49–53, 66, 67t, 212–13, 221
autonomy, 28, 45n, 68, 123

Bendyna, Mary, 6, 9, 12
Bernardin, Joseph Cardinal, 123, 125, 154, 166, 179
Berry, Jason, 121–23
bishops, addressing problems and pressures of ministry, 8, 9, 12, 18, 77, 98, 99, 114; approval of the 31n, 51t, 52; assigning priests, 14, 46, 53, 92, 156, 162, 171, 174, 175, 177; leadership 54, 62, 85, 104; member of the team, 31n, 49, 51t; relationship with the 50t, 53, 67t; spokesperson for the 39; support for priests, 13, 29, 49, 51t, 53, 84n, 106, 113, 131, 207, 221
brother, religious, 28, 78, 116n
brotherhood. *See* fraternity of priests
Burns, James, 142

Canadian priests, 9t, 99, 100–107, 109–10, 141, 192, 228
candidacy for priesthood, 7–8, 188, 190, 192, 194, 201–2, 211, 214
canon law, 13, 84n, 122, 130

CARA, *see* Center for Applied
    Research in the Apostolate
CARA Catholic Poll, 28n
Catholic immigrants, 4, 77, 93–96,
    111; subculture, 4, 5
Catholic population in the US, 1,
    9–10, 14, 70, 72n, 209–10
celibacy, 21, 50t, 61, 63–68, 88, 89t,
    144–45, 195–196, 201, 215; and
    lifelong commitment to chastity,
    50t, 67t; and appropriate intimacy,
    66
Center for Applied Research in the
    Apostolate (CARA), 5, 12, 13, 18,
    28n, 58, 63, 64, 72, 76n, 77, 92,
    97, 104, 120, 138, 208, 209, 215–
    19, 221, 223
century, nineteenth, 207; twentieth,
    1, 9, 207; twenty-first, 204
certainty with which beliefs are held,
    30
change, 1, 4, 8, 15, 17, 26–28, 42,
    55, 58, 76, 80, 81, 87, 89, 98, 102,
    111, 137, 140, 144, 171, 184–85,
    203, 205, 207, 209, 217, 219,
    223–24
chaplaincy, 14–15t
charism, 43, 126, 201
Charter for the Protection of Chil-
    dren and Young People, 120, 125,
    131, 221; and arrested develop-
    ment and immaturity, 128; and the
    bishops, 130; and communal
    residence, 127; and laicization,
    126–28, 146; and response of the
    hierarchy, 120; and turmoil, 159,
    162, 164; zero tolerance, 126–28,
    131–32, 146, 149, 215, 221
children, 4, 23, 30, 34, 36, 54, 103,
    112, 115, 118, 120–21, 123, 126,
    128, 131t, 132–33, 145, 149, 151,
    166, 168–71, 177, 207, 222

clerical, 98, 121–22, 122n, 126, 133,
    145, 159, 172, 181, 197, 206
clericalism, 151, 196
CMSM, *see* Conference of Major
    Superiors of Men
cohort. *See* ordination cohorts
collaboration in ministry, 70, 87–88,
    90–91, 109, 206
community of Christians, 33t, 36–37,
    44t–45, 47, 69, 218, 229
Conference of Major Superiors of
    Men (CMSM), 104, 106
confessions, hearing, 31n, 34–35, 37,
    53, 88–89t
Congregation for the Doctrine of the
    Faith, 141
core values, 38, 43
Council, *see* Vatican II Council
counseling, 75, 124, 127, 144, 156,
    160, 166, 173, 180–81
crisis, 21, 26, 31n, 36, 78, 98, 126,
    148, 150–51, 162, 179, 203, 207,
    213, 215
cultic model, index, 31, 32t, 88, 103,
    187t, 190–92, 191t, 200t, 218–19;
    of priesthood, 31–32
cultural diversity, 17, 92, 94, 96, 110,
    206; in ministry, 109–10; in
    parishes, 93t, 93–95, 109; in the
    priesthood, 96
culture, 4–5, 52, 81, 88, 94–95, 132,
    143–44, 197, 205, 207, 213,
    215–16; and culture wars, 144

deacon, 34, 56, 71–72, 79–81,
    83–84, 89, 126n, 173–75, 206,
    214
death, 34, 115, 157, 227
Deck, Allan Figueroa, 93
DeLambo, David, 72, 84
democracy, 50–51, 213, 221

demographics, changes in, 1, 17;
     characteristics, 1, 8; projections,
     94; trends, 205
dignity of the human person, 151,
     211
diocesan priests, 2–3, 11t, 12–18
dioceses, reorganization of, 58, 60, 84
discernment and spiritual growth of
     priests, 20, 193–94, 198, 201, 213
discouragement of priests, 142
diversity, cultural and multicultural,
     92–96, 109–11; international, 77;
     of viewpoints, 38, 148; racial and
     ethnic, 9, 17, 93, 207
Doyle, Tom, 122

ecclesial status, 187t, 188, 191t, 200t
ecclesiology, 29, 60, 206
educational apostolate, 15t
episcopacy, 184
Essential Norms, 126, 131, 138, 146,
     156, 160
Europe, immigration from, 207;
     priests born in, 9t, 99–110, 187t,
     189, 191t–92, 200t, 228; sexual
     abuse problem in, 141, 144, 151,
     158

Fichter, Joseph, 28, 73
focus group, 20n, 34, 36, 48, 54, 56,
     60–61, 67, 77–78, 80, 84, 87–88,
     92, 94–95, 98, 102, 106, 108–9,
     117, 129n, 130, 132–33, 135, 141,
     144
formation, 4, 6–8, 14, 85, 116–17,
     158, 166, 195–96, 201, 211–212,
     214–16, 224
fraternity of priests, 5, 23–24, 141–
     44, 202–3, 220, 223
frustration, 12, 20, 23, 28, 34, 53–54,
     75–76, 85, 110, 136–37, 153, 172,
     221

Gauthe, Gilbert, 121, 123
generation, baby boomer, 4, 214;
     future, 185; post-Vatican II, 5,
     7–8, 28n, 63, 187t, 190–91, 200t,
     203; pre-Vatican II, 4, 6–9, 187t,
     190–91, 192, 200t; Vatican II, 4,
     7–9, 18, 28n, 43, 187t, 190–91,
     200t, 214; younger, 202
Geoghan, John, 112–13
geographic regions: Northeast, 142,
     210; South, 70, 91, 92, 210; South-
     west, 92, 108, 142; West, 70, 210
Good News of the Gospel, 33t, 36,
     44t, 45, 47, 69, 218, 229
graduate degree, 2
Greeley, Andrew, 3n, 20–21, 25, 68n,
     97, 123, 129n, 143, 185–86, 203,
     213

happiness, 20–21, 23–25, 30–31, 43,
     45–47, 49, 67–69, 197, 203, 218,
     220, 225–29, 231
hierarchy, the, 29, 97, 118, 120,
     136–37, 206; leadership of, 21;
     priesthood as, 6, 88
Hispanic/Latinos, 10, 18, 36, 93–94,
     95–96, 206–7; in Catholic priest-
     hood, 7–8, 10, 97. *See also* Latin
     America
Hoge, Dean, 20–21, 25, 28, 30–31,
     31n, 45n, 68n, 88, 96, 97n, 99,
     103, 190, 209
homosexuality, 60, 127, 144–45, 160
housing, 13, 46; rectory, 4–5, 81, 132,
     146, 149, 153, 175; residence,
     75–76n, 127, 149

identity, priestly, 5, 12, 30–31, 34,
     209–11
ideological, 129; and differences, 103,
     108, 187, 222–23; perspective,
     184, 220

ideology, conservative, 103–4, 108,
     192, 201; liberal, 103, 140–41,
     145, 192; progressive, 31, 32t,
     103, 187t, 190–92, 196–98, 200t,
     218–19; traditionalist, 29, 31–32,
     103–4, 108, 187t, 190–92,
     196–98, 200t, 218–19
immigrants, 4, 77, 93–96, 111;
     German, 9, 97–98; Irish, 9, 97–98;
     Italian, 9, 97; Polish, 98;
     institutions of, 4, 60, 70
India, priests born in, 77, 106–7
infirm priests, 2
institutionalism, 137
international priests, expanding role
     of, 206, 209, 213; studies and
     statistics of, 8–9t, 96–110t, 187t,
     189, 191t–92, 200t; support for,
     222–23, 228; working with,
     73t–74t, 77–79, 83t–84, 93
International Priests in America:
     Challenges and Opportunities, 96

John Jay College Research Team,
     113, 144n; and study and report,
     215–16

Kennedy, John F., 112

laicization, 122n, 123n, 126–28, 130,
     146, 171, 175
laity, 26, 58, 60, 67, 71, 94, 96, 111,
     184, 195–96, 207–08, 226, 232;
     and conflict over controversial
     topics, 61, 73–76, 210; distinction
     from priests, 31, 40, 86–89t, 210;
     effects of the sexual abuse
     scandal, 117, 121, 130, 139, 146,
     154, 161, 183, 229; lay ecclesial
     minister or ministry, 71–72,
     79–80, 83–84, 86–87t, 206, 210,
     214, 222–23, 230; lay leader or

leadership, 71, 172, 214, 230; lay
     people, 40, 70, 81, 86, 91, 157,
     194, 230; sharing ministry with,
     13, 81–82, 86–88, 210, 229–30;
     unrealistic demands and expecta-
     tions, 50t, 58, 66–67t, 73t–74, 230
Latin, instruction in, 6
Latin America, immigration from,
     18; priests born in, 98–100, 103–
     5, 109, 189. *See also* Hispanic/
     Latinos
Law, Bernard Cardinal, 113, 117,
     129, 138
lawyer, 3, 12, 120–22, 130, 139,
     152–53, 166, 176–79
leadership, 14, 21, 28, 39, 51, 71–72,
     81–82, 105t, 115, 117, 122, 140–
     41, 144, 190, 196, 209, 212 214–
     15, 230–31; and decision making,
     52, 104; and satisfaction, 33t, 39,
     44t, 45, 46n; support from, 29
like-minded priests, working with,
     33t, 37, 41–43, 47, 69, 220
liturgy, 29, 33, 44–45, 92, 95, 163,
     218
Liturgy of the Hours, 36
loneliness, 23, 50t, 63–65, 67t–69,
     195, 206, 221
Los Angeles Times Survey of Priests,
     20–21, 25, 56, 129

magisterium, 29, 208
Mass, 14, 31n, 34–36, 40–42, 53, 55,
     59, 61, 73, 88–89t, 92, 95, 98,
     102, 108, 118, 138, 140, 142, 147,
     153, 155, 157, 163, 165, 169, 171,
     176, 178, 193, 195, 197, 231
media, 64, 113, 121, 123, 129n,
     135–39, 142, 161, 163–64, 170,
     178–79, 185, 193, 200t
men, considering a vocation to the
     priesthood, 5, 28–29, 46, 145,

185, 192, 200, 202–3, 208; entering seminary after college, 7; entering seminary and ordained later in life, 1, 29; fewer entering, 1, 28, 99, 185; foreign-born, 99, 102; married as permanent deacons, 71; outflow from the priesthood, 26

mentoring, 173–74, 223

millennial ordination cohort, 5t, 7, 16t, 29, 32, 74t, 83t, 85–86, 87t, 88, 100t, 143, 187t, 190, 191t, 200t, 201, 210

ministry, campus, 14; changing, 217, 222–23; educational apostolate, 15; gift of, 214; hospital chaplaincy, 14–15t, 17, 57, 178; of administration, 224; of vocation directors, 214; one-on-one, 58, 160, 164, 169, 226; pastoral, 22t, 79, 89–90, 212; status, 11t, 13, 100t, 101

monastic model, 7

morale, 20–21, 141–42, 212

motivation, 24, 37, 78, 174

Mouton, Ray, 122

Murnion, Philip, 72, 216

National Catholic Reporter, 115, 121

National Opinion Research Center (NORC), 22

occupations affording satisfaction, 22

OCD, see *The Official Catholic Directory*

Official Catholic Directory, The (OCD), 70, 72

Okure, Aniedi, 96–97n, 99

opportunity, 33t, 36, 38, 41, 44t–46, 68, 84, 110t, 164, 168–69, 178, 183, 206, 223, 227

ordination cohorts, 5t, 16t, 43, 45,74t, 83t, 87t, 100t, 187t, 190, 191t, 192, 199, 200t, 210; millennial, 7–8, 29, 32, 85–86, 88, 108, 143, 190, 201, 214; pre-Vatican II, 6, 73, 186; post-Vatican II, 7, 73, 214; Vatican II, 6, 73, 186, 214

parishes, closure of, 14, 18, 150, 210, 221; clustered, 13t–14, 53, 101, 221, 224; collaboration with, 69, 70, 80–82, 84, 87–88, 90, 109, 206, 209–10, 213, 222, 226, 229–31; large, 18; linked, 14; ministry of, 13–17, 38–39, 58–59, 63, 72, 97, 101, 114, 121, 124, 142, 162, 189, 192, 194, 220; multiple, 57, 69, 205–6, 213, 219; national, 9; paired, 14; reorganization of, 60; small, 59, 64; territorial, 9; twinned, 14; yoked, 14

parishioners, 4, 18, 23, 36, 39, 46, 51, 59, 69, 70, 73t, 74t, 75–77, 81, 95, 114, 117–19, 139–40, 144, 146, 149–55, 159, 162–63, 173, 178–79, 206, 210, 212, 215, 221–22, 227–31

pastoral council, 70, 104–5t, 230

Pastores dabo vobis, 8, 211, 216

pastors, 1, 5, 13–14, 15t–16, 18, 21. *See also* associate pastors

pedophilia, 116, 127, 160, 170, 177–78; heterosexuals and, 145; scandal, 137, 148; serial, 115, 122; tendencies toward, 155. *See also* sexual abuse

Peterson, Michael, 122

Pope Benedict XVI, 111, 141, 151, 172

Pope John Paul II, 7–8, 123n, 141, 172, 211, 216, 231n

population growth, 18

Porter, James, 123

Post-Vatican II, generation, 5, 7–8, 9t, 10t, 28n, 63, 187t, 190–91t, 200t, 203; ordination cohort, 5t, 7, 16t, 74t, 83t, 86, 87t, 100t, 187t, 191t, 200t, 209

PPF, see *Program of Priestly Formation*

preaching, 33–34, 41, 44t, 84, 163, 218, 228

presbyteral council, 51t, 104, 106, 203, 213

presbyterate, 63, 78, 111, 205, 208, 224

pressures on priests, 18, 23, 29, 71, 73, 81, 206, 224

Pre-Vatican II, generation, 4, 6–8, 9t, 10t, 187t, 190–191t, 200t; ordination cohort, 5t, 6–7,16t, 73, 74t, 75, 83t, 86, 87t, 100t, 186, 187t, 191t, 200t, 209, 214

priests, assignment of, 12–14, 16, 53, 68, 101, 139, 167, 174, 221; ontological status of, 8, 30, 88, 210; priesthood, call to the, 21, 40, 90, 111, 188, 193–94, 196–99, 205, 207–8; leaving the, 19, 25–28, 31, 68n, 128, 218–19; permanent character of the, 31n, 86–89

prison chaplaincy, 15t

Program of Priestly Formation (PPF), 8, 216

Protestant, conservative, 21–22t; mainline, 21–22t

psychological issues, 76, 142, 179

psycho-sexual development, 160, 215

Pulpit & Pew Research on Pastoral Leadership and survey, 21–22, 219

recruitment of priests, 71, 185, 203

Religious Landscape Survey, 10

religious communities, 14–16, 37–38, 75, 85, 104, 106, 114, 127–28, 188, 194, 198, 202, 229

religious institutes, 2, 8, 104, 106, 118, 122, 127, 193

religious orders, 17, 23, 37, 39–40, 42–43, 60, 64, 72, 78, 84, 89, 107, 115, 118, 124, 127, 130, 145–46, 165–66, 180, 184, 186, 188–89, 199, 201–2, 229

religious priests, 2–3, 12–16, 33t, 37, 42, 47, 49, 50t, 53–54, 63, 69, 72, 75, 89, 97, 131t, 186, 188, 192

religious sister, 56, 85–86; and nun, 52, 56

religious tradition, Jewish, 181; Protestant, 142, 182, 208; conservative Protestant, 21–22; historically black, 21–22; mainstream Protestant, 21–22

renewal, 6, 203, 230

respect, priestly, 33t, 40–41, 44t, 202, 223

retirement, priests in, 6–7, 11–14, 17, 45, 52, 56, 63, 65, 66n, 72, 73, 75, 89, 98, 100t, 101, 157, 188–89. *See also* active priests; semi-retirement, priests in

retreats, 13–14, 16, 167, 172, 194

rural priests, 63

sacraments, 33–35, 40, 44–45, 55, 75, 86, 118, 123, 151, 218, 228

satisfaction, 17–23, 25–33, 36–47, 67, 69, 184, 186, 188, 206, 209, 218–20, 222–23, 228–29

Schoenherr, Richard, 2

Scripture, 189, 193, 197, 208; New Testament, 84

Second Vatican Council, *see* Vatican II Council

secular, 4, 6, 12, 29, 121, 154, 179

seminarian, 7–9, 24, 42, 116, 195, 199, 202, 205, 211–12, 216, 224

seminary, 1, 4–8, 24, 28, 46, 63, 85, 102, 116, 166, 174, 185–86, 193, 195, 197–98, 201–3, 209, 211–12, 215–17, 224; after college and/or work experience, 7; college (major), 5–6, 98; high school (minor), 4–6, 98; reorganization, 7

semiretirement, priests in, 6–7, 13–14, 100t. *See also* active priests; retirement, priests in

senior priests, 12

servant leader model of priesthood, 4, 7, 31, 196, 209, 226

service, priestly, 22–24, 37, 46, 59, 79, 185, 193, 197, 203, 206, 212, 216, 225–26, 231

sexual abuse, Ad Hoc Committee on, 123; allegations of, credible, 124, 149, 157–58; allegations lacking credibility, 131, 146; bishops, effect on relationships with, 221, 224; causes of, 144–45, 152, 215; and celibacy, perceptions of, 65; difficulties in handling administratively, 157–58, 159, 177; Europe, in, 141, 144, 151, 158; hierarchy, effect on, 52, 138–39; laity, effect on relationships with, 117; media coverage of, 112–16, 121, 123n, 135, 136, 141, 146, 152, 157–58, 161–62, 164, 178, 185; morale, effect on 20, 25, 147; prayer and penance, 120, 127, 146; revelations of, 112–16, 121–22, 148–50; support for accused, 129; victims, reaching out to, 120, 124–25, 159–61, 163–66, 168–74,

179–83; vocational encouragement, effect on, 199–200t, 201. *See also* Charter for the Protection of Children and Young People; pedophilia

sexuality, 195–96

shortage of priests, 2, 46, 48, 50t, 56–58, 60, 71–74, 75, 79, 84n, 98, 199, 205, 210, 220–21, 223, 229; worsening of, 1, 28, 56–57, 90, 92, 185, 206, 209, 213–14

social justice, 4, 43

social service, 15–17, 23

spiritual director, 16, 115, 155, 184, 188, 193–94, 197

spirituality, 21–22t, 24, 30, 34, 35, 43, 81, 193–94, 197; as a factor in happiness, 225, 228, 230

suburban priests, 4

supply priests, 13, 17

synod on priestly formation, 8

theology, 5, 26, 29, 42–43, 50t, 60n, 61, 174, 225n

trends, 1, 8–9, 28, 72, 79, 80t, 84, 88, 89t, 97, 185, 190n, 205, 214; trend data, 14, 88

uncertainty about the future of the Church, 50t, 55, 67t

United States Conference of Catholic Bishops (USCCB), 52, 70, 93, 104–6, 122, 125, 126n, 132, 204n

unity, sense of presbyteral, 78, 88

US Bureau of Labor Statistics, 2

USCCB, *see* United States Conference of Catholic Bishops

Vatican, the, 8, 29, 106–8, 122–24, 126, 137, 141, 151, 172

Vatican II Council, 4–6, 26, 31n, 43, 71, 185, 196, 208; generation,

4–10; and ordination cohorts, 4–10, 16, 18, 26, 28, 31, 43–44, 63, 73–75, 83, 86–87, 98, 100, 186–87, 190–91, 196, 198–200, 203, 208–9, 214, 220

vicar, for clergy, 16, 53, 174; parochial, 15t–16, 79, 102

vocation directors, 193, 195, 202, 211, 214

vocations, considering and discerning, 5, 20, 23, 184–85, 188, 193–95, 197; decline in, 8, 18, 28–29, 45, 71, 98; encouragement/discouragement for, 4, 21, 26, 185–86, 192, 199, 201–3, 207, 213–14; embrace of, 217, 223, 226; indigenous, 8, 99, 102; motivation for, 37, 40, 78; screening and admission of candidates, 211;

understanding of, 43, 96, 190, 204–5, 208

Voice of the Faithful, 172

well-being, sense of, 33t, 41–43, 47, 69, 220

Wenger, Jacqueline, 20, 25, 28, 30–31, 190

wisdom, 90, 202, 212

women, 84–85, 87t, 115, 137, 172, 195, 211; ordaining, 56; religious; 156; working with, 73t–74t, 84–85, 87–88, 103, 210

workload, 4, 56–58, 66n–69, 74–75, 89, 206, 209–10, 230

zeal, priestly, 30, 212–13